Understanding Reality

UNDERSTANDING REALITY

A Commonsense Theory
of the Original Cause

Stefan Hlatky and Philip Booth

JON CARPENTER

Credits

First published in 1999 by
Jon Carpenter Publishing
2, The Spendlove Centre, Charlbury, Oxfordshire OX7 3PQ
☎ 01608 811969

Diagrams by Chrome-Dome Design. Cover design by Sarah Tyzack

ISBN 1 897766 42 4

**Our books may be ordered from bookshops or (post free) from
Jon Carpenter Publishing, 2 The Spendlove Centre, Charlbury, OX7 3PQ**

Please send for our free catalogue

Credit card orders should be phoned or faxed to 01689 870437 or 01608 811969

Distributed in North America by Paul and Company, PO Box 442, Concord, MA 01742
(phone 978 369 3049, fax 978 369 2385)

Printed in England by J. W. Arrowsmith Ltd., Bristol
Cover printed by KMS Litho, Hook Norton

Contents

The Being and consciousness; concrete vs abstract, existence vs activity; science – inner and outer; theology and pantheism: abstract original causes; can God be understood?; Hlatky's view of God, the Being and creation; differences from theology; the whole and its parts; theology and philosophy; the need for mutual love; science and the old traditions; the Big Bang and the problem of the original cause; science and 'why?'; modern science and philosophy; time

The philosophical education of children; the mystical 'I'; 'free' will; human will and Nature's will; the problem of identity; our absolute identity and our 'relative identity'; animals' undivided love of life; unlimited consciousness; is the universe alive? 'life' and 'death' vs conscious and non-conscious; God's activity and the activity of the conscious parts; the need of consciousness: undivided love; the necessity for agreement; 'freedom' from reality?

Can love be one-sided?; can we love an object?; love and preference; helping and understanding; whom can we have exchange with? the bondage of love; identity; the parts of the Being; consciousness and creation; God-consciousness; God: the original object, including his parts; object/quantity and quality; the quantity and quality of consciousness; science and consciousness; the need to understand and to be understood; animals, love and understanding; love or power; use of language: to cover reality or to express oneself; 'who am I?'; children's questions and child-rearing; 'the god within'

Our relationship to reality; a separate life or a common life?; '*agape*' vs '*eros*'; subjective relation and objective experience; philosophical reflection vs thinking; resolving creation's apparent contradictions; a common, concrete start for thinking; checking Hlatky's hypothesis; is creation perfect for its purpose?; philosophical logic; agreeing on axioms; authoritarian traditions or Nature-based logic?; consciousness vs thinking; philosophical reflection; creation is self-explanatory; the axioms; the opposite of an axiom; creation's contradictions; types of whole; equality and likeness; God – the only conscious, living whole; the original cause is self-evident; human vs animal thinking; what is our identity?; subjective and objective needs

Introduction

I N THE WEST WE GENERALLY BELIEVE IN THE NEED FOR A PLURALISTIC society in which each person has their own view of life, and in which tolerance of each other's views, rather than agreement on a common view, is regarded as the most desirable social goal. We tend to look down on societies that are governed by a single worldview, religious or secular. In this climate, Stefan Hlatky's unitary system of thought seems anachronistic. Yet the basis of Hlatky's endeavour is quite distinct from that of traditional religious or other worldviews. Historically, all such worldviews have contained much that is inconsistent, in Hlatky's opinion. This means that they could not be presented rationally, but only in authoritarian ways. In some cases, it was even argued that reality was inherently beyond human understanding. Or, as modern science maintains, it was said that only the 'how' and not the 'why' of reality could be understood – which in Hlatky's view means our understanding would be incomplete.

When Hlatky, who was brought up as a Roman Catholic in Hungary, was himself told as a child that the original cause – traditionally, when viewed as living, called 'God' or some equivalent – could not be understood, he could not accept this. He thought that if God existed, he would have given us the ability to understand him. This was the basis on which Hlatky pursued his own questioning and his own efforts to understand reality. The outcome of his study and thinking is what he first called, in the 1960s, 'The organic view of unity'. The important feature of his hypothesis is that it can be reasoned. Hlatky believes that if we reflect on our total, common experience of everyday life, his hypothesis can be understood by any one of us. So Hlatky is presenting a unitary worldview that is not authoritarian or dogmatic.

The reflection that is required of us, however, is different from the complicated, intellectual thinking that is promoted by our educational system and that we are so used to today. We need to return to the kind of reflection on our immediate experience that we had as children. It is part of Hlatky's thesis that children ask all the right questions to arrive at a logical understanding of the original cause of the world around us, but that they generally give up their quest at a certain point because the grown-ups are confused and cannot answer the children's questions satisfactorily.

Hlatky began presenting his ideas to the public in the early 1970s. He gave many public talks, which included until 1996 a weekly seminar at the ABF Huset, an adult education centre, in Stockholm, Sweden. He has done much writing. Some of this, translated here, has been used in 'exhibitions' devoted to his hypothesis, but none has hitherto been formally published. He himself has used his writing to help clarify how his hypothesis could be best presented and to serve as a basis for dialogue with others. His preferred method, however, has always been face-to-face dialogue – for reasons that are basic to the arguments for his hypothesis [see, for example, the sections in Dialogue 4 entitled 'Agreeing on axioms' and 'Consciousness vs thinking']. He hoped that through dialogue his hypothesis might be taken up and discussed by the main institutions nowadays responsible for education – the church and the various institutions of science, psychology and politics – so that it could be more widely debated alongside its alternatives. This has not happened, hence his agreeing to the writing of this book.

In order to capture something of the kind of dialogue that Hlatky has always sought to foster, we present his ideas and their implications not just as articles, but also in dialogue form. These Dialogues, which form Chapter 2, are based on taped dialogues recorded during 1995. It is difficult to present a unitary system of thought in a neat, linear form, since no element of it stands on its own. Through the format of the Dialogues in particular, therefore, the reader will find themes approached a number of times from different angles so as to convey the picture of the whole. This makes for a certain amount of repetition, but we hope that the reader will find this helpful.

Chapter 1, 'Understanding reality: a basic human need', is a brief presentation of Hlatky's views. This simplified overview serves as a reference point for the reader, as well as an introduction to later chapters. Chapter 2 comprises the four Dialogues between Hlatky and Booth, joined, in parts of Dialogues 2 and 3, by Matilda Leyser. Chapter 3, 'The organic view of unity', written by Hlatky in 1976, examines in detail the major axioms that are referred to throughout this book, as well as some of the implications of Hlatky's view. Chapter 4, 'Are we alike or unlike?', written by Hlatky in 1980, is a fuller, formal presentation of Hlatky's view. Its second part, 'The historical background', presents the answers of five major world religions and the answers of modern science to the major philosophical problems that Hlatky's hypothesis aims to solve. We have tried throughout this book to be clear about where Hlatky's view is similar to and different from other views, and 'The historical background' is intended to reinforce this clarity. Also relevant in this regard is Chapter 5, 'Science, religion and philosophy', a lecture given by Hlatky in 1986, which sets the same philosophical problems in historical context.

It should be said that Hlatky's hypothesis has remained the same since he first proposed it. That means that he has not yet been convinced by efforts to refute it. The terminology he has used to describe it has, however, altered slightly from time to time. This has been in response to the issues that have dominated society at large over the years, and to common confusions about his view that he has met in his dialogues with other people. The word 'organic', for example, has taken on different connotations over the last forty years, so Hlatky now prefers the word 'living'. For a long time he persisted with the word 'consciousness', but has recently come to prefer the term 'ability to experience', to distinguish his view more clearly from prevailing interpretations of the word 'consciousness'.

The sense in which Hlatky uses certain words may seem strange to the reader, but Hlatky believes that he is using them in their proper sense. However, to help the reader with such words, a Glossary has been added. The reader is alerted to these words when they first appear in the text, and they are printed in bold in the Index.

Appendix A on language and Appendix B on the definition of 'dialogue' are occasional pieces written by Hlatky that are too long for the Glossary.

Finally, the reader who is interested in other translated articles by Hlatky will, by the end of 1999, find one or more available on the Internet at the website <http://www.reality.org.uk>. The original Swedish versions of Chapters 3 and 4, along with other articles by Hlatky in Swedish, can already be found at the website <http://hem1.passagen.se/lanor/index/html>.

Philip Booth
March 1999

Chapter 1

Understanding reality*: a basic human need*

Philip Booth

OR HLATKY, A PROPER UNDERSTANDING OF OUR OWN LIVES IS possible only when we have a proper understanding of reality, and a proper understanding of reality is possible only when we have a proper understanding of the original cause* and meaning* of reality. On the basis of the axiom* that activity* can be caused only by a conscious*, living being, Hlatky argues that the original cause of our everyday reality – a reality that we know to be pure activity – must be a single, conscious, living being. Traditionally, the name that has been given to the concept of a conscious, living original cause is 'God' or some equivalent. Hlatky follows theological tradition – Judaism, Christianity and Islam – in using that name too, but he parts ways from theology on major points.

For example, most theories of creation* and of God the creator see God as separate from his creation. Hlatky's hypothesis is based on the idea that God is the invisible original whole* of which we are the original parts*. In this hypothesis, God must create within himself – since if there were something outside him, he would not be the whole.

Hlatky views God – this invisible, original whole with its original parts – as the invisible, omnipresent reality behind creation. On the basis of the axiom that every conscious, living being has the need to be understood as like* and thereby to be loved, he argues that God, as a conscious, living being, must also have that need. It is this need that motivates God to give out creation: he wants to be understood by us, his equally conscious, living parts. This is the meaning and purpose of creation, viewed from God's perspective.

As the whole, God cannot show himself directly to his parts, but he lets us know about himself indirectly through the activity that is creation. He does this by giving us experiences that can lead us to infer his and our own original existence*, as well as to understand him, which means to understand his purpose with creation.

---

* All words marked by an asterisk are further explained in the Glossary.

In Hlatky's view, God does not create us. Each of us is a non-created, unchangeable, conscious, living part of God's original reality – this original reality being traditionally called the Being*. This part becomes connected to a human body that is created along with the rest of creation by God. Hlatky argues that in the original situation in the Being, the conscious parts* have virtually no experience, hence God's purpose in creating creation: so that we can have experience of each other, indirectly through our created bodies, and also of him, indirectly through the whole creation. If we infer God's purpose with his creation, we can start to experience love*: first in relation to God, and then, consequently, also in relation to each other. In this way God's need for love can be satisfied, and ours too. [This central idea is broached in several places. See, for example, Dialogue 1, 'The need for mutual love', p.31.]

So creation is where we can come to an understanding of our original relationship to God and to each other, with huge consequences for the way we lead our lives. Hlatky believes that unless we are conscious of these relationships, it will be impossible for us to escape a feeling of alienation: from the world around us and from each other.

Hlatky argues his hypothesis on the basis of certain axioms which, by the nature of axioms, cannot themselves be argued for, but can only be accepted or rejected by any individual, on the grounds that they are, or are not, self-evident*, that is, they do or do not fit their own total, current experience. These axioms are thus derived from Nature*, and can be checked* against our own total, current experience of Nature, both outside and inside our created bodies. We in fact have to use axioms in much practical thinking – that is, the thinking required for us to be able to deal with our bodily needs and our everyday existence* – but historically they have not been used in discussion in the domain of philosophy*, that is, in relation to the problem of the original cause. Historically, the problem of the original cause has only been discussed in relation to tradition, that is, in relation to what other people say about reality, rather than in relation to people's actual experience of it.

The main axiom [for the principal discussion of axioms, see Dialogue 4] is:

No thing can arise, originate from nothing. Not even activity can arise out of nothing.

On the basis of the first part of this axiom, Hlatky argues that the original reality cannot have arisen out of nothing. On the basis of its second part, he argues that creation, which is only activity, cannot arise out of nothing: there must be an unchangeable thing – the original reality, the Being – behind it.

From this basic axiom follows the next:

That which exists, that which is a real, existent, permanent, and not illusory, something, can never change, become some other thing, or cease to exist, that is, become nothing.*

On the basis of this axiom, Hlatky argues for the unchangeability of the original reality that God is and of which we are parts. Creation, on the other hand, as constant activity, has nothing unchangeable within it.

From these two axioms follows the next:

It is impossible, even for God, to create anything other than activity.

A further axiom, which relates to the idea of consciousness*, and which I have already referred to, is:

Only a conscious, living being who is conscious of its own existence can be active out of itself and thus be an original cause of its activity.

This last axiom combined with the main axiom leads to the further axiom:

Only a living something, body, object conscious of itself and existing unchangeably can be the unchangeable, original cause of activity.

If these axioms – these self-evident statements or basic premises for practical and philosophical thinking – are accepted, then we can argue from them to Hlatky's view that only something existent, conscious and active can be the cause of the activity that is creation.

So creation in Hlatky's view is not a permanent reality. It is only seemingly permanent, existent. It is just activity – what he calls 'abstract'*. In his hypothesis only the original reality, God's Being, is existent – what he calls 'concrete'*. [The discussion of the terms 'abstract' and 'concrete' is taken up in Dialogue 1.] Everything that we interpret with our senses, within creation, as an existent reality is, in fact, simultaneously constructed and destroyed by Nature. Our senses, too, are created and destroyed by Nature.

Hlatky points out that we also know from science that what we see as matter is not matter, that is, not existence in the true sense. He suggests, however, that if we accept the axioms to which he draws our attention, then logically there must be a real existence behind all visible matter, but one that we cannot experience with our senses. This existence is living, that is, it is active, but it can only move, it can only express itself, in the form of vibrations, which, Hlatky suggests – in line with modern physics and also with ancient traditions – is the basis of all other movement in the visible creation. Visible matter, which gives us a distance-based*, external perspective on reality, is created by these vibrations for our senses, so that we can understand the necessity of presupposing an original, invisible existence – the Being – as the original cause behind it.

In Hlatky's view, the whole creation should be regarded as having God's consciousness behind it – rather than as being basically dead and only living and becoming conscious on the Earth's surface, as is the general view. He sees God, therefore, as having an immediate, direct relationship to creation – that is, not as someone or something that created creation outside himself, as we humans create things outside ourselves. If God is seen in the way he is suggesting, Hlatky reasons that humans must function in relation to God, the whole, in a similar way to how the individual cells of our own body function in relation to our own body as a whole. In contrast to our body-cells, however, we have the possibility of understanding the whole, God, and of understanding ourselves in relation to the whole.

Hlatky regards this need to understand the cause and meaning of the visible reality as a basic need of humans. He views it as much more important than the existential* needs connected with our created bodies – even though we can temporarily ignore it, because it is not inescapable in the same way that the existential, bodily needs are inescapable.

The question of the original cause of creation was seen historically – as it is also seen by modern science – as two separate problems: *What is the origin of life, that is, of our own existence on Earth?* and *What is the origin of the whole surrounding reality, that is, of the Earth and of the universe?* Hlatky suggests that the two problems are the same problem. He thinks that if we accept the idea of a conscious, living being behind creation, viewed in the way he is suggesting – in other words, if we accept the idea that Nature is not basically impersonal and meaningless, as modern science would have us believe – then this offers a solution to the problem. He sees the universe as like a single, large arrangement of image-projections. He thinks that, instead of staring blindly at creation's ever-changing image, we can interpret it, if we are guided by the above axioms, and can understand the original, never-changing existence, the Being, and ourselves as original, conscious parts of that Being.

In Hlatky's view, there are two quite distinct forms of understanding. One is mechanical* understanding, which is based on touch, the sense that gives us the experience of matter and form*. The task of coping here on Earth requires us to be able to associate every function* that we experience in the surrounding reality with its correct form, e.g. sunshine with the sun, a bird's song with a bird, and so on. All our experiences start with the ability to experience, which is common to living beings and God. This common ability is in living beings bound by a nervous system to their experience of their own body. The absolute difference between God's experience and the experience of the different species – which also varies between the different species – is that God's experience is bound to the non-created reality and to his need to create.

The other form of understanding is philosophy*, and its goal is to make a total synthesis of all our experiences, with the aim of understanding ourselves and everything else in our visible surroundings as parts in an invisible whole. This requires us to reflect on our everyday experience – but as it actually is, and not in the purely language-based*, theoretical ways in which we have generally been taught to think about it. Hlatky argues that such understanding is human beings' specific goal, in which case the objective* position of standing outside things, of viewing reality as if we were outsiders, is inappropriate. We can be aware* of the visible reality outside us, but we must remember that we are connected to creation through a body, so we must take our consciousness of our body into account too.

Hlatky makes the point that in the past the great world religions tried in vain to help people place their disparate objective and subjective knowledge in the context of larger unitary systems of thought. But this was done in an authoritarian way, so gradually people began to react against it. Nowadays each person tries to fit their jigsaw-pieces together in their own way. It can be said, with a certain exaggeration, that we now have over five billion religions rather than a few great ones. So the problem is not so much the enmity between the great religions. Rather it is that each person struggles independently to make their own sense of life.

This has led to a catastrophic loss of community. That is why, Hlatky believes, we have such a strong need these days for a philosophical understanding of the original cause, so that we can bring our objective and subjective knowledge about creation together. The need for such a philosophical understanding has been suppressed throughout history – because it can be suppressed without existential* consequences for our own lives, though not without consequences for our relationships with other people and for the environment in general. Hlatky thinks that we can answer the question of the original cause in a way that satisfies our need for a common understanding. If we were able to find it logical that even God has the need to be understood as like, Hlatky thinks that this would make it clear for us in what way we are like God, and it would remind us that we, too, have the same basic need.

For Hlatky, logical* thinking starts with knowing the need behind an activity – in the case of God's activity, the whole creation – so that we can check whether the activity is understandable as a consequence of the need, that is, whether the activity is purposeful or not. [For elaboration of this point, see Dialogue 4, 'Philosophical logic', p.133.] Hlatky believes that if the original cause can be understood logically in this way, it will not be so easy for the need for non-authoritarian, logical understanding to be suppressed in our philosophical discussions of the original cause. And he sees the common need to understand logically and to be understood on a logical basis as the key to a feeling of community and love.

To set Hlatky's views briefly in historical context, I quote him:

'Greek philosophy was the first public attempt to use scientific thinking to anchor religion. But after the full emergence of Christianity, the Church took control of philosophy, and it did not become a public matter again until the twelfth century when the first university was founded. The Church was then forced to argue the background of Christian belief. In the absence of logical argument, it decided to limit the field of philosophy by valuing a particular form of human experience, 'revelation', as absolutely true perception not requiring the support of logical reason.

'In the sixteenth century rationalist scientists, such as Galileo, Kepler and Francis Bacon, laid the foundation for modern science by dividing up everyday experiences of reality into the non-measurable (subjective) and the measurable (objective). Only the measurable was regarded as scientific. The subjective – that is, the basic part of our experience – then fell outside the scope of science. 'Warmth', for instance, was seen at that time as an example of subjective* experience: before the thermometer was invented, warmth could not be measured objectively.

'The more techniques were developed, the more confidence in exact, objective science grew. When Wöhler succeeded in creating an organic substance, urea, out of inorganic components, this was interpreted as scientific proof of atheism and of the idea that life is a mechanical process driven by necessity and chance.[1]

'Gradually more of the subjective has become measurable and has been transferred to objective science. But at the same time there has been a growing realization that there must be a fundamental mistake in this view. My hypothesis is an attempt to correct this fundamental mistake without falling into irrational, and therefore authoritarian, alternatives.'

---

[1] In 1828 Friedrich Wöhler synthesized organic urea out of inorganic ammonium cyanate. The discovery that there is no boundary between inorganic, 'dead', and organic, 'living', matter, was taken as proof of the mechanistic* nature of the universe and as an argument against the existence of God. For further discussion, see particularly Dialogue 2, 'The need of consciousness: undivided love', p.68.

Chapter 2

Dialogues

Stefan Hlatky and Philip Booth

Dialogue 1

EXISTENCE, ACTIVITY AND THE ORIGINAL CAUSE

The Being and consciousness

Philip: The first chapter, 'Understanding reality: a basic human need', is my attempt to summarize your views. In later chapters we have other articles written by you, in which you present your ideas more fully. Where do you think we should start with these dialogues*?

Stefan: I think we should start with the concepts of 'the Being' and 'consciousness'. These are the two most difficult concepts to understand, and they lead to the most confusion.

P: They are used differently by different traditions, aren't they? Could you define how you use them?

S: By 'the Being' I mean the original, non-created, unitary, unchangeable, concrete and conscious reality that I hypothesize as being behind the changeable reality that we experience. The changeable reality I view as 'creation', since I view it as created by the power of the whole non-created, conscious Being – which I call 'God'.

P: Sometimes you use the term 'relative Being' to refer to creation.

S: Yes, in which case the non-created Being is 'the original Being', or 'the absolute Being'.

P: And your definition of consciousness?

S: 'Consciousness' I view as the absolute quality* of the original Being, and the only quality that we – whom I view as original parts of the Being – can experience. Consciousness is primarily the ability to experience, interpreted as an ability in itself, independent of that which we experience. It is also, but secondarily, the ability to act purposefully in response to what we experience – which requires a body to act with, and, for the original parts who act in creation with a created body, also memory of earlier experiences and thinking.

P: We will need to come back to your idea of consciousness, which is radically different from the modern idea of consciousness...

S: Yes, the modern idea is linked to the secondary ability of consciousness, the ability to act on the basis of memory-based thinking.

P: ...but for the moment I would like to understand your idea of the Being. I know that in your conversations over the years, you have found your concept of it a difficult one for people to grasp. Why do you think that is?

Concrete vs abstract, existence vs activity

S: I think it is because historically – that is, in the theological traditions, Judaism, Christianity and Islam, and in the pantheistic and pantheistic-like traditions, Hinduism, Buddhism, Taoism and Confucianism – concepts of the Being have usually been based on our experience in creation, rather than on philosophical reflection* on that experience. Confusion has arisen from the fact that we can have two mutually exclusive experiences of creation: the everyday experience and the so-called transcendental, or, as it is also called, the mystical, experience, which is available through the turning of our awareness within. The confusion has been caused by the fact that the transcendental experience has been interpreted by every tradition, not as experience of another level of creation, but as experience of the non-created, original Being. This 'original Being' has then been interpreted as the cause of 'creation' – with 'creation', in this view, restricted solely to what we experience in our everyday lives.

Because in the transcendental experience there is no experience of solid objects, as there is in our everyday experience, this original Being was considered to be 'abstract'. The everyday experience – 'creation' in their view – was considered by contrast to be 'concrete'.

P: Whereas in your view the whole original Being is concrete, and is the cause of the *whole* creation, both of what can be experienced transcendentally and of our everyday experience?

S: Yes. Their 'original Being' – what I think of simply as what constitutes the transcendental experience of creation – is, seen mechanically, in my view only the created precondition for our everyday experience of creation. The original Being, as I construe it, is both the conscious – that is, the purposeful – and the mechanical cause of the whole creation – that is, of the reality that it is possible to experience either transcendentally or in an everyday way. In contrast, it must be impossible to have an experience in creation of both the original reality and the created reality mixed together at the same time. Creation has to substitute for its cause.

P: So this question of whether the original Being is concrete or abstract is a central one.

S: One of the most central, because there is a lot of confusion with the words 'concrete' and 'abstract', both in philosophy – which has to do with the question of the whole reality's identity* – and in psychology – which has to do with the question of the human being's identity. Everyday experience of creation is generally regarded as based on matter, and matter is generally interpreted as something 'concrete' – in spite of the fact that it is changeable, and so can't fundamentally be concrete. This so-called 'concrete', 'existent' matter is then seen as expressing innumerable activities, which are interpreted as qualities or properties of different forms of matter, such as light, sound, copper, and so on, or even life – whereas in fact these are, along with all forms of matter, different forms of activity that exist only in creation. And this visible and tangible matter is regarded as being experienced in different densities, on a continuum from solid, to liquid, to gaseous, and finally it is imagined as 'abstract'. This last, 'abstract', is generally used to describe a quality or property that we imagine neither as an activity nor as the quality of something concrete – but rather as an existent thing in itself, though an existent thing that we can't experience with our senses. In philosophy and psychology, 'spirit' and 'soul' are the most important examples of what are generally considered to be such 'abstract' existent things.

P: So, in contrast to your view, theories of the Being have usually seen the Being as 'abstract', based on this interpretation of the everyday and transcendental experiences of creation?

S: Yes, with only one exception, and that relates to the other typically human way of investigating the background of creation.

I am referring to the investigation that even children undertake, based on the dissection of every tangible part of creation. In contrast to mystical or transcendental or spiritual science, it is called matter-based science – or simply science – because it is a straightforward extension of the knowledge or science that everybody has, based on light and on tangible matter. This tangible matter is experienced and interpreted as the opposite of the intangible, 'the intangible' being the absence of resistance, the 'experience' of which gives rise to the feeling of emptiness. In relation to the total visible manifold*, this boundless emptiness is spontaneously interpreted via language as an 'abstract', existent whole, an endless, empty space.

P: What is your interpretation of this 'empty space'?

S: The impression of empty space is necessary because the distanceless, coherent, continuous original reality can't be present in our experience at the same time as the distance-based perspective on creation. It is the same practical problem we have in being unable to sleep, dream, meditate and be present in our daily activities all at the same time. If the necessity for the impression of empty space is not philosophically understood this way, but instead is interpreted in a spontaneous, unconsidered way, then the final aim of the external investigation of creation – that is, going behind the surface of creation by dissecting things, rather than by meditation – becomes to find the original cause of all changeability in a definitively resistant part behind all the destructible parts.

This was the aim before Democritus, and not just after him. All that Democritus did was to give a name to such indestructible parts – atoms – and to create the first known philosophical tradition based on the idea of mechanical necessity. This was expressed in his theory by a combination of invisible atoms, invisible empty space and an original cosmic whirl, which were seen as the mechanical origin of all movement. The practical problem before the invention of the microscope and telescope was that this matter-based investigation, which had been realized since time immemorial, couldn't verify the spontaneous, general belief in non-created, indestructible, concrete parts, because it ran up against the natural limits of the senses.

It has been easy, therefore – also since time immemorial – to move the philosophical question of the original cause from the tradition of 'concrete', matter-based science to one of the other contradictory, disunited traditions based on the impression of an intangible, non-concrete reality only visible to a mystical inner sight. This reality can't be compared with what matter-based science investigates. As I've said, it was interpreted as the original background to the whole creation – but in different, incompatible ways. Theology introduced the idea of a non-created reality, God, but seeing God as a part, a participant, a perfect outsider in this original reality – which they called Heaven. And pantheism operated without the idea of a non-created reality, considering there to be only developable parts, developable outsiders.

P: You mentioned the invention of the microscope and telescope. Are you saying that the question of the original cause was moved from these other traditions back to our matter-based science after the invention of these means for expanding the natural limits of the senses of sight and touch?

S: Yes, that's what I mean. The start of modern thinking is generally related to Copernicus. But he only corrected an old mistake made by Ptolemy. The first attempt to move back to our everyday experience was made by the Greek philosophers, but they couldn't free themselves from the other traditions. Since the beginning of the seventeenth century, everybody has been engaged in the expansion of these two senses – sight and touch – and in the development of a new technology based on this expansion. The philosophical problem nowadays is that the spontaneous, original aim of discovering Democritus' atoms has been changed to the theory of energy and quanta, mathematically formulated as an ambivalent relation between matter and movement – in place of matter and empty space, and without Democritus' hypothesis of a cosmic whirl.

P: Do you mean that the theory of quanta and energy is a reversion to pantheism?

S: Yes, the idea that everything is in flux. But pantheism is founded on the transcendental experience of creation – rather than, as in external science, on the experience of the sense-impression of empty space and matter. Pantheism sees the transcendental experience as an 'abstract', intangible original of the tangible, 'concrete' matter that constitutes our everyday experience of creation. It interprets it as a non-created, 'abstract', but existent, potency that is active out of itself – similar to Einstein's 'energy' – and as the original Being – similar to the way scientists started seeing energy as indestructible from about 1840 onwards, when Mayer defined the first principle of thermodynamics. In contrast to Einstein's energy, however, pantheism's original Being, its original endless flow, is ruled not only by impersonal mechanical laws, but also by some of its developable parts. These developable parts, these gods in the making, are governed by the impersonal mechanical laws and, in relation to each other, also by ethical laws.

Science introduced the idea of the Big Bang as the origin of space, matter and time, instead of Democritus' whirl, which was in relation to *existent* space, matter and time.

P: Whereas your interpretation of the so-called original, 'abstract' reality...?

S: In my view, everything in creation is activity. That means that the whole creation – as it is experienced both concretely and transcendentally – with its constructive and destructive changeability, is abstract: it can't exist in itself, without something that is active, something that expresses the movement that creation is.

P: So your view is radically different from all three views: the pantheistic, the monotheistic and that of modern science?

S: Yes. In my view, it is the original Being, and not creation, that is concrete. The original Being is existence, it is existent, in the sense of unchangeable. It doesn't even change as a result of its activity, creation. This is in contrast to activity, which is changeable and which does not in itself have an existence, that is, it does not exist in the sense of 'exist unchangeably'. In my view, the word 'abstract' should be understood as referring only to activity – that which is going on, and which gives rise to our idea of changeability, temporariness and time. So creation, the relative Being, is in my terms abstract, because it is only activity – whether we are talking about our everyday experience of it or the transcendental experience of it. There is nothing truly concrete in it. Nothing in it has in itself a concrete, unchangeable background, nothing remains recognizably the same, everything changes all the time.

Activity can't be separated from the concrete, from existence. It should, therefore, always be seen as relative to, that is, as caused by, something concrete, something unchangeable, something absolute. The original reality can't change, develop, be more or less, produce or reproduce itself, become something else over time – otherwise we would not be able to have a basis, a start, for our understanding.

P: So where does the idea of the Being come from?

S: Like all language-based human ideas, it comes to us through language. It's up to us whether we use such ideas or not, or how we use them. So the phrase 'the Being' was either used or not used by people responsible for tradition. In German now, for example, 'das Sein' is used more, and is therefore more familiar, than 'the Being' in English. And the term can be used in different ways. It means 'that which exists', 'what is'. But even then, it can be used to refer to both objects and activities that 'exist' within creation as a meaningful* illusion for our senses.

P: The illusion being that objects appear permanent?

S: Yes... the impression that objects, bodies, existent things give that they are objects, bodies, existent things. That is the illusion – the impression they give of being permanent, non-active, still, showing the opposite of movement, the opposite of activity. That is the illusion – because creation is activity, creation is in flux.

P: Which brings us back to the distinction between concrete existence and abstract activity again – which I know is an important distinction for you.

S: Yes, it's quite crucial. In my interpretation, I distinguish existence – an existent object or matter or mass – from its ongoing activity. It is important, however, to understand philosophically the relationship between existence and activity or movement. It is an axiom, it is self-evident, that activity can't exist by itself, but only as the activity of something existent. But because activity can begin, can exist for perception as long as it goes on, and can end, but is not tangible in itself, activity is relative to, is caused by existence. In contrast, existence can never be relative to, can never be caused by activity. So activity is all that can ever be created. In other words, something existent cannot arise out of activity.

And modern physics has confirmed that creation is only activity, after Einstein's introduction of the idea that energy is the origin of what we experience in creation as matter. This reality that we experience day to day – as living bodies and objects of different densities – is only activity.

P: So are these examples of the way you use the axioms that I referred to in the first chapter to argue your hypothesis?

S: Yes, they are. I argue that science has shown that the whole creation is activity, and I argue for the belief that the cause of creation must be existent on the basis of the axiom that activity in itself cannot be a cause, and so cannot be the cause of creation. That's why I say that the reality that we experience transcendentally cannot be the original cause of our everyday reality, but can only be its 'cause' in the same way that the manifold appears to be the cause of its own interaction.

I argue that the original cause must also be conscious on the basis of another axiom: that existence can create activity only if existence is conscious. It is our experience in creation that only conscious beings are capable of originating activity.

P: Which means that the conscious beings in creation must be existent. Yet you have said that creation is only activity.

S: It is the created bodies of the conscious beings that are only activity. The non-created conscious part behind the body is existent. This original, existent, conscious part of God's Being becomes connected to a body in creation. This is my view.

P: So, reiterating: the Being is concrete existence, whereas creation is activity, and, therefore, intangible in itself. So creation is abstract, the opposite to concrete.

S: Yes. We experience creation, either in an everyday way or transcendentally, and creation is activity. What is confusing for us is that we don't experience the concrete, existent source of creation: the whole conscious Being of the creator. We don't experience it because we can't experience a whole that we are parts of, that we are inside. We can't have the relation to the whole that activity, movement in creation, allows us to have to creation.

P: And we must be inside it, if it is the whole?

S: Yes. So only the whole can experience and use the Being as a whole, as its own existence.

P: If we agree then with the axioms you are proposing, the activity that is creation can't be understood on its own. There has to be an existent, conscious being that is its source. But isn't it also confusing that in our everyday lives we don't actually *experience* creation as activity?

S: Yes, without philosophy, it can be confusing. We *experience* creation starting from a manifold that seems to our senses to be existent. But if we *understand*, philosophically, that the manifold, the diversity*, the multiplicity*, is not existent in a real sense – which means that creation is only activity – the confusion falls away.

P: So for you the Being and existence are the same thing?

S: Yes. And the Being or existence is not changeable. It has the same identity all the time. In contrast, activity is ever-changing: it has no identity in itself.

P: And creation goes on inside the Being, in your view?

S: Yes. Because creation is activity, and activity can't be separated from the thing that is active. And if the thing that is active is the whole, then the activity must be going on inside the whole.

P: Your usage of the word 'abstract' to describe activity is unusual, nonetheless, isn't it?

S: Yes, it is, but I think that the general usage is illogical. Generally, 'abstract' is considered either the opposite of 'concrete' or the alternative to it.

When 'abstract' is used as the *opposite* of concrete, it means 'the absence of matter'. Then 'abstract' is just another term for 'nothing', 'the absence of everything' – both the absence of activity and the absence of existence. This is the confusing idea of 'empty space'.

When 'abstract' is used as the *alternative* to concrete, it creates another confusion, due to the fact that we have no unequivocal experience of the concrete – because of creation being basically activity. As I have said, 'concrete' is regarded as being experienced as solid, liquid or gaseous. Taking this further, 'abstract' is regarded as something finer than gaseous: as neither a solid nor a medium, but as between 'something' and 'nothing', as an *existent* yet *immaterial* something – a contradiction in terms, in my view. Because this notion of 'abstract' is illogical, it couldn't be discussed.

P: You mean that because it is illogical, it couldn't be rationally discussed so that people could agree upon it? It just had to be asserted?

S: Yes. That's why the claim, made by both the pantheist and the theological traditions, that the original cause is abstract – in the case of pantheism, an abstract original reality, in the case of theology, an abstract God in a community with abstract beings – had to be upheld in an authoritarian way. It is no surprise then that priests say that their abstract God is beyond human understanding, and the pantheists that their transcendental experience – which, as I've said, they interpret as experience of an abstract original reality – is beyond description.

P: But – if I can just be clear about this – you use the word 'abstract' as a general term to describe every activity. Are thinking, remembering and imagining, for example, 'abstract'?

S: Yes, because they are activity. The whole creation, in my view, is abstract. It is only to our senses that it appears to be concrete, as a temporarily existent, meaningful activity intended to create for us the illusion of permanence – because we couldn't experience it as only activity. In my view, only the non-created, original Being, including the parts, is concrete. So 'abstract' also means 'created' – with reference to creation, as a meaningful activity created for our created senses by the concrete, non-created Being.

Science – inner and outer

P: I would like to discuss other traditions more now, because ideas about the Being, God and creation are there in different forms in different religions, and have a long history.

S: Yes. People have grappled with these ideas throughout history in their efforts to explain the whole reality – which means explaining the whole of causality, how everything is caused. The tradition of modern science has tried to explain the whole reality, too, though in the beginning it consciously restricted itself to mechanical causality and left aside the problem of life and the question of why creation came about. Its original aim – which became actual after the construction of the microscope in 1590 and the telescope in 1609 – was to use Democritus' theory of mechanical necessity to explain the mechanical construction of the whole visible reality behind the mystery of life on Earth.

P: So at its inception, modern science didn't seek to explain the mystery of life, only the background of the mechanical laws in the whole universe?

S: Yes, the mystery of life was left to the Church – at least at that time.

P: How would you characterize the main differences between the approach taken by modern science and the explanations of the pantheist and theological traditions?

S: With modern science, the idea arose throughout Europe that it is possible empirically to discover the mechanical background of everyday reality completely and to describe it precisely with the language of mathematics. After the construction of the microscope and telescope, external investigation of the background of everyday reality was no longer restricted by the natural limit of the human senses. For the first time in history we could go beyond that limit and, with the help of technical* instruments, extend the development of externally-orientated, or extraspective, mechanical science. Objective science – as it then came to be called – had always been developed before then, but only up to the limit of the senses. Before then inner, introspective science – the traditions whose research methods were based on meditation – was always regarded as the real science. That was because of its claim to be able to experience directly the original background of everyday reality, through transcendental experience. In other words, it already claimed to be able to go behind the surface things that the unaided human eye could investigate. This inner, introspective science was continuously developed, in every generation, by initiates.

It was always a problem, however, that it is impossible to communicate the experiences generated by introspection in everyday language – by which I mean the language that we use to communicate our common, everyday experience of reality. So the 'inner scientists' were forced to develop a special language, which others regarded as mystical. When the new or modern science began its development, more and more investigatory technology was invented. The more that was invented, the further it was possible to see beyond the natural limit of the senses. So extraspective science hoped to be able to explain the whole of reality in this way, and it hoped that its precise, mathematical language could replace the mystical jargon of introspective science.

P: But modern science hasn't achieved its aim of explaining the whole of reality, has it?

S: No – in spite of its continuous growth and development. It hasn't been able to find the origin of matter, nor the origin of life, nor the origin of the Big Bang. But in my view, introspective science hasn't achieved its aim of explaining the whole of reality either. Unlike modern science, however, it believes it has. As I have said, in my view, the reality to which the inner scientists gain experiential access 'transcendentally' is not the original reality, but another part, an earlier, more original, state, of creation – one that is, seen mechanically, the precondition for our meaningfully realized part of creation, but not its original cause. In my conception, the original cause of both parts – of the transcendental part and of the part of creation we experience in our everyday consciousness – is the unchangeable, original reality: the Being.

P: What about those people who say that they 'meet God'? Isn't that rather similar to those who believe they have experiential access to the original reality?

S: Yes, it is. Theologians and religious people – those who believe in one God – say we can 'meet God'. They claim he can be met in Heaven, of course, but also even while we are still on Earth, in so-called mystical experiences. I view this as simply another interpretation of the transcendental experience of creation.

Many people say 'I have met God'. What I say to such people is: 'If you really believe that we are participating in God's creation, everybody meets God all the time' – if, that is, you believe in God in the way I am suggesting: as the whole inside which we live, as the Being of which we are parts. Obviously, if you don't have this belief – as theologians and religious people don't – then all you think you are meeting when you meet creation is this general picture of the multiplicity or manifold that creation is, without God directly behind it.

P: Well, you don't believe we really meet God directly in creation, do you? Isn't it that you see creation as God's expression, so that we meet God indirectly through creation?

S: Yes, yes. And we meet each other indirectly too, mediated by the same creation. We meet God as the whole, the whole Being, indirectly through the whole creation, and we meet each other as parts of the Being indirectly through created human bodies. I think that if we want to have a proper understanding of what 'meeting God' and what meeting each other means, we have to imagine my conception of the Being – the unchangeably existing reality, God's 'body', behind creation – and to regard that Being as the kind of whole we find in creation in every living body, that is, a whole in which there is a constant, distanceless relation between the whole and its parts.

Theology and pantheism: abstract original causes

P: You talked earlier about the European development of extraspective science. But if we look globally, what was going on in parallel in the rest of the world?

S: The situation was the same in the rest of the world as it had been in Europe before the invention of the microscope and telescope. People everywhere have always tried to develop an understanding of the whole reality. And there have always been two different ideas of the whole reality.

One is the belief in a non-created, 'unbegotten' creator: God. That view is some form of theology. In theology, our everyday reality is seen as 'creation' and as starting from one existent, that is, concrete source, but considered 'concrete' in an 'abstract' form – with again this contradiction in terms.

P: Whereas God is really concrete, in your view?

S: Yes, though that is not the only difference from my view, as I am sure we will come on to.

The alternative to theology has been the belief that there is no creator, and therefore no 'creation', but only activity. This activity has never started, but it has been and is endlessly ongoing, and it is governed by impersonal laws. This view is some form of pantheism. In pantheism, both the original reality or Being, out of which our everyday reality is fashioned, and our everyday reality itself, are interpreted as abstract. Within this view, created, born, 'divine' human beings have to construct their own meanings, and a corresponding social order, out of the basically meaningless activity that is determined only by the impersonal laws.

Variations and combinations of these two contrasting theories – the theological and the pantheistic – have been developed throughout history.

P: I think this is an important point, because one rarely finds a pure form of either belief these days: there are many theologians who have pantheistic elements in their beliefs, and many pantheists who talk about God.

S: Yes, this is so. But I think it makes it all the more important to be clear about what you call the 'pure forms', so as to be able to contrast them in a clear way with my hypothesis.

P: Does your idea of a concrete, conscious Being that is the starting-point of creation represent the main difference from these historical ideas?

S: Yes. Historically, the original cause was interpreted in every tradition as abstract. In theology, God is seen as conscious and existent, but existent in an abstract way rather than in a concrete way. In pantheism, the Being is seen as impersonal and basically non-conscious and abstract, but out of this Being consciousness is seen as being able to emerge and develop further. The contrast I am making – between those views of the original cause and my view of a conscious, really concrete Being as the original cause – has never been made in history in the way I am making it.

P: But if we accept the axiom you put forward earlier – that activity can be caused only by something existent, something concrete – these ideas of an abstract original cause can't logically explain the activity of creation. Theology's God is existent yet abstract; and pantheism says activity is existent, in other words, the abstract is concrete. How did they get round this problem?

S: Because of the illogicality of their views, they both had to create the idea of a potential power – which is what the term 'potential energy' means – a sort of dormant force or potentiality, a pre-existing activity that is for the moment non-active, but which can start to be active. In theology, this is regarded as an undetermined *living* potentiality, God. In pantheism, it is regarded as a *non-conscious* potentiality determined by impersonal laws, and is interpreted as different interacting, abstract 'elements' representing different types of non-conscious potentiality. In theology, God is regarded as almighty. That means he has all power and his power is not ruled or bound by anything. In pantheism, the elements or powers were seen as being controlled objectively by pre-existing, impersonal physical laws, and in human societies, by pre-existing, impersonal ethics* and moral laws.

P: Today we are familiar with the idea that impersonal, physical laws for objects can pre-exist, without any originator of them, because we have such an idea in modern science. Pantheism's idea of impersonal, pre-existing ethics and moral laws for subjects is less familiar, at least in the West.

S: It was needed because all the old traditions – unlike modern science – also had responsibility for organizing people in society. They couldn't, therefore, avoid having moral laws, in order to control people's behaviour. But the pantheists couldn't do what the theologians, with their idea of God, could do and say that God was the origin of those moral laws. The pantheists had to say that the moral laws just pre-existed in the same way that the objective laws pre-existed.

P: You say that in the theological view God was seen as abstract, but most people's idea of God is very concrete. Isn't God also referred to – in the Bible, at least – as a person whom people meet, so that the image of him there is of something concrete?

S: Yes, but you use 'concrete' there in terms of our experience of the 'concrete' in creation, not in my sense of a non-created existence. That idea leads to all these human images of God. Children – before they are given the ideas of 'abstract' and 'death' – always imagine God as something 'concrete'. But they imagine him as another part like themselves or anybody else, only with a different external appearance. But they don't imagine him as the only whole. In other words, they imagine him in the way we experience parts as 'concrete' wholes in creation. They imagine him as a 'concrete', if absent, being – somewhat similar to their parents, with the difference that God cares for everybody.

P: But you think that we need to distinguish between what children might think and what the theological traditions themselves say?

S: Yes. The theological traditions actually consider God to be abstract in some concrete, existent way. They talk about him as a basically spiritual being, in the way that we talk about humans and angels as spiritual beings. I think it is this idea of God as 'abstractly existent' that forces those who hold the idea to say that God is beyond human understanding.

Can God be understood?

P: Whereas you think God can be understood?

S: Yes. I think that it is their particular idea of God as concrete, existent, in an abstract way and as also undetermined that is not understandable, for several reasons. The first is that we can't imagine a living being that is abstract – because all the living beings that we experience manifest a meaningful relationship between a visible, living whole and its invisible parts. The second is that we can't imagine that anything abstract – that is, a thing that is not in any way concrete

– has power. And the third is that we can't understand an existence that has a free, arbitrary will to act – that is, whose will to act is not determined or constrained by a need and the need to satisfy that need practically. Such an existence could change its mind at any moment.

P: So we couldn't count on its purpose remaining the same?

S: That's right. I think that when children are told that God is an almighty spirit and beyond human understanding, they lose their first belief in him as something real, without being given the correct idea of 'concrete' that I mean: that is, of an unchangeable existence. Children are also taught that not only God but also human beings are spiritual beings – that is, they are not just a body, but that they are basically a spirit and have an imperfect, developable soul. God is then imagined as a part, like other human beings, and not as the whole – but a part whom, if so-called mystical experiences are excluded, we can only meet in Heaven.

P: Let me be clear. You think that children are very open to your suggestion that God is a really concrete whole, but because they are told that God is an almighty spirit, they either give up their belief in God as 'concrete' and think of him as some kind of ghost, or they hold on to an irrational idea of him as an outwardly 'concrete' – in the mistaken sense of 'concrete' – basically spiritual part, whom it might be possible to meet from the outside?

S: Yes. And that goes with the idea they are given that the whole creation is 'concrete' and that we are created as 'concrete', spiritual beings who are different from one another – as opposed to my idea that we are similar conscious parts of the original, non-created Being. What they are taught about us being created in this way contradicts the axiom that only activity can be created.

P: There is also the idea that humans, though created, are at the same time permanent, existent, because it is believed that we live on, in some spiritual, 'abstract' form, after our death.

S: Yes. It's always the same mistake: because we interpret creation illogically as concrete, we have to make, in language, irrational ideas as to what the reality behind creation is.

P: And you think the idea of an almighty God is untenable?

S: Unconstrained by some need, the almighty God of the theological traditions can't be a starting-point for rational thinking. But he can easily be a starting-point for irrational imaginings, leading to anxiety.

P: ...such as that God is angry with us, punishes us, and has all the intentions that we humans can have, that he could destroy me or the world whenever he fancied?

S: Yes, those would be examples. In my view, God is concrete – which means he can be the personal originator of activity. As a whole – the whole Being – he has all power, but that power means power over himself, over his own existence, and it is bound by the need for love, which is the need to be understood by the parts of his own existence.

P: What makes you think God needs to be loved?

S: Because he is a conscious being, and every conscious being needs company, needs to be understood as a precondition for being loved. This is another axiom. Nobody wants to be hated or unnoticed.

P: So you think that the idea of God having that need makes God understandable?

S: Yes. In my view, not only God, but also creation *can* be understood, *can* be thought about rationally – if, that is, one thinks of God as concrete, as the invisible, non-created, original, conscious whole, and of ourselves as invisible, non-created, original, conscious parts of this invisible whole; and if we also think of God's power as bound by the need for love; and, finally, if we think of God as having created creation so as to fulfil his need to be loved by his conscious parts.

P: Why, in your view, does he need to create creation in order to fulfil his need for love?

S: Because in the Being, the parts can't be conscious of God, because of the original distanceless relation that they have to him in the Being. Through creation God gives us the experience of distance, and an indirect perspective on the whole, on himself. Without the experience of creation, we couldn't be conscious of God.

P: Would you say that children lose interest in the question of why God creates, and in other questions about God, too, because they don't get a logical answer on this point of why God creates?

S: Yes. If you can't answer logically the question as to why God creates, you can't answer logically any other question about God.

Hlatky's view of God, the Being and creation

P: I think we need to hear more about your view of the relationship between God, the Being and creation.

S: God, in my view, *is* the Being. That is, the Being is his non-created 'body' – though obviously not the kind of body that we have in creation, with organs and so on. Logically, as a conscious being he must have an immediate, subjective relation to the Being, similar to how we generally experience our own created body, that is, without distance. But God can't get distance from the Being, he can't get free of it, in the way we can become free from our created body – at night, or when we die, or in some exceptional situations such as near-death experiences or meditative states. He is primarily dependent on the Being, which he experiences as his own existence. That means practically that he experiences us and has the same feeling for each of us – undivided love* – as we are parts of his existence. As a conscious, living being, he must have the need, as we have, to be understood, as the necessary precondition for the full experience of love.

P: You have talked several times now about the need 'to be understood'. You don't mean that phrase in the way that modern psychology uses it, which involves understanding the particular peculiarities of a person, do you?

S: No. I mean quite specifically to be understood as like: as like us who are also conscious, living beings – and not as definitively unlike, so not as the almighty creator.

P: What difference does it make to understand God as like us or unlike us?

S: You can understand that somebody is unlike, but that 'understanding' is not the same as the understanding of somebody as like. The first gives rise to feelings of anxiety, or fascination, or admiration, or to feelings of inferiority or superiority. The second gives rise to the feeling of love. The question is: is it possible for us to understand God and each other as likes? There is a difference depending on whether we think of God as the whole and ourselves as parts, or whether we don't take this view. If we suppose that the whole has the same nature as the parts, then we have to regard God as having basically the same nature as we ourselves basically have, that is, the ability to experience, and the need to be understood by other conscious beings as like in this respect.

Having said that, there is, in my hypothesis, a categorical difference or unlikeness between God and the parts, and that is in respect of the ability to create: only the whole, with its unlimited potentiality, can give out, can create creation. But this definitive unlikeness is not alienating, because we can understand God's meaning with creation. Creation is not then foreign to us.

On the other hand, if we believe in God, but not as the whole with the need to be understood by its parts, then the only alternative is the theory that God is a mystical* part without relation to a whole, or a mystical whole without relation to parts, and in both cases alone, before creation, as a mystical being. He therefore creates other parts in order to have company. In that case, we don't regard God as basically being in an original, living relation to his parts, and as having the need to be understood, but as an independent, perfect, almighty, mystical existence, who basically has the ability to create anything, independently of any purpose – also out of nothing or out of his mystical self. With such a being we can never experience likeness. We can't experience likeness with each other either, because we don't then see ourselves as basically conscious, living, experiencing beings who have the need, in common with God and each other, to be understood as like.

The only alternative then is to see our ability to experience as our ability to create expression, either perfectly or imperfectly, without any other background than moral rules*, that is, without experiencing the common need for love as the practical background. This leads to the idea of development – towards some conception of perfection. Within theology, the development is moral development. Within non-theological – that is, pantheistic – views, it is the development of knowledge and creativity*, with the aim of becoming like God: independent, perfect, almighty. Either way, the idea that we can develop means that we cannot be like.

On such a view, we can only be like when our ability to develop has been fully developed, when our development is complete – in other words, when we are perfect.

P: So God wants us to understand him as like, and thereby love him?

S: Yes.

P: And to be understood comes first, because…

S: …you can't love something you don't understand. You can perhaps admire it, and you can certainly be afraid of it. But if it is alien to you, you can't love it. And because God is the whole reality, he has nothing outside himself, and can only be understood, therefore, by the conscious parts inside him. God has the need, therefore, to give out creation for the purpose of giving the parts the opportunity to understand their relation to him, the whole, and their relation to each other – both relations that never change. In this way, he is also, but only secondarily, dependent on creation. God's creation, God's activity, is determined by the purpose creation serves – so God can't be arbitrary in his activity, otherwise creation won't serve its purpose, it won't be perfect for its purpose.

Differences from theology

P: Your interpretation of the Being as God's existence, God's 'body', seems to me an important difference from other views.

S: Yes, it is the most important difference. Another difference is that, rather than saying, as the theologians do, that God creates out of 'nothing' or out of himself, I argue that he creates using the potentiality of the whole original reality, this Being. The original Being, including its parts, is the only thing that is concrete, non-created, unchangeable. Everything else is activity originating from this Being.

P: When you say God is creating 'using the potentiality of the whole original reality, this Being', how is this different from creating 'out of himself'?

S: Because in the theological view, the Being that God creates out of is interpreted as abstract. God is interpreted as creating out of his abstract self or out of nothing. In my view the Being is concrete. There is a concrete relation of the whole to its parts.

P: And the relationship between the Being and creation is different too in your interpretation and theology's – even though theology also has a God and talks of God's creation?

S: Yes. In the theological explanations the creator is not directly connected to his creation, as he is in my view. In theology, creation is seen as a separate, concrete Being or reality created by God, at 'the beginning of time', outside his own non-created, yet abstract – which, as I have said, is to my mind contradictory – Being. In my view, God, as the whole reality, is creating all the time, out of himself but within himself, in the same, permanent, ongoing way. And in my view he can't create anything concrete, only activity. So creation in my view gives the experience of a relative, abstract Being – relative to the original Being, that is – rather than the separate, concrete Being of the theological view.

Also, if God is a mystical, independent, abstract part outside creation, as theology suggests, then we can only think of God as we generally think of each other: as another conscious object or body not bound to any need, not even to the need to be understood. That is different from my idea of him as the whole, in the way I interpret 'whole' – that is, like the wholeness of a living body in creation, in which there is a constant, distanceless relation between the whole and its parts. In such an 'organic'* whole – as distinct from the totality* that an object in creation represents – the whole needs the parts, just as the parts need the whole, and the whole is forced to satisfy the needs of the parts, just as the parts are forced to satisfy the needs of the whole.

There is a crucial difference, however, between the organic wholes we find in creation and the living whole that God is: the non-created whole, God's Being, doesn't have any existential needs – that is, for light, warmth, air, water, food, movement, reproduction, and so on – because it is not a body like our bodies. God has only the need for mutual love, which is common to every conscious being, and which can't be satisfied by force, that is, from one side.

P: You said a moment ago that theologians see God as a 'conscious object'. This is an odd combination of words.

S: Yes, but both subjects and objects are represented in creation by a seemingly existent, objective totality that we call a body – in the case of subjects, a whole, where there is a meaningful relation between the whole and its parts, and in the case of objects, a sum of similar parts. An object is the idea of a body that has no needs and no experience of relation, either to itself – its own parts – or to its surroundings. Theologians see God as living, as conscious, but the idea of 'conscious object', rather than the idea of 'subject', does apply to their conception of God. In their view, God has no original relationship to any parts, nor to any surroundings. If God is outside his creation as a mystical, abstract something and creates us, as the theologians say, then God cannot experience us before creation in the way I suggest: as conscious parts of his conscious existence.

The whole and its parts

P: And in the theological view, God is without a body of any kind – since he is abstract or spiritual?

S: Yes. It is possible – if we take as the basis our relative ideas of solid, liquid and gaseous – to imagine an 'abstract' something, a spirit, that in practice represents a potential power. But then it is as a sum of similar parts, rather than as a whole in the way I am suggesting. And then you don't have the idea of something that experiences, receives and has needs – as I think of God. Instead you have the idea of something that only expresses: expresses power and has the power to do anything.

But the main point is that in theology God is seen as an independent part in itself without a surrounding whole – which doesn't make sense. What is a part without a whole? And yet he is also seen in theology as a whole, which makes him a whole part – if such a thing could exist – who is originally alone, without any relation, and without any other parts, conscious or material. That doesn't make sense either. What is a whole part or a whole without parts? In reality, a whole and its parts are indivisible.

P: You mean that the word 'whole' is used only of something that has 'parts', and the word 'part' implies a whole that the parts belong to, that the parts are part of?

S: Yes.

P: Don't we experience parts by themselves in creation?

S: But not – as we generally see them – independently either of the whole or of other parts. The parts in creation are dependent both on their own parts and on other parts in the surroundings. There are no real parts in creation. In creation – which is just activity, activity that doesn't reveal its origin – we can experience existence as separable, because of the experience of space. We can't experience the whole creation as a whole, only as 'parts' seemingly separated by space. But the 'parts' themselves we can only actually experience as wholes: we can never actually experience them as parts.

P: So, for instance, when we meet another human being, we experience them as a whole, and not as a part of the whole creation?

S: Yes. We can interpret them as a part of the whole creation, but our actual experience of them is that they are a whole. And if we try to find the original part of the original Being that the human being with its created body represents, we can't find it – because it must be impossible to find the non-created part as a part in itself separated from the non-created whole. In its origin the part is a part of the Being. But in creation we don't actually experience existence proper – that is, the original existence, the Being – either as a whole or as a part. In creation we experience only the quality of the original Being, which is the ability to experience – which is what makes the whole Being, including the parts, alive, active. But generally we believe we are experiencing existent parts in creation – though, as I've said, if we think about it properly, this is an illusion, since nothing in creation is existent, that is, unchangeable.

P: But God, on the theological view, is alone?

S: Yes, because the theologians don't see God's Being as a living whole which has a relation to its living parts. They see God as only a part without any relation. So then he has to create parts, in order not to be alone. But as soon as he is seen as creating parts, he himself becomes a non-created, 'eternal' part, among other created parts. In theology, these other parts are imperfect, developable and mortal. Thus, according to this theory, God made imperfect parts who have to become perfect parts like God. This idea gave rise to the problem of theodicy: *Why does a perfect, almighty being create imperfection?*

P: And it is a further difference in your view that, as you said earlier, you do not think God creates us?

S: That's right. In my view, he creates only our bodies, and we, as conscious parts with the ability to experience, are, like God, non-created.

P: Why do you think that?

S: Because the hypothesis that we are original, non-created parts of God is the only alternative to the hypothesis that God created us. And, from my point of view, it makes God's need and purpose behind creation understandable. It also makes the whole creation understandable for us – because it's only possible to understand an activity if we understand its purpose. [For discussion of this point, see Dialogue 4, 'Philosophical logic', p.133.]

P: Do both theology and you see God as eternal?

S: Yes, but 'eternal' is a time-based concept. In theological explanations, creation, as a separate Being, was made in time – in a single period of seven days. Since then it has been running outside God, in time, as our creation. For me, creation occurs inside God's Being, where time is not relevant, because time implies 'changing', and according to my view, neither the Being nor the meaning of creation ever changes.

P: I am confused. Do you mean that if the Being didn't change, but God's purpose with creation did, that would give rise to an experience of time?

S: No. The experience of time derives from our experience of ongoing activity – in other words, from our experience of certain things as changing, as active, against a background of our experiencing everything else for a time, temporarily, as not changing, as non-active.

The question is what we identify with. We generally identify with time, history – that is, with our memory of Nature's activity – because we are identified with creation as a contradictory, meaningless happening, and because we don't understand God's purpose with creation. If God changed his mind, we couldn't understand God, and that has nothing to do with time. So if we woke one morning and God had changed the purpose of creation, then we would have to understand everything again as something new. If God was free to change his mind and kept changing it – in other words, if he had free will, that is, if he wasn't bound by anything and could do whatever he wanted, and therefore could also act in an arbitrary way – then we would never understand him, we would never understand the original cause. That's also why we don't understand each other: we live with the idea that we have free will and can change reality, rather than understand it. It's as impossible to live with a God who has free will as it is to live with people who are constantly changing their minds.

Time is simply the idea we use within creation for practical purposes. It derives, as I've said, from our experience in creation that things change, and from our need and ability to remember how things can change, that is, our need and ability to understand causality within creation.

Doesn't 'eternal' anyway just mean 'non-created', 'unchangeable', 'concrete'?

The theologians don't use this formulation, as I do, because they don't talk about God's original Being, the original existence, as concrete in the way I do.

Theology and philosophy

P: Earlier you contrasted your view of creation with theological views…

S: Yes, some theologians followed St Augustine's emanation theory and said that God created out of himself.

P: …which, as you've said, is different from your idea of God creating out of his own existence, the Being.

S: Yes, because Augustine believed in an abstract God, and not, as I do, in a concrete, existent, living God who has a relation to his living parts. This emanation theory, which originated from Brahmanism, dominated Christian thinking until the introduction of Aristotle's ideas through Aquinas in the thirteenth century. Other theologians said God created out of 'nothing'. That is, instead of my idea of a concrete potency, the Being, they say God took its opposite, 'nothing', and made something – a separate Being – out of it.

P: And you think that both these theological views are illogical?

S: Yes. Both views make creation mystical, incomprehensible: Augustine's, because creation is activity, and activity can only arise from something existent, and Augustine considers God abstract; and the other, because nobody can imagine creating out of nothing. So the theological traditions can't answer children properly – that is, logically. But the theologians maintain that everything is possible for an almighty God. Therefore, you have to believe that God can create out of nothing. '*You* can't create out of nothing,' they say, 'but *God* can create out of nothing.' But because nobody can imagine how God does this, they then say that we can't understand how God makes creation. The last part of that I agree with, though I say that we can at least understand that the absolute whole's creation must logically start as three-dimensional activity – what we call 'vibration' – since it creates within itself. That's the only rational way we can imagine it.

P: Three-dimensional as opposed to…?

S: As opposed to the one-dimensional movement in Euclid's system of movement. Euclid's system starts with an absolute part seen as a point without dimension, that is, as an abstract, not-existent part which can only move ahead as a line or a ray in empty space, in relation to something else. But as the absolute part of the idea of absolute nothing, it cannot vibrate immanently, in itself, as an existent three-dimensional whole – like an earthquake, for example. The absolute whole can move one-dimensionally but only in time – Einstein's fourth dimension – but not in relation to something outside itself, nor towards its own parts.

In practical life, one-dimensional, 'linear' activity is represented by the movement of objects. Then there is the two-dimensional activity represented by the movement of a surface, such as waves on the surface of water.

But how the whole's three-dimensional activity culminates in what we experience in creation as objects, that it is impossible to reconstruct. All we can say is that creation is created in such a way that the invisible whole Being's three-dimensional movement – what we regard as Nature, or, since Einstein, as energy – must become focussed into 'matter', energy-potencies, that further partly organize and partly disorganize matter. These energy-potencies, seen from the outside as matter, then build up the universe as one absolutely interacting order, simultaneously creating and destroying the meaningful picture of the manifold.

P: But though we can have only this limited understanding of the 'how?' of God's creation, you think we can understand the 'why?'

S: Yes, on the basis of this hypothesis of a non-created whole. Then, out of this understanding of 'why' the whole creation is being created, we can also logically understand why the surface of creation, the universe, is made the way it is.

The need for mutual love

According to my view, it is self-evident that God must love the parts of his own existence. Because everything belongs originally to God, God can experience only undivided love, that is, he loves the whole of himself, which includes the parts. It is natural* for everybody to love the parts of their own body.

P: But some people come to hate parts of their body, or even the whole of their body.

S: Not without some idea that makes them hate it. And for people there can be many reasons, because our body doesn't belong to us in the same way that God's belongs to him. We can have the idea of changing parts of our body or the whole of our body, because our body is part of creation and not part of the original existence. We can then have the idea of changing it for the better, and so not love what we have.

But God must also, as I have argued, have the need to be loved by his parts. That's why God must give us, through his creation, the opportunity to understand the unchangeable relationship between him and us. In my view, God doesn't want to be adored as an incomprehensible, almighty technician: he wants to be understood as like, as a conscious being with the need for love. And I think that God's need to be loved and the necessity he has to create creation make him understandable, and not in any way less perfect.

P: Your idea that God has the need to be understood, as a precondition for being loved, makes your view radically different from the theological view.

S: Yes. The theological traditions did not have this conception of the need for mutual love between conscious beings, so they had to order people to love – to love God and to love each other. But ordering people to love makes the idea of love one-sided, and it reinforces the generally accepted, but, in my view, mistaken, idea of love as something that we give and take. It's impossible to love on command anyway – which everyone can check against their own experience.

In my view, love is a question of understanding each other as like. And we *are* like if we consider each other, not as mortal parts in a mystical creation, but originally as immortal, conscious parts of God's conscious Being. In my view, only if we have this understanding – that we belong inseparably together in this way – can love function, as a constant understanding of God and of each other.

A further difficulty for me with the theological view of love is that I don't see how we can love God if we don't understand him. Just as, if we don't understand each other, how can we love each other?

P: But every tradition talks a good deal about love. For example, the theological traditions say that God created us 'out of love'.

S: Yes, it is said that God makes us and creation out of love for us. But is it logical for God to love us before he has created us, as this formulation implies? It's self-evident that it's impossible to love if one is alone: one can't be loved just by one's own existence. But if one says that God *makes, creates* human beings so that he can love them and be loved by them, this makes it like when children imagine they are loved by their man-made dolls or stuffed animals. Children do imagine that as an enjoyable game, but I think they know very well that what they imagine is not love. They know that they are just imagining the precondition for love.

P: In other words, that the dolls or stuffed animals are alive?

S: Yes. From their own experience children can remember that they experience love in relation to conscious beings who love them. So if they imagine this in relation to their dolls or stuffed animals – that the dolls or stuffed animals are conscious and love them – children can feel love towards them. But if the grown-ups reinforce the idea that what the children imagine is really love, by telling children, for example, 'Teddy loves you' or 'you love Teddy', children can become confused about the difference between imagined love, based on their memory of the precondition for love, and love itself. The theological traditions, too, confuse people about what love is by creating, in my view, an irrational belief about the relationship between God and creation.

P: By saying that God created us?

S: Yes.

P: What about the idea that God created once, 'at the beginning of time'?

S: This leads to the problem of whether God is interfering in creation or not. If we take the Christian view, God has the same relation to his creation as we have to the things we ourselves create – that is, he is outside it. According to my view, God's creation and what humans create are not comparable. That's why I have the idea of the non-created reality, the Being, as the 'material' that God uses for his creation, whereas we can only use for our creating what God provides in creation.

P: But you think that a belief in your hypothesis of the relationship between God and us and creation makes God and that relationship understandable, and therefore makes love possible?

S: Yes. Mutual love is possible only if we can agree that God is present through his creation. Only in this way can it be experienced that creation is a meaningful whole – in the sense I have described – and only in this way can creation be loved as a whole, that is, undividedly, as the creation of one conscious being – even if you are suffering, which is the story of Job in the Bible.

If you don't understand reality as one whole, you see it as parts, and then you can only prefer one part to another part. Then you can experience love only in relation to the things and relationships that you prefer. That makes the idea of love comparable. Love becomes connected in our mind with particular things and situations. This makes us think we can give and take love: we remember the things we connect to love and the situations in which we loved, and we give or we want to own those things, or we try to recreate those situations. This makes love 'rememberable', because it is bound to these preferences*, which you have to remember and which you see as various preconditions for love.

P: Whereas, if you love the whole undividedly, as a living unity, love is always present, so there is nothing special to remember?

S: Yes. We don't then have to remember the things we connect to love and the situations in which we loved. It's only because we don't love undividedly that we can have an experience of the absence of love at all, and hence can have the idea of recreating love, using our memory of situations in which we were able to experience love.

Love can't be made, because the ability to experience can't be made. The ability to experience is the basic state of existence, of the whole Being, and love is the basic quality of the ability to experience. Not even God can create or make the ability to experience, and not even God can make love. It's impossible to create anything other than activity. Love is not a thing, a substance. There is no thing that one can give or take. Love can become actual only through meeting another conscious being. As long as there is no reservation – that is, fear or anxiety – on either side, then love is the natural feeling of this relation, independent of any objective activities the conscious beings express or don't express. Either we experience love spontaneously when we meet another conscious being, or we don't experience it because another temporary feeling overshadows the basic feeling of love. When we lose the feeling of love, we then experience the need for love, the need for the natural state. But we can't make love happen. In order to experience undivided love, we have to create its precondition, by philosophically reconstructing the original cause and meaning of creation.

God's problem, and the problem we have in common with God, is that we can only believe in God, but can never meet him in creation in the same way we meet each other in creation, through one unitary body. So love between God and us can function only when we understand God as, like us, a conscious being, and as behind his creation, which we meet all the time.

P: And what about love between human beings?

S: The problem of love is the same between humans. The difference is that we humans don't have to be conscious of the fact that God – that means, another conscious being – is behind the whole creation. We can deny this. In other words, we can deny that it is a meaningful creation. But we can't deny that we meet another conscious being when we meet another human being.

P: On the other hand, when we meet other human beings, we don't have to be conscious of the fact that we are meeting our likes in them.

S: That's right. We can be confused by the fact that we just meet men and women – and can think that we have to get to know each other as different species. If we let the division of the sexes confuse us, we begin to see human identity in every form of possible unlikeness and in the development of every possibility for difference. In doing that, we can only become, individually or collectively, more and more alienated from one another – which makes love, a meeting without any reservations, impossible.

P: Just as we become alienated from the whole reality, too, if we don't conceive of a similar consciousness behind it?

S: Yes. Love can only be experienced between conscious beings who understand that they are likes.

P: So why does God create our human bodies as different, then? Is it because we couldn't tell each other apart if we all looked the same?

S: Yes, on practical grounds. We wouldn't know whom we were talking to otherwise. And, of course, it's also because we can't be joined to creation in the unchangeable way we are joined to God's non-created reality as powerless parts.

Science and the old traditions

P: Can we return to the relationship between science and the old traditions?

S: Yes. The two explanations of the old traditions – the abstract God of theology and the abstract Being of pantheism – existed before modern science. And then came modern science, at the start of the seventeenth century, with a total revolution. The ability to go beyond the natural limit of the senses – principally the senses of touch and sight – and to see things that humanity had never been able to see before, made people completely hubristic. The old tradition based on introspective science was regarded as absolutely nothing compared with the new science. '*Now* we can begin to discover and explain the background of reality, the whole of causality, in everyday consciousness, not in the old mystical way.' The historical belief in traditions – the past – was suddenly turned into a hubristic belief in the future. This led to the century of the Age of Enlightenment: 'Now the *true* Enlightenment starts. We don't need to believe in these inward-turned, introspective scientists any more.' And this enormous revolution became global. So it confronted every old tradition in the same way, wherever it went: Africa, Asia, America, all over the world.

P: So the theological traditions and the pantheist traditions were all confronted by this new science?

S: Yes, but in the beginning only theoretically, as a dream, since the new science hadn't realized its hoped-for goal of explaining the whole causality on the basis of invisible, indestructible parts.

P: But no one doubted that it would be able to do that?

S: That's right. So though the confrontation with all the old theories – which were all originally based on introspective science – was only theoretical at first, it was immediate. There was an immediate break with the past. Even the Church was paralysed, because it talked about the original cause in an authoritarian way, which science threatened. And yet the Church believed in science. It was only later – as more and more highly refined technical instruments revealed new forms of microscopic life, and as the idea became current that life originated from so-called non-living matter, and was not, as the Church held, created by God – that the confrontation with the old theories became a practical confrontation. Unless we understand all this, we will never understand our time. We have to see our time in the light of this enormous technological* revolution arising from science, a revolution that is still going on.

The Big Bang and the problem of the original cause

P: So is the theory of the Big Bang science's attempt to replace God and all the other old theories of the original cause?

S: Yes, but not a satisfactory attempt – in spite of a widespread public opinion to the contrary and the views of some scientists within astronomy who interpret the Big Bang as a theory of the original cause. The Big Bang in my view is just a theory of an event: it doesn't offer any explanation of the original cause. I heard scientists talking on a television or radio programme about the Big Bang, and a 10-year-old boy asked: 'Who made this explosion?' And the scientists answered: 'It was so far back in time that we can probably never reconstruct what the cause of this explosion was.' Stephen Hawking writes: 'As far as we are concerned, events before the big bang can have no consequences, so they should not form part of a scientific model of the universe. We should therefore cut them out of the model and say that time had a beginning at the big bang.' [*A Brief History of Time*, Bantam Press, 1988, p.46.]

P: Hawking allows, then, for events preceding the Big Bang, but says that their effects don't extend past the Big Bang, and so as a scientist he is not interested in those earlier events? In other words, he is not interested in the original cause?

S: Yes, that's right. Scientists today say that time and space started with the Big Bang, that our whole reality came about through an explosion. But though they don't say anything about an original, non-created reality that might have caused the explosion, they do operate with the ideas of space and time following the Big Bang as representing something of an existent reality in themselves. But 'space' is simply the word given to our experience of distance, and 'time' simply the word given to our ability to remember everything that changes. Neither of them represents an existent reality. If they are interpreted as existent, space is then the irrational idea of an existent 'nothing'...

P: ...'irrational' because the idea of a 'nothing' that is 'existent', that is, a 'nothing' that is 'something', doesn't make sense?

S: Yes. And 'time' is the irrational idea of the one-dimensional movement of the three dimensional empty space and of the ever-present, and at the same time ever-moving, ever-changing, creation from a non-existent 'future' to an 'existent' past – that is, from a mystical, non-realized state into a realized state in our memory, which we then form, using human language, into history. This one-dimensional movement of empty space and creation – time – is then imagined as something in itself, because the supposedly existent background to creation – the three-dimensional, 'ever-present', non-moving, empty space or 'nothing' – is also imagined as something in itself. This moving 'nothing' – time – is seen as going on infinitely, alongside changing creation...

P: So time and 'nothing' are seen as equivalent?

S: Yes, time is seen as the one-dimensional representation of the three-dimensional empty space. So while 'time' – the movement of this 'nothing' and of creation – goes on infinitely, empty space, 'nothing' itself remains the inactive, non-moving background to the ever-present, seemingly existent, not obviously* changing, but active, moving creation.

But 'nothing' does not exist, and neither the future nor the past is a really existent reality. So how can 'nothing' and 'time' be the original reality and the cause of 'something', or of movement, or of activity?

And, to come back to the Big Bang, what is the explosion in itself – that is, if you don't take into account how it started, its cause?

P: Yes, what is it?!

S: It's ongoing activity, enormous activity – activity that creates what seems to our senses to be existence, what we call 'matter'. Some scientists say that the activity comes from the other side of the Big Bang, from an original atom that detonated. This is again some sort of idea of an original cause. So are the ideas of anti-matter and black holes, which scientists also talk about. Black holes, for example, are seen as absolutely, or almost absolutely, dense matter. This is a mechanical version – that is, one that excludes consciousness – of my idea of the absolute Being.

P: Don't some scientists think of energy as a sort of original cause of creation?

S: Yes, that is another idea. Since Einstein, science has talked about energy as an abstract original cause of everything that appears concrete to our senses, that is, of all matter. This is similar to the pantheistic interpretation of ancient introspective science, which also referred to energy and vibrations as the original reality.

P: So what are you saying about the Big Bang?

S: That it's wrong to think that it's an explanation of reality. The Big Bang offers only a limited, technical, mathematical or other symbolic description of creation. It excludes not only the question of what gave the explosion, what released the energy – that is, the question of the original cause of creation – but also the question of why it is given – the question of creation's meaning. It is only children who ever ask about these questions nowadays – without getting any answers. Scientists merely refer to the agreement, suggested by Francis Bacon in the seventeenth century, not to deal with the philosophical question of meaning, but to concentrate solely on describing every purposeful activity in Nature as a mechanical process. Modern science came to be based on this agreement, and it is used globally nowadays as a common system of thinking. The result is that we have as many individual searchers after the meaning of life as there exist people. That is because, if we don't yet know the cause and meaning of creation, each of us has to create a meaning for his or her own life – since it is impossible to live without meaning.

P: So you think that a different agreement is needed?

S: Yes, we need a common agreement about the original meaning, instead of a spontaneous, unconsidered agreement that there is no original meaning. We need to agree that there is an inseparable connection between the original cause of the objective universe, which is the problem that global science addresses, and the original cause and meaning of life on Earth, which generally is viewed as each person's private, subjective problem. It's my view that you can't understand the meaning of your own life without understanding the original cause and meaning of creation.

Science and 'Why?'

P: But I thought you said that modern science was not interested in the original cause, whereas just now you have said that it's the problem that global science addresses?

S: Yes, let me be more precise. From its inception, modern science hoped that it could solve the question of the original cause, but only in the future. It saw the dissection of creation as the method by which the question 'how?' – how everything is constructed or made – could be answered. It hoped to be able to get down to Democritus' indestructible atoms. The hope was that, when the answer to the question 'how?' was found, we would also understand 'why?' So only the question 'how?' needed to be pursued for the time being. [For a modern reference, see the quotation from Hawking, p.41.]

P: So modern science managed to put off the question of the origin of creation, both as regards the ultimate 'how?' and as regards the 'why?'?

S: Yes. Before modern science, the question couldn't be avoided. All this creating by life on the Earth's surface, all this activity that is moving all the time, must have started somewhere. Every child asks about its start. So every tradition had to give an answer. And either the answer was that 'God' was the original cause – but then in the irrational, therefore authoritarian, way I have pointed out. Or it was thought that the original cause was what was experienced in inner, transcendental science. That experience is available to anybody who meditates systematically and was regarded as giving omniscience or wisdom. But it requires you to accept the authority of initiates – you have to believe that they can lead you to this omniscience. At the same time, you have to accept the idea that activity can exist by itself and the idea that activity can be a cause. The problem common to both theories was that neither could give a rational answer to the questions of how or why creation started.

P: Modern science is also concerned now with how or whether creation will come to an end, isn't it? It doesn't know whether the expansion of the universe will just continue indefinitely, or stop, or turn around and end in a big collapse, the 'big crunch'.

S: Yes. All theories, even those predating modern science, had to be concerned with this question. That's because everything that starts is activity, and all activity can end at any moment. Can it be otherwise? But only the theological traditions – and, in certain interpretations, Brahmanism too – had to answer this question about the end, because only they talked of a start.

P: Are you thinking of the idea of the final judgement in theology?

S: Yes. But the pantheistic traditions could avoid answering the question, because for them there exists only infinite activity, which has neither a start nor an end. They symbolized this sometimes as an open circle, that is, a spiral.

The other logical question that always arises is: can an activity start without there being a conscious potency who can start the activity and who can stop expressing it? And because a conscious potency is always purposeful in its activity, every child asks logically what the reason for the start of the activity is and what the reason for stopping expressing it could be. But from the theologians and the pantheists they get only authoritarian answers, and from modern science, no answer at all: 'Nobody knows'. And this makes further checking by logical thinking impossible.

P: If activity is what starts and stops, would you say that existence doesn't start or stop, it just is?

S: Yes.

P: But isn't the idea that there is something existent that never started impossible to imagine too?

S: Generally, we tend to think of either 'nothing' or activity as the original cause. We think of 'empty space' or 'space' as being the background to everything that we experience as existent. Because of this, we tend to say that 'nothing' is the cause of everything. But we can't actually defend this, either philosophically or scientifically. Alternatively, we can think that activity creates existence, or that existence creates activity, and ask which is more logical. We can only think that activity creates existence from the example of human beings being able to make objects. We can even think that our activity brings about reproduction, via insemination – in other words, that we create human beings. But this assumes that what is created is existent, which we know it is not. And it ignores the question of what caused us, or what caused the sperm and the egg. It ignores the fact that Nature's ability to create cannot be compared with the ability of animals and human beings to construct and make objects – in other words, it ignores the question of the original cause.

P: I remember you saying that you got stuck on this point when you were talking to a group of farmers, who were insistent that humans create life.

S: Yes, even when I asked them whether, therefore, they were also the creators of calves when they artificially inseminated cows!

As long as we leave out the question of the original cause, then everything in creation can be regarded as a cause, or as an effect, that is, as being caused by something else. So humans can be regarded as the cause of both insemination and reproduction, for example.

P: That explains how the alternatives to something existent as the original cause are impossible, but isn't it still difficult to imagine something that has never started and will never end?

S: Don't people who believe in 'nothing' as the original cause in fact imagine that that 'nothing' is an existent oneness, a oneness that never started and will never end?

P: Yes, that's true.

S: And if you imagine 'activity', not as something going on from one point to another point, but as cooperation or interaction, then can't you also imagine activity as an ongoing oneness, which has neither a start nor an end?

P: That's true too. So the traditions give either, in the case of theology, the idea of God, an active creator – but without a logical reason for creating...

S: ...and therefore with only commandments or rules for behaviour.

P: And by that you are implying that, if we understood God's purpose in creation, we would know how to relate to creation, including other people – we would know how to behave and wouldn't need rules? [See Dialogue 2, 'Human will and Nature's will' and 'The problem of identity' for elaboration of this point.]

S: Yes.

P: ...And in the case of pantheism, the traditions offer the idea of infinite activity ruled by non-conscious, unchangeable physical and moral laws that bind humans but that don't operate out of a particular purpose?

S: Yes. And without a logical reason for creation, both frameworks leave humans free to create their own purposes and to seek to adapt creation to those human purposes.

Modern science and philosophy

P: I would like to come back to the relationship between philosophy, as you conceive philosophy, and modern science. Could you say more about that?

S: Before modern science, the answers to all philosophical questions were regarded as being in the past, in tradition, and as given by the founders or reformers of the different traditions. After the invention of the microscope and telescope – that is, from the late 1500s onwards – the answer has been regarded as being in the future, dependent on the development of modern technology. In my view, the answer is in the present, in space – where reality is – and not in time. We can solve the problem of the original reality, but to do so requires us to discuss the original reality, and not just – as is generally the case today – the experiences that people have of all the causality in creation. The philosophical problem is just the problem of the original Being as the original cause.

P: So philosophy doesn't deal with the mechanical causality that is going on as cause and effect in creation?

S: No. That is a scientific problem. In general life, everything can be a cause and everything can be regarded as an effect from a practical point of view, from the scientific point of view. Philosophy is concerned only with the original cause, which must be the cause of everything, the whole creation. But – and this is the main point in philosophy – this can't be done from the position of an outsider, that is, from the position of a neutral observer of mechanical relations.

P: ...which is the position that modern science adopts?

S: Yes. Philosophical considerations require a constant consciousness of our immediate, subjective relation to the whole creation. This immediate, subjective relation is what gives us, firstly, the subjective feeling of the natural need for love – love being the feeling of community, of belonging together – which every conscious being has; and, secondly, the subjective feeling of the equally common, natural needs of the human body. This immediate, subjective relation to the whole creation is what gives us the opportunity, through philosophical reflection, to understand God's unchangeable relation to us in the original Being.

P: Why can't we understand the original cause if we see ourselves as outsiders in creation?

S: If we entertain the idea of the original cause at all, it must be as something conscious, because only a conscious being can act by itself. But if we see ourselves as outsiders in a basically 'dead' creation, we see consciousness as being present in creation only in ourselves and other so-called 'living things'. Then we can only have the idea of other relative conscious parts within creation, not the idea of a conscious whole we belong to as conscious parts. And then we are interested only in the causality in creation, which we separate into two categories, 'living' and 'non-living'.

P: I want to come back to what you were saying about the Big Bang. When you said that modern science had been unable to find the origin of the Big Bang, were you using that as an argument against the scientific view?

S: No, I just wanted to point out that scientists have consciously limited themselves with the declaration – which marked the start of the discipline called new or modern science – that they are not concerned with the question of meaning, 'why?', or with the traditional theories of the original cause. They are interested in mechanical, technical functions, the question 'how?': 'How is visible reality constructed?'

As regards the Big Bang, scientists never ask philosophically how it was caused. They put the question only technically – if at all. For example, Stephen Hawking, as I quoted earlier, and others say that even the technical question is irrelevant, since space and time – that is creation, what science is dealing with and wants to describe – started with the Big Bang. Other scientists ask 'why?' only technically: what preceded the Big Bang and what technically caused it?

P: But you are not saying that they should continue to pursue the technical question?

S: No, not in relation to the original cause – because it is impossible to discover technically the origin of creation if the whole is that origin. We could never 'meet' the whole. We have to be separate from something if we are to be able to meet it.

P: So you're saying that scientists should ask philosophically, 'What caused the Big Bang?'

S: Yes. We have to explore whether it is possible to reconstruct through philosophical considerations the creator's meaning, motive and aim in creation, without our being able technically to meet the creator and ask him. The technical answer does not solve the philosophical question. Stephen Hawking is dreaming when he says in the last lines of his book: 'However, if we do discover a complete theory, it should in time be understandable in broad principle by everyone, not just a few scientists. Then we shall all, philosophers, scientists, and just ordinary people, be able to take part in the discussion of the question of why it is that we and the universe exist. If we find the answer to that, it would be the ultimate triumph of human reason – for then we would know the mind of God.' [*A Brief History of Time*, Bantam Press, 1988, p.175.] It is a very nice dream, but it is a dream – because a mechanical theory can never be a complete theory of creation: it can never answer the question 'why?'

Time

P: Is time something technical, rather than philosophical?

S: The idea of time comes from Nature organizing things so that we are able to remember earlier experiences: time and remembering are the same thing.

P: As an aside: are you personifying Nature there?

S: Yes, because I interpret Nature as creation and, therefore, as God's purposeful activity.

So – going back to time – we just make of memory a theoretical idea: the past. And then we have a problem with the future. History is remembering. What we can know about history is as much as people can remember from their earlier experiences, and that is what people read about. It is the communicated memory of reality. Then we have the immediate experience of reality, which is the truth. The immediate experience of reality always represents the truth. If the stars were to start moving in a 'stupid' way, you would have to take it as the truth. But if we live instead in the past and in the future, we leave out the problem of philosophy, which deals with the question of the meaning of the whole present – I would say, ever-present – reality. Only if we know the purpose of creation can we understand it as a purposeful order, a purposeful interaction. Otherwise, creation would be – as the pantheist theories say – just like an abstract, ever-changing, running river without origin or end. That notion leads to the idea of time.

Science can never answer the philosophical question 'why?', and is therefore bound to the idea of time, and to continually examining the past in order to try to foresee the future. I say that I can in principle foresee the future the moment that I understand creation as a purposeful order, an order that is changeable on the surface but not fundamentally.

P: You mean that, because the purpose of creation never changes, the basic order never changes?

S: Yes …no matter how much we interfere with creation on the surface, by polluting it, destroying forests and so on. We can confuse the order on the surface, but the order will always eventually reassert itself, from the very moment that we stop confusing it with our own creativity that is blind to Nature's creativity.

P: But if we don't think creation has an unchanging purpose…?

S: Then two different sets of principles rule the future. The first set of principles is that which actually rules the order of Nature. This set is determined by God's need to be understood and therefore by his purpose in creation. The second set of principles derives from the meanings created by human beings, who have to organize themselves in some way – since life is always interaction, which includes interaction with other human beings.

P: And as people nowadays are generally educated by modern science without any agreement about the order of Nature, they can't see the virtue of being ruled by the order of Nature?

S: That's right. And in that case they can't avoid having to agree about and be ruled by the different meanings or purposes human beings create, even though that process invariably brings endless conflict – which is why it was always said that wars are inevitable. And nowadays such competition about meanings – which is inevitable when there is no agreement about Nature's meaning – has even been made into a virtue by the ideology of the market economy.

Dialogue 2

CONSCIOUSNESS AND IDENTITY

The philosophical education of children

Philip: We mentioned earlier that children lose interest in these philosophical questions if they are given illogical answers to their questions. Can you say more about that?

Stefan: The philosophical education of children nowadays starts with their being told that the Earth is moving in empty space – which means in 'nothing'. This is the view that science incorrectly comes to, and it corresponds to the spontaneous view of children, which is based, as science is, on sense-impression and fails to take into account our immediate subjective relation to the whole creation. It's a view that doesn't make sense philosophically, if you take our immediate subjective relation to the whole creation into account. It only frightens children. But science is only interested in the problem of how creation is made, whereas philosophically the main question is why the creator made creation.

The mystical 'I'

And then comes the next word that makes children confused: the word 'I'. They get confused when they understand that grown-ups interpret this grammatical word 'I' as human identity. What is 'I'? Grammatically, we have to have this 'I' – or other personal pronouns such as 'we', 'she', 'he', 'you'. We need them in language for practical purposes. But then we take the word out of its grammatical context in language and use it to make an identity out of it.

P: ...so that 'I' becomes more than a practical way of referring to oneself?

S: Yes. When children first use the word 'I', it's quite straightforward and practical. It's simply an alternative to the proper name for themselves, which they've already learnt. So sometimes, for example, when a child knocks on the door, and the people inside ask, 'Who's there?', the child will reply 'It's me!' – because the child doesn't distinguish between its proper name and this new identity, 'I' or 'me'. It's just practical. Children see that everybody calls themselves 'I' or 'me', so they use that too. At first they connect it to their surface appearance, in the same way that they connect the name of another person to the surface appearance of that other person. But then after a while, the child comes to understand something quite different by this 'I'. What do you think that is? – it arises from communication with grown-ups.

P: You mean grown-ups start to use 'I' to refer to something other than the surface appearance, such as when they say, for example, 'So-and-so doesn't know *me'* – by which they mean 'so-and-so doesn't know what kind of person I am'? A young child would never say that.

S: Yes, 'I' becomes something mystical. And it takes children a long time to get the idea that grown-ups are referring to something invisible. And so later children come up with the question 'Who am *I*?', which shows they have accepted this identity 'I' as different from their physical appearance and that they think of themselves as invisible. 'My own parents don't know me!' It's a terrible discovery for children – at least in the beginning, before they learn to utilize and enjoy this anonymity. Then they think – and they can enjoy the thought – that each person is free to define themselves. The negative side of that is that they *have* to do this defining of themselves, otherwise they think they will remain unknown, which is what everyone's basic anxiety is. Underlying it is a feeling of loneliness, a sense of alienation, an unsatisfied need for relation, for love. They suffer more and more from the sense of anonymity. 'My own species doesn't know me. Some people just care about me, but nobody knows me' – that's what people think.

So what do children eventually come to understand grown-ups to mean by this identity 'I'?

P: Do they see it somehow as the essence of the person?

S: But what is that essence?

P: They don't know.

S: That's right, because it's interpreted differently for everybody.

P: ...whereas you define 'I' as the same for everybody: as a part of God's Being with the ability to experience?

S: Yes. But as it is traditionally used, 'I' is never defined in a common way, but only personally, as something unique and individual, which is interpreted as different. It's something mystical. It's like time: nobody knows exactly what it is, but everybody talks about it. But how do children interpret the grown-ups' talk about the 'I'?

P: I don't understand what you're getting at.

'Free' will

S: They interpret it as 'free will'. They think: 'Nobody knows me, so I have to tell everybody and show everybody what I am capable of and what I want, in order to be known.'

P: Oh, I see.

S: And the 'personality', when each person nurtures and develops it individually, that is, differently, is a consequence of this anonymity interpreted as free will that is taught to everybody in childhood. Hasn't it been discussed in every age whether every individual in the human species has free will: whether they are 'undetermined', or, like objects and the other species, which get lumped together, 'determined' – without any regard being paid to the difference between biological necessity and mechanical necessity? [See this Dialogue, 'The need of consciousness: undivided love', p.68, for further discussion of this point.] In Christianity, it began with Paul's mention of predestination. [In his Epistle to the Romans 8:28-30.] It was most strongly defended by Augustine, and later by Calvin at the time of the Reformation in the sixteenth century. It was the big difference, for example, between Protestants and Catholics.

P: Didn't Calvin think individuals had free will and yet were predestined – a sort of double bind?

S: Yes, that is right. The idea of free will 'as the best thing humans know' arises because nobody can enjoy meeting, nobody can love, a living power, an authority, whose background they don't know and who is therefore a foreigner to them. If we don't know in what way the person we are meeting is an authority, if we don't know their capacities, their will, their purpose, their aim, we can't enjoy meeting them. Because that is so, there is a spontaneous global agreement that we have a common natural need to defend ourselves, individually or collectively, against our own species – in the same unreasonable, power-based way that we defend ourselves against other dangerous species.

Similarly, because of the lack of any agreement that we are like, that we belong basically to the same Nature, we are forced to use human language to express only our unlikeness and to verbally manipulate others. That's why every society is required to have a police force to restrict the power of its unreasonable members and an army to defend it against unreasonable neighbours. Theology transfers the same irrational idea of an absolutely free will, combined with the idea of absolute power, to the idea of God, because they don't declare God's background: his purpose and aim, his will with creation. They can't question God's free will, as they question humans' free will, by restricting it with moral rules. They say that God's purpose with creation is love. But love is relation between likes and has nothing to do with power. Therefore they have to say that God has created humans as his likes. But because God's creation starting from the non-created whole cannot be compared with the possibilities for creating that humans have, they can't say in what way God and humans are 'like'.

P: What is your view of so-called 'free will', then?

S: I see the will as arising from the need for activity. Consciousness – which I interpret as the ability to experience, prior to all knowledge – is our basic quality. The need for activity – the need to understand and to act – arises from what we experience, that is, from our knowledge of biological and mechanical necessities. So the will is always dependent on what we experience. It is therefore senseless to talk of a will that is independent of experience. The will is never 'free' in itself: it always has preconditions and consequences. However, humans have human language that covers, gives a name to, everything we can remember, and this enables us to discuss the whole of causality. This everything-covering language*, however, also gives us the possibility of having a purely language-based, theoretical experience of reality that is independent of our practical experience of reality.

P: What do you mean by 'purely language-based'?

S: I mean based on language used to express only people's 'own reality', that is, their ideas about the future, and their own history, that is, their own rememberable past. This gets joined to other people's own realities, that is, other people's different ideas about the future, and to other people's histories, that is, other people's different rememberable pasts. Language used in this way creates a purely theoretical experience of reality, based on our ideas about reality and not on reality itself. We are then free to choose this purely language-based, theoretical experience of an absent reality in place of our practical experience of the ever-present reality. So unless we agree about the natural purpose of human language – which, in my view, is to understand the original cause and meaning of the ever-present creation…

P: Do you mean that God gives us the need of an everything-covering language and the possibility of constructing such a language in order that we should be able to reflect on our experience of creation and come to an understanding of him?

S: Yes, as the original cause behind whole Nature's activity. So unless we agree about the natural purpose of human language, human beings will work with two experiences of reality. One is this purely theoretical one, based on our formal impression of creation and on language used in this way, and originated by human beings. The other is the practical experience of an active reality, originated and determined, via biological and mechanical necessities, by reality itself, as the purposeful, active creator and, as such, the originator of the truth. And this practical experience is common to us all – which is why it is the basis of 'common sense'*. It is also actually the basis of modern science, since modern science doesn't accept any theory unless it is relative to our common experience of all the unavoidable biological and mechanical necessities.

Human will and Nature's will

We have a basic choice as to which of these experiences of reality to make primary: the immediate experience of Nature's own biological and mechanical information, or the purely language-based information that comes from human beings. What we choose determines which reality we love: our own, or the common reality. If we choose our own reality, we live by our own will and creativity in cooperation or conflict with the will and creativity of other people. If we choose the experience of the common reality, we live by the will and creativity of the common reality, to which we adapt our own will and creativity. The choice – between people's own will and the will of the common reality – is absolutely free. But whichever we choose to make primary determines absolutely our own will, what we want to do, that is, our thinking and our activity. In neither case do we have a 'free' will.

P: And again, is your personifying of reality here – as you personified Nature earlier – because you see God as behind creation?

S: Yes, I see God's consciousness of the non-created reality, with his need to be understood and loved, as an understandable background to creation.

P: So this choice comes down to a choice between relating to Nature's creativity, God's will, or seeking to impose human creativity, human will, either our own or other people's?

S: Yes. Either we are conscious of and believe in a creator, whose purpose in creation we understand, agree about and consciously adapt to. Or, unconscious of, but alongside, the natural meaning of creation, we use language to create and realize innumerable meanings of our own on the basis of an illusorily free, creative, human will, in cooperation with the illusorily free, creative wills of other human beings. In this latter case, either we seek to impose our own will on others, or we have to adapt to their will.

P: But let us assume that we can agree about God's overall purpose in the way you suggest, is there still not room for disagreement about what would be in accordance with God's will in any particular instance?

S: There would be no room for disagreement, but there would still be a permanent necessity for agreements. This is because bodies in creation are definitively unlike – not even two leaves on the same tree are identical – and bodily needs are the same for the different bodies only in principle. So the way of satisfying bodily needs is definitively different for each species, and within the same species can be different over time and between individual members of the species. But all needs come continuously to individuals, and the satisfaction of all needs takes place in the common surroundings. So animals, too, have to agree. But everything-covering language makes it possible for humans to agree in a specifically human way in any particular instance about all the problems of the life that we have in common. This can work satisfactorily, however, only if we fundamentally agree about God's need and purpose for our common life in creation. Unless there is this agreement, we have a situation in which different wills that are not permanently conscious of a common background but are conscious only of different, personal backgrounds, are confronted by each other. All they can do then is either, like animals, fight or reach a compromise about their differences, without having any fundamental agreement, or act together on the basis of different communities of interest, that is, with some temporary or partial, but not fundamental, agreement.

P: Could you say more about how this relates to the historical debate about predestination?

S: The problem of predestination, in its religious meaning, originates in a blind, authoritarian belief in God that takes no account of God's experience of his reality – that is, his experience of the Being. In my view, God's experience of his reality is the origin of God's will. The traditions talk of a God who has an absolutely undetermined will. They say nothing about his need for activity based on his experience of his own existence.

Predestination is the idea that this God has decided everything from the beginning. In this view, all behaviour is determined by God. But if one takes this view, humans are left without responsibility. So the question arose as to whether the will and behaviour of human beings could be an exception. This religious question was increasingly treated as a political and psychological question after modern science was established. It became a question simply of how freedom applied to the relationships among human beings and to the relationships between human beings and the universe, without any reference to God. Human beings were no longer seen as determined by religious rules and as responsible for those rules and for carrying out God's will. Their will came to be seen as undetermined, free, or as determined only by the common biological, bodily needs and the mechanical laws that science was beginning to formulate in its exact, mathematical language.

After Wöhler's discovery of the unity of Nature in 1828, the discussion took on a new form.

P: You mean when Wöhler demonstrated that inorganic matter could give rise to organic matter, so that Nature could no longer be regarded as divided into the two?

S: Yes. Thereafter in education the categorical distinction between physical determination by powers or forces, and biological determination by needs gradually stopped being made. Through the new education, people's view of the whole of Nature became the same as that borrowed from Democritus by modern science at its inception: Nature functions mechanically without any meaning, that is, without any reason, purpose or aim previously determining it.

P: So instead of drawing the conclusion from Wöhler that Nature was all-living, they drew the conclusion that it was all-dead, all-mechanical?

S: Yes. And from that the spontaneous conclusion was drawn that the meaning, the purpose of the apparently free human ego, the mystical 'I', is to give meaning to basically meaningless, 'animal' life. From a practical point of view, this meant developing every possible technology in order to try and make Nature function according to the human ego's 'free' will.

P: Was predestination also discussed in traditions other than Christianity?

S: Yes, in every tradition. It was discussed without people ever being able to solve the problem. But no tradition could escape the problem, since it relates to the problem of responsibility, that is, ethics. Since humans are free to create their own meanings, and can't live without meaning, ethics is inescapable. We can't escape the question of the meaning – that is, the need and purpose – of human behaviour.

P: You mean that, in order to get by in life, we have to be able to make sense of other people's behaviour?

S: Yes. And we have to discuss what meanings should guide our own behaviour, and agree about them publicly, so that people will feel responsible for them and follow them.

The lack of agreement on the question of predestination – that is, whether humans have free will and therefore responsibility – has lasted and is still current. The reason for this, I think, is that no tradition clearly distinguishes, as I do, the ability to experience as an ability in itself.

P: Why does making that distinction solve the ethical problem?

The problem of identity

S: Because it solves the theoretical problem of identity.

P: Okay, but how then does solving the theoretical problem of identity solve the ethical problem?

S: Well, let me discuss the problem of identity first. The problem of identity is confused by the fact that every tradition talks about human identity as imperfect, changeable and developable. They do this either in relation to a perfect being – such as the non-created, absolute God of theology, whose moral rules we should follow; or they do it in relation to a changeable, developable reality – as in pantheism or, as it is called nowadays, New Age – by developing knowledge of causality in creation, so as to be able to develop creativity as an end in itself, that is, so as to change and improve that imperfect reality, without any notion of what the end-state would or should be.

P: But if you want to change and improve something, you have to have some purpose, some goal in mind, don't you? It can't be just as 'an end in itself'?

S: Yes. But those goals are arrived at through our considering details of reality to be imperfect. So we change details of reality, without taking other details into account or without taking the meaning of the whole creation into account. The ideas 'perfect', 'imperfect' and 'developable' are understandable only in relation to a purposeful meaning. As no tradition talks clearly about creation having a purposeful meaning, we can only try to understand creation mechanically, that is, with regard only to how it is constructed. If our interest is only in the changeable details of reality, we can never have an idea about reality itself having an identity. The same is true of human beings: if our interest is only in their changing and developing, then we can never have an idea of human identity either.

P: How so? Do you mean that then we don't regard humans as recognizably the same, or reality either?

S: Yes. 'Identity' comes from the Latin *idem est*, 'what is the same'. The identity of something is what is the same about it, what is unchangeable about it.

P: So to talk of a 'changing identity' is a contradiction in terms?

S: Yes. This applies to theology. The theological idea of an absolute God is not understandable at all, because theology doesn't say anything rational about what God's nature is, that means, what God's identity is. They talk about God as being an almighty creator, but 'almighty' means 'arbitrary', 'not bound by any meaning'. The term 'arbitrary' contradicts the idea of 'identity', which is about remaining the same in some sense.

I interpret the ability to experience as every living being's, as well as God's, basic, never-changing identity, which is always recognizable as the same. In the case of God, what remains the same about him, in my view, is not only the quality of consciousness – the ability to experience – but also his experience of the whole non-created Being and his meaning with creation.

P: And in the case of humans, what remains the same about us, apart from the ability to experience, is that we are original parts of that original, non-created Being?

S: Yes.

P: Okay, so now how does your view of God's identity and our identity solve the ethical problem?

S: Because it gives an understanding of the meaning of the whole creation and thereby an understanding of the creator on the basis of the same need that every conscious being, including God, has: to be understood as like, and thereby to be loved in an undivided way, that is, without any reservations. And because we meet each other face to face in creation through our created bodies, we need this understanding of God's similar need in order to be able to relate meaningfully to each other as participants in the same creation, and to experience undisturbed love for each other and the whole creation.

In my view, we are joined together, we are parts in the original non-created, conscious reality – the Being – in a way that is not satisfying for us, because we don't experience each other there, and satisfaction for conscious beings starts through meeting other conscious beings as likes, because they are conscious of the same reality. This satisfaction is the experience of love. And the lack of this experience when we meet other human beings gives rise to the problem of ethics, because we don't know how to behave towards human beings who only want to know and agree about their so-called 'own reality', their own meanings, and who deny *a priori* the existence of any responsibility for a common meaning given by common Nature.

P: Do you mean that understanding someone as like – and therefore knowing how to behave towards them – is the precondition established by Nature for both love and ethics?

S: Yes, if you mean by 'understanding as like' the insight that we have the same need – because then we know how to relate to each other, which is what the problem of ethics is.

P: What did you mean when you said a moment ago that the ability to experience is 'never-changing'?

S: By 'never-changing', I mean that it is independent of the different consequences of that ability: it is independent of what a particular living being
experiences from moment to moment. The ability to experience is subjectively
experienced by every living being as consciousness. From an objective viewpoint
– that is, when it is seen from the outside – consciousness is called 'life'. To be
alive means to be conscious, and to be conscious means to have the ability to
experience: to experience one's own body, through one's nervous system, to
experience the needs of that body, to experience the abilities the body has to
satisfy those needs, and to experience an impression of the surrounding reality,
through the body's senses. Being conscious then means, secondarily, to be able
to act purposefully according to the bodily needs and to what one experiences
in one's surroundings.

P: How does this relate to the question of free will?

S: I have to develop this further and give the whole picture for that to be clear,
so let me continue. Our created body gives to our ability to experience the possibility of action. Action needs thinking: we must think in order to understand and
control causality in our surroundings. Thinking needs memory: we need to be
able to relate our present experience to our earlier experiences. Through
language we can communicate our experience of the present reality, our memories, our histories, our evaluations* – the values we connect with things and
activities – and our practical conclusions about how to control different causalities. Simply to experience, simply to be conscious of the present reality – without
our mind being on memories and without our experiencing any need for activity
– is every living being's basic ability. It is the undisturbed enjoyment of being.
Using language properly, this undisturbed enjoyment should, in my view, be
called 'love'. It is the basic state or identity – we can also say the basic need – of
every conscious being or life. Because it is the basic state, it can be disturbed only
temporarily. But this state of undisturbed enjoyment, this state of love, can't be
given or received. It can only start to be disturbed or stop being disturbed.
Within this undisturbed experience of being, there may be a need at any moment
for different, purposeful activities, but these don't have to interfere with this
identity, this basic experience of love of existence, love of being.

P: You say 'every living being'. Does that include animals?

S: Yes. But for animals, the need for different activities and the need to control
causality are given solely by Nature, through bodily needs and through physical
conditions in their surroundings. We have the same biological needs as animals,
and our need for activity and for controlling causality is also conditioned by
biological needs and physical conditions in our surroundings. The only difference
is that human beings have a language that covers everything – which means that
we can discuss activities and causality in the whole surrounding reality without
reference to our biological needs. If there is no traditional agreement about the
natural purpose of human language – which in my view, as I have said, is to

understand the original cause and meaning of creation – then we don't experience our need to control causality as given for a purpose by Nature.

P: That purpose being to meet our existential needs?

S: Yes. But if we don't interpret it this way, then the need to control causality – that is, the seeking of knowledge – is interpreted either as a forbidden possibility [see, for example, Genesis 2:17: 'But of the tree of the knowledge of good and evil, thou shalt not eat of it: for in the day that thou eatest thereof thou shalt surely die'] or as a free and arbitrary need to develop knowledge, as an end in itself, as the need to create meanings and to develop the technical power required to realize those meanings, and thereby 'change' reality and 'create' our 'own' reality – which is how pantheistic development-theories and the modern science-based idea of developing knowledge are interpreted.

P: Doesn't this extend to the efforts people make nowadays to 'make themselves', to create their own unique 'personality'?

Our absolute identity and our 'relative identity'

S: Yes. The problem is that we don't distinguish in general language nowadays between our absolute identity and our relative identity.

P: Using the term 'relative identity' loosely for the moment, in view of what we said about identity being unchanging?

S: Yes. Our absolute, common, unchangeable identity is our ability to experience – that is, our everyday, common awareness of our own body, which allows us, through the senses, to experience the whole, ever-present, common creation. Nature is meaningful, in this view, and forces us to relate meaningfully to its meaning. If Nature is not interpreted as meaningful, then our relative identity in relation to humans becomes actual. We have to create and communicate our own meanings, which we then try to realize. This relative, personal, developable identity is our differently, individually developed ability to evaluate, think, remember, control, change. These are the abilities that we need to develop in order to create technical things – which is all we can create, since we can't create or control life from its origin. So human creativity becomes based only on the physical laws, and not on a common, undivided regard for whole Nature, that is, for Nature's original cause and meaning.

Our absolute identity is the same for all of us. It is common. Our own relative identity we can contrast with the relative identity of other human beings, because it is different for each person. And such contrasting is always competitive.

P: So when we consider ourselves to be our relative identity, we don't see ourselves as conscious participants in a meaningful creation?

S: That's right, and we forget that we have an immediate connection to a created, living body and its existential needs. We only think about our own technical creativity, rather than relating to life's creativity, and this gives us the illusory feeling that we are free and independent of biology, that we are dependent only on physical causality, which we use for our own purposes, without any conscious regard for life's creativity.

P: But we can't forget our own body and its existential needs.

S: No, of course not. But we don't see them then as meaningfully enjoyable. We start to see them as a burden, as something 'animal'. It is impossible for us not to relate to them, but we see them as getting in the way of our completely identifying with our own creativity.

The feeling of being free of the whole reality, the feeling of not belonging inseparably to the whole reality, is obviously a dream, just a theory. But it is unfortunately a fundamental theory of human identity that has been discussed in every age. There has never been any agreement about it though, because it's impossible to agree about something that doesn't exist in reality.

In my view, all that is free is the theoretical question of what we prefer. We can prefer to continue the tradition of discussing the theory of free human nature. The consequence of this theory is that we feel ourselves to be outsiders, we feel we don't belong to reality. From this position it seems logical, instead of relating to reality's meaning, to put our efforts into trying to control the whole causality through our own power, in order to create a better life. And that is to fall in love with, become obsessed by our own power, and to adore, envy or hate the power of others. Or we can start to use language in consciousness of the fact that we belong absolutely to the whole. And that is undivided love. We then discuss and try to agree about the creator's meaning or purpose with the whole creation, seeking in this philosophical way to understand both the creator and creation. That is the basic choice: power versus love; time, memory and history versus presence in the ever-present reality; identification with thinking on the basis of the human ego's historical view of an existent past and a not-existent future, versus identifying ourselves as conscious parts of God and relating to each other in consciousness of God's and every living being's basic need and in consciousness of the purposeful, understandable meaning that God, as the non-created, original reality, has with creation.

P: And God does not have free will either, in your view?

S: No. But throughout history, theology's discussions about God's free will have been bedevilled by confusion about the nature of love. And human free will has been vainly discussed in the same way. I say that God is not free, but is bound by the same things that every living being is primarily bound by: his experience of his Being and the need for love. The difference is that the creator, considered as the conscious whole behind creation, disposes, rules over the non-created, unchangeable, original reality as his existence. That is God's experience. So God knows everything about himself, including that we are parts of him, so he does not have the need to understand and to love – that is, he has no problem with it. And because the Being is unchangeable, and doesn't therefore need to be maintained, God has no existential, no survival needs. So the only need that God has is the need that every conscious being has: to be understood as like, which we experience as the need for love. And this will remain a mystical, unsolvable problem for us as long as we are identified with our 'outsider', surface view of creation – which, via Nature, is purposefully based on absolute unlikeness – and with the idea of a free human ability to create more and more unlikeness, without any regard for the meaning of the impression that we have of absolute, surface unlikeness.

Animals' undivided love of life

P: What about animals' need for love?

S: In my view, animals can't but love the whole creation. They are not conscious of the origin and the end of life, so they can't experience the feeling of anxiety in relation to life that is characteristic of humans. Humans can't avoid the question of the origin and the end of life. It comes to every child through language: they are told about it. And if the traditions can't offer children a logical solution at the time that children hear about life and death, children can't continue to love life as they did before. To solve the question about life and death, we need everything-covering language. Animals don't have this, because they are not the highest species and so can't be interested in the whole causality, that is, in the question of the original cause of the whole creation. We on the other hand are the highest species, and so we can't avoid being interested in the whole causality.

P: Do you mean that if there were a higher species than us – from another planet, for example – we would not be interested in the original cause?

S: That's right. Our interest would temporarily stop at that higher species. We would want to learn about them, about what makes them a higher species.

P: Yes, I think that's true. It could also explain why there is so much interest in extraterrestrial life: we no longer have much interest in the original cause.

S: Yes.

P: So coming back to animals: they can't suffer anxiety in the way we do if we fail to understand the original cause?

S: That's right. Because they are not the highest species and therefore don't have our language, animals can't communicate their memory of reality. They can only think on the basis of their needs and on the basis of their present surroundings. So they can't think in a purely memory-based, theoretical way. That means they can't have a purely memory-based, theoretical or historical experience either of reality or of causality. They can't have an experience of time, for example.

P: But surely they have an experience of intervals between things happening?

S: Yes, but that is not the same thing as having the idea of time, that is, past and future. They can't become identified with the past and future. And animals can't have an experience of their memory-based reality that is separate from their actual experience of the ever-present, common, whole reality. We can – when we think about or talk about history.

P: And that allows animals to live in what you call 'undivided love'?

S: Yes. If no difference is made by language between a living being's own reality and the common whole reality, then undivided love is experienced. The feeling of oneness, the feeling of belonging absolutely, indivisibly to the whole, is then self-evident. So animals live with unlimited consciousness and undivided love for life – because the feeling of belonging absolutely together within the whole can never be questioned without human language.

P: So you argue that animals live with undivided love simply on the basis of this conclusion?

S: Yes. And also we don't find any sign that animals experience themselves as separate from the surrounding reality.

P: What about when they are suffering? Do they still love life then?

S: They still love life then in the same undivided way.

P: Even at the very moment of suffering?

S: They have to learn to avoid suffering in the same practical way that they learn to satisfy their needs. They don't hate life or reality because of their suffering, because they can't associate the cause of their suffering to the whole creation, the whole Nature. They can't have the language-based idea of the whole creation to make the association to. Nor can they have the language-based idea of death, and nor, therefore, the idea of suicide as a way of ending both suffering and life.

P: And the feeling of everything belonging absolutely together…

S: …gives animals the impression and the feeling of a living whole, and that gives this feeling of undivided love, the same feeling for the whole as for their own existence. This feeling becomes broken for humans when we learn language without a satisfactory theory of the original cause as the whole – because language forces us to give a name to everything in reality that we can separate out, and so to experience everything as separate, as connected to the sound-combinations that we call 'words'. Without a satisfactory theory of the original cause, we can't bring these separate words together into a whole again theoretically, that is, through word-combinations, so that we can understand the original whole – the absolute belonging together – and the meaning of its activity, its creation. [See the definition of the use of language in Appendix A.] Failure to do this leads to the idea that we can change creation. And that idea forces us to act as separate parts and separate creators and to develop our creativity. In this identity, the idea that we 'belong together', with other creators, gives a completely different feeling. Then we are dependent on other human beings – those who want to change reality in the same way that we want to change reality – in a hierarchy, in which there are superiors and inferiors, but no one is like. And we are confronted with other groups who may wish to change reality in a different way. Then we have either to defend our view or cut ourselves off from the other groups. And so there will always be anxiety associated with the feeling of 'belonging together' in such cases. There will always be a feeling of alienation if we want to change reality, alienation from both reality and each other. If you love something, you don't want to change it.

Unlimited consciousness

P: What do you mean by the phrase 'unlimited consciousness' that you used in relation to animals a moment ago?

S: In creation every participant's ability to experience is basically unlimited...

P: 'Unlimited' in what sense?

S: You don't know where the beginning and the end of creation are. Our experience – whether we look inside objects or inside ourselves, or whether we look outside ourselves – is that we don't reach an ultimate, indestructible limit, any permanent part or building-block of creation. So in relation to creation, we don't know where its beginning or end is – either in the direction of the whole, or in the direction of the details and the participants.

P: I see. But we still ask the question.

S: Yes, but generally only the technical question 'how', not the philosophical question 'why'. And science asks the question only in relation to the whole manifold: when and how did the visible whole begin, and whether and how it will end. They think it started with the Big Bang, but they don't know if it will continue to spread in empty space without a limit, or if it will end in a big crunch.

P: But science looks for the end of creation in the direction of the details of creation too, surely?

S: Yes, but only in order to try and answer the question about the whole manifold. It only needs to know about the smallest details in order, it hopes, to be able to work backwards to how the whole manifold began.

P: Okay, but then isn't science interested in the origin of life, too, the origin of consciousness – in your terms, the origin of the parts?

S: Before Wöhler's famous discovery in 1828, only the rationalist philosophers were interested in it, but not scientists. Since Wöhler, scientists have been interested in it, but without seeing any basic difference between life and mechanical activities. They can't avoid the question of the origin of life because of biology, but they are interested in it only in a general and mechanical way, that is, they are only interested in the mechanical origin of life in general.

The general population is interested in the question of the origin and end of their own particular life – that is, in the start and end of one part, seen as a person. Mainly this comes down to the question of whether life continues after death, and if it does, how. And for each person, any interest in the whole is generally restricted to the question of how to exploit it for the realization of their own purposes. The bigger question of the origin and the end of the whole is delegated by the general public to science – just as before modern science it was delegated to monks, initiates, wise men or churches.

P: So are you saying then that generally each person is barely conscious of the whole, but is conscious of only a small area of creation as it relates to their own creative activities?

S: Yes. That means that they identify with the ego and their thinking – the interest in mechanical causality – and that consciousness is regarded basically as the ability to create, not as the ability to experience.

P: So how do you see this question of 'unlimited consciousness'? Does it mean that we are not conscious of any limit within creation – at least when we are born?

S: Again, it is a question of identification. Through learning language we become conscious of and are reminded of, in a typically human way, all limits and all the differences between things, because we are forced, through expressing the names of all the things, to pay special attention to them. Animals – and children, too, in the beginning – experience and remember limits and differences. But without language animals can't understand, experience and remember their knowledge of limits and differences in a theoretical or intellectual way, just for the purposes of communication. So animals can neither limit, nor develop through language, their actual knowledge and memory, their earlier experiences, of the whole reality. That is, they can't limit their consciousness, what they are conscious of, through identification with memory- or language-based experiences of a past reality. This identification is possible for humans, and it creates the typically human anxiety in the face of an unknown future seen as dependent on original, arbitrary human creativity.

If the tradition of language doesn't give information about the original cause and meaning of creation, so that every child can understand it, or if it gives irrational information by not making a clear distinction, which every child can understand, between the creativity of the original creator and the creativity of humans, then it becomes impossible for humans to relate meaningfully to creation.

P: How does that follow?

S: If there is no agreement about the original cause and meaning of creation, there will be definite disagreement about it and, in practice, no consciousness of it. If that is so, identification with human creativity – which means having regard for human creativity alone – is inevitable. Then there will be an unavoidable problem with the need for undivided love and the need for predilection*. This will arise from Nature – because we can't avoid living together, and living together actualises either ethics or moral rules. It won't be possible to resolve the conflict between human beings' dual responsibility: towards Nature's creativity and towards the creativity of other human beings, which is linked to the common need to organize society. It won't be possible to solve the problem of whether to be guided by ethics – that is, undivided love for the whole reality, which represents the truth – or by moral rules. If there is not ethics, then moral rules are needed in order to avoid the use of power in deciding between human beings' conflicting wills – because, when there is confusion about the truth, these will be guided solely by personal interest based on personal predilection.

And because nobody can have the idea of starting a new creation alongside the established creation, all that humans can imagine applying their creativity to is to altering and changing the established creation, from the point of view of our surface relationship to it. The more we learn to change, the more we become convinced of our power to change. In the end, this creates the idea that we can perhaps change creation from the bottom, or at least from the start of its biological creativity on the Earth's surface, from the so-called start of life.

P: So we can get ideas like having our bodies frozen when we die, to be brought to life again after the further advancement of science, as happens in the United States? Or there is the present interest in gene manipulation?

S: Yes. The more we teach children to identify with – which means to limit themselves to – human creativity, by producing more and more ideas about how to change life, how to make life better, the more difficulties we create for everybody in recognizing the original creation, God's creation, with life on Earth. And the more difficulties we have in talking about our responsibility for our choice as to whether to adapt with all our intelligence to Nature's creativity or to adapt primarily to all human creativity, seeing it as superior, and only secondarily to Nature's 'inferior' creativity.

P: So Nature's creativity just gets buried beneath human creativity, in the same way that the concrete jungles that humans have created have ousted Nature in many major cities?

S: Yes. The negative consequences of this identification, of this limiting of identity, accumulate…

P: …in the clashes of 'unlike', 'superior' and 'inferior' 'creative wills' and in harm to the environment?

S: Yes. But all that gets discussed is who or what is responsible for the negative consequences of human creativity. There is never any discussion of the general disagreement about the cause and meaning of the original creation.

P: But isn't it logical, within that framework, that people should blame each other? They see everything as being down to human beings.

S: Yes, it is. But fundamentally I think this situation has arisen because the age-old disagreement about the original cause and meaning was changed – in the light of the new science and at the beginning of our modern identification with human creativity – to an agreement that there is originally nothing: there is neither a cause of, nor any meaning to, creation; there is just disorder or chaos. I think this must be how this has come about, since without such an agreement this modern identification with human creativity – which has replaced the age-old pantheistic identification with human creativity based on so-called inner or transcendental light – could never have occurred. This agreement about nothing or about a mystical, mechanical cause without a meaning – 'mystical' since a mechanical cause, that is, a cause without a meaning, is not a cause – is based on our impression of an unlimited whole, what we interpret as 'empty space', behind our visible impression of the original creation, which we see as if from the outside when we see the surfaces of separate parts. We have a free philosophical choice as to whether to interpret this absolute interaction as a meaningful, and therefore understandable, order, or as meaningless, interacting 'matter' that we can use for our creativity.

'Unlimited consciousness' is given by creation: we experience creation as a limited manifold against a background of unlimited space that offers no visible resistance. And 'no resistance' means 'no limit', because it is resistance – resistance for our eyes made by light, and resistance for our skin made by the mechanical impression of bodies and objects – that gives us the impression that something is existent. If we are to think, we have to limit our consciousness to, 'concentrate' our attention on, something existent. So if we don't, based on philosophical considerations, concentrate our consciousness on the existent, non-created whole – which means in fact extending it rather than limiting it – then creation limits our consciousness through the manifold, that is, through the many visible objects in creation. Then we have to choose which part of the manifold to take as a temporary starting-point for our thinking, that is, for our understanding of causality. This can go on *ad infinitum*, as science demonstrates and even claims. This is pluralism*: many original causes. [See Chapter 3, 'The organic view of unity', for an extended discussion of this point.]

P: Which is why specialization is necessary in science education, to study the endless number of starting-points for thinking?

S: Yes. The only way to understand the whole causality is from the point of view of the original cause, which is the single cause of the whole creation. If we have the hypothesis of the existent whole – rather than the hypothesis of not-existent empty space – it's not a problem whether reality is limited or not. We don't then think of reality as the separated-out manifold. The separated-out, cooperating manifold is just creation, behind which the original indivisible reality, as a conscious whole, exists as the permanent start of creation. The parts of the indivisible existent reality can't create, they can only interact with creation – when joined to a created body.

So if we have this hypothesis, the question of identity is solved. Both the whole and the parts have the same identity, the ability to experience – which is the precondition for the experience of being and for the experience of relationship.

The philosophical problem is then purely practical: to enjoy life together in a permanent consciousness of the creator's need and purpose in giving out creation.

P: But, going back to this question of 'unlimited consciousness', are you saying that it represents a problem for us that we have to solve?

S: Yes. It makes us ask the question about the origin of the whole creation.

P: So would you then say that you deal with this problem by saying that, if we limit our consciousness by extending it to the whole – the whole, non-created Being of God, which includes our being and the whole creation – the problem is solved? But to limit it to anything less than the non-created whole is unsatisfactory?

S: Yes, because to limit consciousness to the whole is to limit it to the original cause, and that is the only way we can understand the whole of causality, that is, the indivisible oneness or singularity of causality. Of course, we can't experience the whole itself. We would need to be outside it to be able to do that. The purpose of creation is to free us from the absence of experience – except perhaps of ourselves and of an immediate feeling of a resistant, surrounding reality – that we probably have in the Being, and to replace it with distance: the experience of 'empty space'. Distance is a precondition for awareness of something that is outside us. But in the original situation, in the Being, God has an immediate relation, without distance, to us, the parts, similar to our immediate relation, without distance, to the cells that belong to our own body. We can't have the same immediate relation to the whole Being as God has, just as one of our cells can't have the same immediate relation to our body that we have. As parts in the Being, we can only experience God's existence as resistance. Creation frees us from this.

P: You mean it stops enclosing us, so that we have distance? Creation creates seeming distance between God and us, and this seeming distance frees us to have interaction?

S: I wouldn't say it stops enclosing us. We can't leave our original situation as a part in the whole, in the Being. Creation offers us an illusory alternative. Through creation God gives us an illusory, indirect perspective, both on the whole and on the parts.

P: But you are not saying, are you, that because the perspective on the whole and on the parts is illusory, then relationship is an illusion too?

S: No, I am not. The relationship to our own body and to other bodies and objects in creation is an illusion, not the relation to God or the relation to the conscious parts behind creation. But we don't usually make a distinction between the non-created conscious part and the created body.

P: You mean that we tend to think of relationship in terms of relationship to the body of another person?

S: Yes... even though we generally experience a loss of relationship when someone dies, in spite of the fact that their body remains. That should remind us that our relationship is not to their body, but to the conscious being through the body.

P: I just want to be clear what you mean, Stefan: you are not saying that in your view creation itself is illusory?

S: No. Creation itself is not illusory. It is real activity. The illusion is that creation is shown to us as if it were existent, and not as pure activity. But it is shown as temporarily existent. We can understand, therefore, that this aspect of creation is illusory. Consciousness of being, the feeling that we exist, the ability to experience, is not illusory, but it doesn't belong to creation except temporarily when it connects to a created body there. Therefore, we can think of it as present in the three different so-called states of consciousness: everyday awareness, dreams and deep sleep.

Is the universe alive? 'Life' and 'death' vs conscious and non-conscious

P: How is your view similar to or different from certain modern ideas about the universe being a living organism?

S: There are quite a number of theories of that kind, and nowadays a lot of them can be found on the Internet. The difference is that I take the whole conscious Being behind creation, rather than the whole creation itself, to be a living organism. But, as I've said, the Being isn't comparable with the living organisms we experience in creation, which have a heart, a stomach, limbs, and so on, because it's not constructed, it's not created. That means it's unchangeable, and so it doesn't have to be maintained. In my view, the whole Being – the whole and its parts – is conscious, and therefore, because it is conscious and existent, we must interpret it as a living body, a living whole. By that I mean that it is not the kind of whole that is the sum of its parts, which is what a mechanical object is. As I have said, it is a whole in which there is a constant, distanceless relation between the whole and its parts, similar to the organisms we experience in creation, which also demonstrate the ability to experience and a constant, distanceless relation between the whole and the parts of that whole. The whole creation is just a technical expression of the whole Being's, of God's, creative activity. It only seems to be living, that is, acting from itself, because God, with the power of the whole non-created Being, is behind it, expressing it all the time. And, of course, what is confusing is that we, as parts of the Being, are also expressing activity within creation, as participants there.

P: But you are not saying, on the other hand, that creation is dead?

S: No, because God expresses creation. But I don't say either that creation is living. Creation in itself is activity, and activity in itself can be neither dead nor alive. Generally, we consider that causes can be either 'dead' or 'alive'. But in my view, a cause cannot be 'dead', nor strictly is it 'alive'. 'Alive' is a less precise word for 'conscious'. We use 'alive' in relation to bodies on the Earth's surface that manifest an ability to experience and to act by themselves, in contrast to objects, which we call 'dead' – which means that they have no quality or property at all, that is, they don't have the ability to act by themselves. Yet we know that they, too, are active by themselves – out of numerous created qualities or properties. That is chemistry and mechanics. So we have to think that consciousness is also behind their activity. So in my view a cause is 'conscious', that is, it must have the ability to express purposeful activity by itself.

P: So when in creation there is activity that seems not to be caused directly by a conscious being – for example, a landslide, an earthquake, the wind, waves, things that would generally be considered accidental – you would say in fact that God is the conscious being behind them?

S: That's right. God's consciousness is behind all activity, so God's consciousness is behind all these phenomena.

P: And where do the original conscious parts of the Being fit into creation?

S: They come into God's activity at a certain point – when the necessary bodies have been created. This point or limit is what we experience on Earth when we meet the biological system that is built up on the Earth's surface by innumerable species, as a closed, living order managed by needs. This system culminates in the human species. This living order managed by needs is a continuation of the seemingly needless, that is, seemingly meaningless, mechanical order of the whole creation, which is generally interpreted as being ruled by physical powers.

P: Are the powers generally interpreted as physical powers because generally people don't see the need and purpose behind them?

S: Yes. In my view, the whole of creation is ruled basically by the need of consciousness, which is the need for understanding and love. All human activities, too, are ruled basically by the same need.

P: Even if we can be confused about this?

S: Yes.

Matilda [Matilda Leyser participated in parts of this Dialogue and Dialogue 3]: I want to be clearer about the difference between your view and these other views that say the universe is alive. In your view does something that is alive have to be conscious?

S: 'Life' and 'living' should be interpreted as 'conscious', because what we experience in the 'living' surroundings on the Earth is consciousness: the ability to experience and then act meaningfully in accordance with what is experienced. We talk about 'life' and 'consciousness' as different qualities because we don't think philosophically.

P: By which you mean that we don't allow our thinking to be spontaneously guided by the need to understand the original cause and meaning of creation?

S: Yes. Philosophical thinking requires human beings spontaneously to make a clear distinction between understanding the meaning of an activity and learning to control it – that is, to change and affect things by power in order to reform them, make them better, be a better creator, as we do with our own creations. Collectively it also requires there to be a publicly communicated agreement about this distinction at the start of typically human thinking, that is, when children learn to use human language. We know that the cause of creation can't be an unconscious object or nothing. It must be a conscious being – which gives the ancient idea of only one God and his likes, but not the idea of gods. So God's consciousness goes through the whole creation. We have to understand that there is absolute continuity: there is no boundary between 'life' on Earth, the Earth and the universe. It's not that God's and humans' creativity comes into it at a certain point. Creation is one system. It is not two: that is, one dead, without consciousness, and a second, on the Earth's surface, where consciousness starts. That creation is one system is what Wöhler discovered. This insight led some people, identified with Democritus' atoms, to say that the whole of life is chemistry, that is, basically mechanical activity, and others to say the opposite, that the whole universe is alive. This is this confusion between 'dead' and 'alive' and 'conscious' again.

P: Are you saying that the distinction between 'dead' and 'alive' is a meaningless one?

S: No. For practical reasons, the distinction has to be made between bodies that can move by themselves and other bodies or objects that don't have this ability. Even animals have to make this distinction. In human language, this division is made by describing a body or object as 'alive' or 'dead'. But it is wrong to talk of 'dead' objects. We use the word 'dead' originally in relation to a 'living' body that 'dies'. That is our experience of 'death'. But to apply the term 'dead' to natural objects that have never 'lived' doesn't make sense. And even objects actually express a function, an activity. We can say that they act by themselves. Chemistry acts by itself, in the same way as living bodies do. When a 'living' body is 'dead', then everything that 'living' body previously expressed disappears. But that is not what happens with natural objects. We can't kill natural objects; we can only break them down. And then they continue to express the same quality.

P: So copper remains copper, even if you break it into pieces?

S: Yes. What we experience as a boundary between chemistry and biology is the point at which the original, non-created conscious parts of the non-created Being start to interact with God's activity – creation – which itself starts from, originates in and also takes place within, the non-created whole, the whole non-created Being.

M: So it is misleading, for example, to call a table 'dead', because it has never been 'alive'? And when we are 'dead', our 'dead' body is still 'alive', as 'alive' as the table – that is, chemical processes continue to express activity in it?

S: Yes, but if it is misleading to call a table 'dead', then it is also misleading to call – as pantheists do – dead bodies 'alive'. Both confuse the interpretation of the word 'consciousness'. Certainly your body, when it dies, becomes part of the ongoing chemical activity. But the situation is that you then stop expressing your activity through this particular body that you had. Chemistry takes over then. But it is not you who express chemistry after your death, just as it is not you either who express chemistry in your body during your life. What we have to fully appreciate is that there is nothing that is non-conscious in creation, because God's consciousness – his ability to experience and to act according to what he experiences – is behind the whole creation. The parts of the original existence, on the other hand, can never be present in creation in the same total and original way as God, but only in a partial and relative way. And then they can adapt to God's purpose with creation or not.

The pantheists say 'the sun is living', 'the Earth is living', 'everything is living'. 'Living' is their basic category, and for them 'life' means 'activity'. They only believe in activity. For them there is nothing existent that expresses that activity. Activity is the cause of activity.

P: But some pantheists do talk about God, don't they?

S: Yes, but only about a resting, inactive and only conscious God, a so-called transcendent God, who is at the same time creator and participant in everything. That means God is outside his creation in a passive, impersonal way, and inside his creation, in a transcendental form, in an active, personal way. For them, even God is as abstract as activity. He is conscious, but he is not an existent being as such.

The pantheists talk about activity as life, because they see consciousness as relative to life. They don't see life as relative to existence, as I do. For them life is not a meaningful, actively ongoing consequence or result of what consciousness experiences. Instead, life is seen as the cause that develops consciousness. For them it is not life but consciousness that is changeable and that can grow and develop or regenerate – in relation to original, impersonal laws, that is, objective and subjective necessities.

I say that creation in itself is not 'living'. Like every activity in itself, it is technical. Except on the Earth's surface, where life becomes obvious*, creation is always active in the same way, as if it were purely technical.

P: Are you thinking of celestial bodies?

S: Yes, including the matter that constitutes our own celestial body, the Earth. But because creation as a whole, including biology on the Earth, is one purposeful order, we have to assume that there is a single consciousness with an original, non-created being behind it – which pantheists don't do. It's just that generally we don't connect the activity to God, because the connection to God's Being is not obvious in creation.

P: Why did you say, a moment ago, 'except on the Earth's surface'?

S: Because it is only on the Earth's surface that the parts of God's existence interact with God's creation, so their consciousness affects God's creation there. We aren't forced to think that God's consciousness is behind the whole creation, but, as I've said, we can't avoid thinking that not only objective and subjective necessities, but also an organizing consciousness must be behind the meaningful activities of the biologically organized bodies that are anchored to the Earth's interacting surface.

P: Is activity always a sign of 'life'?

S: Yes. Either of God's life or of that of the parts. That is why to have the words 'life' and 'consciousness' mean two things is confusing. They are the same thing. In the general view – that is, other than mine – if we interpret an activity as neither living nor conscious, then we call the thing that expresses that activity 'dead' and describe the activity as mechanical. If we interpret an activity as living, but not conscious, then we call it 'alive' – this relates to plants and animals. Only our own species do we interpret as both 'living' and 'conscious'. But in my view, with God behind the whole creation, there is the same consciousness behind everything in creation, so the distinction 'dead'/'alive' – a distinction we still have to make on a day-to-day basis for purely practical purposes – does not exist.

M: So is a table alive or dead?

S: Philosophically, it is neither. Through science we understand that a table is activity, and if you reflect philosophically, it is impossible to create anything other than activity. Being, existence, must exist behind all activities, behind the whole creation, because only Being can act.

M: Does everything that we call 'alive' have a bit of consciousness in it?

S: Not 'in it'. There is consciousness behind every activity, whether we call it 'alive' or 'dead'. What is behind plants? With plants we start to get the idea of consciousness. In chemistry we don't get the idea of consciousness, even though chemistry acts by itself. And the sun also acts by itself. But the activity of chemistry and the activity of the sun don't seem to us to change, so we don't generally think of there being consciousness behind them.

P: But because they are active, there must be consciousness behind them?

S: Yes. So we have to think that God's consciousness – and God's Being, God's existence – is behind them. But the big problem is that God, because he is the whole, can only be active within himself, in a three-dimensional way, as I suggested before. So as participants in creation we can't technically follow an activity which starts from the whole of God's Being, because we can only follow activities that emanate from created objects when these activities travel one-dimensionally, that is, linearly, or, like a wave on the surface of the water or a snake on the ground, two-dimensionally. Light, sound, and an earthquake are typical examples of three-dimensional movement. They go on in all directions. We can experience them because they start from objects, but we can control them only as one-dimensional movement – like a ray, for example, in the case of light.

P: So we can experience the three-dimensional activity of the whole as one- or two-dimensional within creation, but we can never experience the source of the activity because it is the whole. On the other hand, we can experience the sun and the stars, for example, that are the source of the three-dimensional movement of light. In other words, since God's activity, creation, is coming at us, as it were, from all sides, we can't say where it is coming from, although we conclude that it must be coming from some whole that we are in?

S: Yes. So we can't understand how God creates. Nor can we go through the reverse process of technically tracing an activity back to the whole – that is, we can't learn or reproduce how God creates. That's why, incidentally, it's wrong, in my view, to think that the experience of our senses – whether we turn our attention inward, or whether we develop technology so that we can see more in an outward direction – can lead us to the original cause, to a total explanation of creation, which is what we are all expecting from science. Both processes – tracing an activity *from* a whole or *back to* a whole – are possible only in relation to the created manifold, where we experience matter in all its different destroyable forms as the origin of activity.

P: So within creation we can technically follow an activity starting from a whole – like a 'whole' human body that initiates activity, such as, say, throwing a stone, or, say, a 'whole' billiard ball that hits another billiard ball. And we can trace an activity back to a whole – like a bird's song to a 'whole' bird, or the movement of a billiard ball to some 'whole', a person or object, that moved it?

S: Yes. And we can, for example, technically follow how we take a watch apart, and so be able technically to reconstruct it.

P: So is it because God is the whole behind Nature that we can't technically understand and technically construct Nature-made 'living' parts: we can't do with a flower what we can do with a watch?

S: Yes. And because the whole creation is basically one order, which has the same autonomous creator, God, behind it, we also can't construct Nature-made 'objects' – neither living bodies, nor parts of living bodies, nor objects, nor parts of chemistry – because we can't find or make the original cause that we would need as a start for such creativity.

With our senses we can neither perceive nor control anything that goes on in the original Being. This possibility is cut off for us, as a meaningful necessity, by the indirect impression we get of empty space. It is replaced by the distance that we experience in creation to each other, through our created bodies, and to the whole, as the creator, through the whole diversity. Consequently the whole diversity, along with our own bodies, is shown to our senses as relatively solid, liquid and gaseous, and as changeable between these states and ultimately destructible: that is, as existent and not-existent at the same time. So the identity, the real existence of the original Being, as a living relation between its whole and its parts, is not a technical question, but a philosophical, a purely theoretical one – that is, it is a question of belief. That doesn't mean that this belief is non-empirical, or that it requires the development of a special knowledge, some special form of enquiry – like science or meditation. So it doesn't require a blind belief in authorities. What we have to do is to recognize God and each other on the basis of our basic ability to experience and our common need to be understood as likes in our common relation to the same creation, with God as the only creator and us as participants on the same natural condition given by the need to be understood as like, which is the precondition for mutual love.

P: And not to identify ourselves and each other with unlikenesses?

S: Yes. But we should also stop wasting time trying to understand what perfect knowledge is without relating it to a purpose – which is what we traditionally do when we regard the perfect conditions for a creator as the possession of perfect knowledge.

P: As can be traced in Jewish, Christian and Islamic interpretations of Genesis?

S: Yes, and in the theories of Greek philosophers or in innumerable mystical pantheistic or mythological sources.

The purpose makes every activity understandable, and simultaneously also makes the cause of every activity understandable. We understand every species, because we know the purposes behind their activities, and we know their purposes because we have, by Nature, to fulfil the same conditions.

Perfect knowledge without knowledge of its purpose, without knowing what it is perfect for, knowledge that is only believed or supposed to be perfect for everything, that is, for anything at all, can only frighten. As long as we have this idea and this aim of 'perfect knowledge' as the basic condition for a perfect creator, and as long as we see such 'perfect knowledge' as the aim of philosophy, the only result can be the typically human anxiety in relation to God, as well as in relation to our own species.

P: So going back to what we were saying about our inability to construct Nature-made objects: it is obvious that we couldn't make a piece of granite, for example?

S: That's right. We can only set up certain conditions so that Nature's creativity can operate.

M: But is a plant an activity, or is it conscious in its own right?

S: In my view, the plant has no consciousness. Your body has no consciousness. Your consciousness is *behind* your body, it rules your body, but your body is not conscious. Your body is activity, part of creation. All creation is activity that basically reflects God's consciousness and only relatively the consciousness of the parts.

M: What is the difference between a table, then, which we call 'dead', and a tree, which we regard as 'living'?

S: It is just a practical limit, which helps us in our practical behaviour. It helps us to know that we have to treat tables differently from plants and animals.

M: So there is no actual difference?

S: No. That is what Wöhler showed. It's the same, single system. But because of our practical need to know how to behave towards the different things, we draw this boundary, we make this division.

It's wrong, in my view, to think of consciousness as being *in* creation. God's consciousness is *behind* creation. And the conscious parts of God's existence – which are also *behind* creation, in the Being – come into creation in varying degrees of so-called incarnation – though 'incarnation' is a confusing term, because it suggests 'in' rather than 'behind'. So the consciousness of the parts becomes more and more apparent to us, in the biological activity on the Earth's surface. That is where we experience the objective expression of consciousness. But it is wrong, in my view, to think of consciousness as being *in* bodies or objects. Consciousness is not even in your own body.

God's activity and the activity of the conscious parts

P: What is the relationship in creation between the activity that originates with us, as conscious parts of God, and the activity that originates with God?

S: God's consciousness expresses the whole Nature and this whole ecology on the Earth. But the conscious parts interact with this ecology. The conscious parts create activity that interacts with the meaningful activity of God's creative consciousness, that is, interacts with God's original creation.

P: So we humans interact with God's activity?

S: Yes. We can interact in two ways. We can do it consciously, by which I mean being conscious of God's existence and his purpose in creation. In that case, we act in harmony with God's activity. Or we can do it unconsciously, that is, being unconscious of God's existence and purpose. In that case, we are confused and we disturb creation. We might say in that case that we interfere with creation, rather than interact with it.

P: But with regard to the original parts of God – in the original situation, in the Being – are you saying that in creation some of these parts become connected to human beings, others to animals, others to plants and so on?

S: No. Philosophically it's wrong to give different names to different objective expressions of the same quality, consciousness, that is, to call some of them plants, some animals, some humans and so on. The whole has the quality of consciousness. And the quality of consciousness is the same for God as for the parts of God's existence – it is the ability to experience, to take in. When it comes to 'giving out', to expressing, plants differ from animals, and animals differ from human beings. And human beings can differ from one another, because of the differing, individual, free interpretations humans can make of creation, which they communicate through speech and action. But the impression of reality, mediated by Nature, that we each have all the time as human beings is the same, independently of what we take in and of what we express through language. Our body informs us of our existential needs – light, heat, air, water, food, reproduction – and the possibility of satisfying them in the surrounding reality, and we are also informed of the need that consciousness has, that is, undivided, undisturbed love, the need to be understood by other human beings.

The need of consciousness: undivided love

P: How are we informed about the need that consciousness has?

S: In the same way that our consciousness is informed about our bodily needs: through desire. Consciousness is informed about its own need through our common desire for relationship. It is desire that binds our consciousness to all our needs. This bondage in itself is invisible, because what experiences the desire – consciousness – is invisible. But because the things that our consciousness is bound to by our bodily needs – food, water, air and so on – are obvious within the material, objective reality, bondage to our bodily needs, as conditions for the body's survival, is generally interpreted as operating mechanically, rather than biologically.

P: How do you mean?

S: Because mechanical force is inescapable and biological needs are inescapable, and because biological needs are generally interpreted as a biological *force*, we experience them in the same way that we experience mechanical necessities. We generally connect biological needs in our mind to the body, which we interpret as forcing us, physically, to eat and so on. We generally think of it as our body wanting food, rather than our consciousness wanting food. We don't trace things back to consciousness.

P: It should be clear that our body does not want food if we consider that a 'dead' body does not want food.

S: Yes, quite. The only way to escape our bodily needs is to die or commit suicide. But we can never escape the need for love, which for the original parts involves both the need for understanding and the need to be understood. But if we think that it is our body that wants food, then we feel forced by the body's needs. As I said earlier, we see our bodily needs as a burden, as forced upon us by Nature, because we are identified with our own creativity, which we want to force on Nature.

The other view – my view – would be to see our bodily needs as part of the enjoyable, created reality that we can never escape. There is only one reality: the original one with its activity, expressed as what we call Nature. We shouldn't try to escape it or to change it according to our own wants or wills. In other words, we shouldn't relate to it as meaningless, non-conscious, dead, as acting only mechanically.

P: So, going back to the need of consciousness itself...

S: Yes, the need of consciousness itself is different in that it can't be satisfied by meeting reality only objectively – which is how we generally meet reality: as non-conscious objects ruled in a meaningless way by mechanical and biological necessities. The need of consciousness can't be satisfied by meeting reality only objectively because the need of consciousness itself is not a desire of the metabolism. It is not the desire to enjoy the satisfaction of the existential needs, but the desire to experience love through meeting another conscious being, another subject, in mutual understanding. Because the need of consciousness is not mechanical – that is, it requires not just a meeting between bodies – nor is it even biological – that is, it doesn't require an exchange of food that we need and that we can give to and take from each other – this particular need, the need of consciousness, can easily be considered mystical. It *will* be considered mystical if we don't make the clear distinction between biological causality, which operates through a desire, an attraction of the consciousness to something in the environment, and mechanical causality, which operates, in our objective experience of reality, through power. This is a distinction that we ought, philosophically, to make. As I have said, after Wöhler the distinction between biological and mechanical causality was eliminated. His finding was generally interpreted as evidence for there being no creator, no mystical God's finger behind life on Earth. It was seen as scientific proof of atheism. In fact, with the first so-called synthesis, he did no more than discover the natural conditions for Nature's creativity – similar to the way humans discover the natural conditions for agriculture. But thereafter matter, which was regarded as non-living, was generally interpreted as the cause of life. So since Wöhler we have tried to understand everything, including life, in terms of objective, that is, mechanical, causality.

P: Because with Wöhler biology came to be reduced to chemistry?

S: Yes – chemistry interpreted as mechanical causality, without consciousness behind it. Our experience of mechanical causality is a product of our distance-based, objective relation to creation. If this is interpreted as absence of bondage, it gives rise for humans to the feeling that they are free from reality, as well as to the idea that we have power to change reality. And as long as we dream about being free from reality and about our power to change reality, we can't be interested in the whole creation as a relationship to an unchangeable order made by a conscious creator, God. We become satisfied with a mechanical explanation – the Big Bang – without asking what the biological cause and meaning of this mechanical event is. At the same time, we can never be rid of our experience that we are alive and that there is life on the Earth, nor of our desire to understand life's meaning in the context of our unavoidable cooperation with everything.

In my view, we have to actualize the question whether the meaning of life is to change reality or to understand the creator's purpose in creating. And, as I've argued, unless we understand the creator's purpose, we can't understand either the creator or ourselves – because it is impossible to understand a conscious being who has neither a need nor a purpose behind its activities.

P: ...which applies to both God and us?

S: Yes. If we don't understand the creator's purpose, the word 'God' or 'creator' remains anonymous. It is just an empty word for a powerful, 'almighty', living Being – which tells you nothing. It is like the word 'I', as 'I' is generally interpreted. We can attach to it whatever meaning we want. In that case, we will remain confused about how to satisfy our need for love, both in relation to each other, whom we will see as arbitrary egos, and in relation to the whole of creation, which we will experience as basically changeable, rather than as a basically unchangeable order that is only changeable on its illusorily existent surface.

P: You are going a little too quickly for me here. Why do these consequences follow?

The necessity for agreement

S: A mechanical answer to the question of the cause of an activity can never satisfy us. We need also to know the meaning of an activity. That's why an authoritarian answer to the question of the original cause – that is, one that can't give a logically understandable answer as to the meaning of creation – is never a satisfactory answer. We can't love the whole of creation if its original cause is considered to be matter, that is, something non-conscious, non-living, an object. We can't love an object, because an object can't have experience and act by itself and be responsible for its activity – so there can't be mutual relation with it. Similarly, we can't have mutual relation with other humans, we can't love each other, as long as we want to be creative out of ourselves, rather than out of our common consciousness of reality. If we want to be creative out of ourselves, by ourselves – because we are not interested in understanding reality's meaning – we want to change reality. But we can't get rid of our responsibility, both to Nature and to humans, for our own creativity, for our 'independent' 'own reality'. Unless we can agree that we are all responsible for the two different uses of language predetermined by the choice that faces us – to interpret reality as God's meaningful creation, or as the product of human creativity – we remain anonymous to each other: we can't know, we can't understand another person until we know what the particular ideas behind their creativity are. When we do know one such idea, the anonymity stops, but only a certain sort of limited love can start if we agree with only that one idea and the way to realize it – 'limited' because it may be disturbed by all the person's other ideas that we don't know about. If we discover other ideas they have with which we disagree, then our love becomes divided.

P: You mean: we love them when they express the idea with which we agree, but not when they express the idea with which we disagree?

S: Yes. Or they may change their mind about the idea or ideas that we love them for, and then we can't love them any more.

P: If we don't agree with them at all, what then?

S: Then either we tolerate them or we fight against them. But we can't love them.

P: So, in your view, love can be permanent only if we experience reality basically as one conscious existence, and if we understand other people as inseparable parts of that invisible, conscious existence, who become temporarily engaged in a meaningful creation to which we all have to relate in a common agreement about its purpose?

S: Yes... by remembering that everybody is connected to creation, by the common need of consciousness – the need to be understood, the need to experience mutual relation – and by the common needs of their own body.

P: So you are hardly a pluralist!

S: No. If you believe in the original cause in a logical way, then the whole creation is one. There can be only one truth, which we experience as one Nature. But we have to agree about it publicly, and continuously communicate it to the next generation.

P: Do you believe you have the truth?

S: No, I can't have it, because I can't prove it. I can only hold my hypothesis as a belief, which means theoretically. To 'have the truth' would mean to have knowledge-based, that is, sense-based, evidence for the truth. All I can do is present my belief in language and invite other people to check the consequences of this belief. They are welcome to criticize it. If they really criticize it and don't find any argument against it, then of course they will believe it too. The more they check it, that is, the more they try to criticize it while still not finding that they can refute it, the more they will become convinced of their belief – at least, that is my experience.

P: So love is the basic need for everybody, because love is the need of consciousness.

S: Yes. And consciousness is the basic quality that everyone has. This consciousness, this unlimited consciousness, gives us relation to the whole unlimited reality when we come into creation. Doesn't everybody experience their consciousness as unlimited as soon as they are born? And don't they spontaneously start to use their senses to acquire awareness and experience of this new reality, these new surroundings? They use their senses to take in the image of the universe, and they coordinate themselves with their bodily needs and with the circumstances on Earth. Isn't every person then aware of the whole creation experientially in the same way? Does a person lose their consciousness of the whole creation just because they are concentrating on drinking a cup of tea? No, I acquire it as a child, and then I have it and can remember it throughout my life – unless there is a catastrophe with my brain, so that I completely lose my memory.

P: But I suppose that when people get their own ideas about reality, they live in those ideas, and not in the ever-present reality?

S: Yes. But people don't have any clear ideas about 'reality', because generally nobody distinguishes between the ever-present reality on the one hand and the memory of reality or history on the other. People generally say that reality is both these put together. The memory of reality, or history, is a reality, of course, but it is particular to the person remembering it. It is different from the ever-present reality, which, as a whole, is common to us all.

'Freedom' from reality?

P: So in practice people can't leave the ever-present reality? They are always exposed to an impression of the whole?

S: Yes, but most of the time people are disturbed by it, because they prefer to live in their memory of reality and history. They have to set their consciousness of the ever-present reality aside all the time, because it creates anxiety for them.

P: Because they don't understand the original cause?

S: Yes. The only alternative then is try to overcome the anxiety by seeking to control reality. So they distance themselves from it, otherwise they can't achieve the idea of 'freedom', the feeling of being independent of reality, of not belonging to it, of being outside it. They become totally identified with this position, hoping that from it they can control the whole reality. Yet they know – everybody knows – that we all belong one hundred per cent to reality. There is no possible way of leaving reality. Everyone knows this. But you can't live according to the idea that you are independent, free, unless you set this knowledge aside.

P: You can't have the illusion of free will if you are conscious of the whole reality?

S: Nor can you have the illusion of free will if you remember that you are bound in a distanceless way to reality through your bondage to your own body.

P: But we say of people that they are 'out of touch with reality'.

S: But it's a wrong way of putting it. Such people try to isolate themselves from reality, but in fact they are in touch with reality all the time – even though they don't want to be.

P: But when we are with somebody who is like that, we feel they are less present, that they are 'absent', or 'absent-minded'.

S: Of course, long self-isolation, long-term living in the memory and in history brings such results. You can't make contact about the ever-present reality with such people unless you tell them your belief about the ever-present cause of their presence in creation and of the whole ever-present reality. But you still can't force any interest in the ever-present cause and the ever-present reality. Not even God can. That is the problem with any understanding that living beings have to do – whether it relates to understanding the activities of objects or the activities of other living beings: they have to do it by themselves.

Dialogue 3

OBJECTS, SUBJECTS AND LOVE

Can love be one-sided?

Philip: You said a little earlier that we can't love an object, because we can't have a mutual relation with an object... [See p.71.]

Stefan: Yes, objective experience, that is, the experience of objects outside us, is always one-sided.

P: ...and you said that subjective relation is always two-sided, and love is two-sided. But can't love also be one-sided: when we love another person and they don't love us?

S: Yes, it can also be one-sided in that way, when it's not certain that the other loves us too. I can also believe that I am loving when I am not.

P: What are you referring to?

S: For example, when we 'fall in love' or admire somebody. Admiration is based on unlikeness. We admire someone for being something we are not. Love can never function as long as we feel unlike. And 'falling in love' is between unlikes, because generally it is accepted that the other gender is unlike, and today even that everyone is unlike, everyone is unique. When the 'falling in love' is mutual, it is one-sided admiration on both sides. Each admires something in the other. But this is not love.

If people don't meet on the natural basis I have talked about – in which they identify with their common consciousness of the ever-present whole – then love can't function. People can then only meet on the basis of an identification with some detail or details of the common consciousness of the ever-present whole.

P: So one flower-lover will feel they have something in common with another flower-lover, or one Beatles fan with another Beatles fan, or one historian with another historian, and so on?

S: Yes. And they will develop their knowledge of the particular detail they are identified with and experience that detail as their own, personal reality.

Matilda: How is your view different from the common conception that one 'gives love'?

S: You can never give love. Not even God can give love. God can give creation, but God can't give love. It's impossible to give or to take love. There is no thing, no substance – 'love' – that you can give or take.

P: So when you, Stefan, from your point of view, say 'I love this person', you don't mean 'I am giving love to this person'?

S: If you were to say that you are giving love to a particular person, then from my point of view you are confused about what love is. Love is only possible if we have a proper belief in God. If we don't have a proper belief in God, that is, if we don't have a proper understanding of the original cause and meaning of creation, then we can't have a proper understanding of anything – which makes it impossible to understand what love is.

P: So what is the situation with human beings who believe in God in the way you are suggesting, and who say 'I love the other, but they don't love me'?

S: The full feeling of love is when we also feel understood, because love is a relation between two conscious beings. Each must understand the other.

M: But from your point of view, if you love another, and they don't love you, you don't feel hurt by that?

S: No.

M: Do you feel anything? Doesn't it matter?

S: It's not that it doesn't matter, because in the same way that God desires love – that is, desires to be understood as like – everybody desires love. Only one does not then start 'treating' the other person in such a way as to 'get' love. One knows that it is impossible to demand or force love. One tries rather to actualize this understanding – of God and so on – in the other person. But one never tries to 'treat' the other person, because we know that treatment and love are two different things. Treatment is to have power over, to control, and it's what we do to objects. Love is between subjects, and then only between likes. And as long as people want to have power, they are locked into a hierarchy and there are no likes. It's self-evident. Power is 'over' someone. In a hierarchy you are either 'under' someone or 'over' someone, but never 'like'.

M: It's because love is so bound up in common culture with the ego that it's quite confusing thinking of it in this way.

S: Yes, if someone experiences their ego as their identity, it is impossible to love. Nobody is confused about the *desire* for love, but then everybody has this quite sure conception of themselves as being able to 'give love'. And because of that, love stops. But people try all the time to give love. Or to take it. 'Taking it' is the same idea: 'I give so that I can take.' Love can only function if we understand each other as complete likes, which means thinking of each other as conscious parts of the same reality.

M: Love is a state, in a way.

S: Yes, it is a state of consciousness, the natural state of consciousness. But it is displaced by anxiety when we learn language if there is not a logical tradition about the original cause. Then we desire infinite knowledge and power and the ability to control creation, instead of understanding its meaning. We become objects that think mechanically, as Descartes suggested we are, impressed by modern science's perfect, so-called exact, objective investigations of mechanical relations.

P: You say thinking 'objects' because then we don't see ourselves as driven by either existential needs or by the subjective need for love, but just by the desire for objective power?

S: Yes. We no longer act from our identity as a conscious part of the whole, but identify with ourselves as a thinking being. We see ourselves as an ego that develops knowledge of causality, both mental and physical, in order to have either greater mental power – what we call 'charisma' – or greater physical, mechanical power – what we call energy resources.

Can we love an object?

M: I am still puzzled when you say we can't love an object.

S: You can prefer one object to another, but you can't love an object – because love is only possible between subjects who can understand and act according to what they understand.

M: Can we love somebody, a subject, who is behaving like an object, that is, a subject who experiences themselves as a thinking object?

S: If I experience the subject behind the object, then I can love the subject – even if he or she is behaving like an object. Behaving like an object starts when people have turned away from their original consciousness, their identification with their original ability to experience, and act as egos, identified with the possibility for memory- and language-based thinking. I can prefer one ego to another, but it's impossible to love an ego, because preferring and love are different things.

Every culture has talked about these problems: the difference between undivided love and preference, predilection. And preference or predilection was always said to be mixed with suffering – passion, in the old sense of the word.

M: We love creation…

S: …if there is not this fundamental anxiety.

M: But surely in loving creation, we do love objects: a tree, or a stone?

S: Yes, because we generally don't make the distinction in language between preferences and undivided love. I mean loving creation with an undivided love. You can only love creation as a whole, connected to God. Unless you love it that way, undividedly, all you can do is prefer – that is, prefer some parts of it to other parts of it. You can't have the same feeling for an object as for a subject – but we don't make a distinction in language between these two feelings either. Love is only possible between two subjects.

M: But you said one-sided love is possible.

S: One-sided love is possible, if I think of God as behind all these objects. Just as if I also think, in relation to all these objects sitting in chairs here – I mean human beings – of a conscious mind behind each. Then I can love in a one-sided way. If the other has the same idea about creation and my body, then two-sided love is possible.

P: So if you just see a stone with pleasure, and you don't think of God as behind creation, then you prefer it, you don't love it?

S: Then you prefer it for some practical reason, but it is still impossible to love a stone.

M: But if you see God behind it, then you love it?

S: Not the stone. One is loving God, for and through his creation. As it is impossible to separate a cause from its activity, it is impossible to separate God from his creation. And the more we have checked that creation is really made for the purpose I am suggesting, the more we love God for his creation or, more precisely, the less often our love for creation is disturbed – by what is generally seen as evil, for which God is blamed.

P: It's the same with people, isn't it? If you think there is a conscious mind behind them, you can love them, and then you love their bodies too.

S: Yes. And then you can check if these other people want to know about their consciousness, their ability to experience, or only want to be thinking objects – because which they want makes a difference to their behaviour. If they want to be thinking objects, we don't know what the needs and purposes behind their behaviour are, unless they announce them. And if they announce them, either we can accept them, if they don't disturb us, or we are disturbed by them. If they don't announce them, we generally feel confusion and anxiety when we meet such people. People who see themselves as thinking objects are always experienced by us as anonymous, and we feel alienated from them.

M: Can you have a two-sided relation with animals?

S: That is all you can have with animals, unless the animal is dangerous, and then the relationship with it is disturbed. But you always have two-sided relation with animals, because you know their needs.

M: Are you loving them or God?

S: Both at the same time. I am loving God for their existence, as I love the whole creation – because there is God's consciousness behind the activity that is their physical body, and there is the consciousness that is connected to the animal's body, which directs that body as a whole.

M: Is that different from a stone again?

S: Yes, of course, because I meet only God's consciousness behind the stone.

M: What about with a tree?

S: It's not the same as with an animal. I can't have the same objective relation with a tree that I can have with a dog, because a tree doesn't react immediately to my behaviour. It's just different if you play with a dog. The dog responds. A tree responds only if you give it water and so on, and it takes a long time to respond! However that may be, as soon as we suppose 'life' to be there – that is, as soon as there is a sign of consciousness – there is an experience of two-wayness in the relationship, and three-wayness when you believe properly, without contradictions, in God.

Love and preference

P: But let's say I feel this undivided love for creation, and that includes other people, it may still be that I like some people better than others, and I don't know why?

S: You don't need to ask or say why. There is no reason to ask the question. We are forced by practical life to make choices. Preference exists because we must make choices. But we wrongly experience our 'likes' and 'dislikes', our preferences, as an expression of 'who we are', of our basic identity. We become identified with them. We don't see them simply as choices that we each can and must make because of unlikenesses that also belong to Nature.

But we don't want to meet people who behave in a completely different way from us, or people who don't want to know about reality at all, or who want to know about reality in a completely different way. We don't want contact with criminals, for example. And criminals want to have contact only with criminals. It is obvious that we want to have contact only with those who have the same, or not contradictory, ideas about life.

P: Whether we take your view or not?

S: Yes. Unless we agree about, or at least are interested in, the original cause and meaning of the whole reality, it is impossible to get rid of this alienation from each other and from reality.

Helping and understanding

M: What if I wanted to have contact with criminals in order to help them?

S: 'Helping' is possible only in relation to physical problems. In psychological terms, it is not a matter of 'helping', because only each person alone can help themselves to change their identity – that is, to realize what I believe to be their true identity: their human identity.

M: Can't I help a criminal stop being a criminal?

S: Yes, but you can't stop them feeling alienated, in the way people – criminals or non-criminals – feel alienated. You can only try to discuss with them to find out if they are interested in their human identity, rather than wanting to be an ego.

M: But it may be so rare that someone treats them as a like.

S: But it's impossible anyway to 'treat' someone as a like. As 'likes' you don't treat one another. You have mutual communication through language. You experience mutual relation with a like. 'Treatment' involves unlikeness. Then we use language to 'treat'. We can use language in many different ways to 'treat' each other, but such use of language is a misuse – although it's the only way language is used today.

P: But it may be that when the criminal is with you, they feel that you are different from other people, they have a different emotional experience, and that may lead to them asking a question.

S: Yes, if they have some idea of an alternative, and if they want to get rid of their identity as a criminal. But let's say the criminal asks me something, because they experience me as different, and I give an answer: if they don't ask me from their human identity, my answer is never directly an answer to what they ask. That is often my problem: people don't interpret my answers as answers. With my answer I want to put people back to the human identity, to our common, natural consciousness of the whole reality, in the hope that there they can come to the insight that language, if we want to use it for communication, must be anchored in the common reality. But they often ask from the personal ego, and they say I have not answered. But I have answered.

P: Is this the problem of people asking about the details of limited situations, whereas you always want to discuss the details in relation to the whole situation?

S: Yes. They ask me about my views on something particular, without understanding that I always talk about something particular in the light of the whole.

P: So this could happen with the criminal too?

S: Yes. But if they show a real interest in the whole, then the dialogue starts. But it can't be a dialogue [see Appendix B for an expansion of this definition of dialogue] until they show this real human interest, without preconceptions. And that's the only problem. But it's a constant problem. I used to give invited lectures that were attended by people who hadn't heard me before, among them atheists. The atheists often left the room saying that it was impossible to talk with me. They said I was unfair, because I didn't want to discuss their questions. Yet I always answered them, telling them what I thought their view missed or lacked. But I answered with this other consciousness. I tried to get them to understand that I don't talk from an atheistic basis, but they wanted to discuss things on an atheistic basis.

P: I suppose people sometimes don't realize which philosophical viewpoint on these questions – about the original cause – they are coming from, because the questions are not discussed in society nowadays.

S: I think that is often the case. But if people don't want to change from this ego identity to their identity as a human being, I can't do anything. And often people don't want to because they have this ego that regards itself as completely free from Nature and which sits in preferences, not in the basic state of undivided love. That is 'personality', identification with unlikenesses. And each personality is different. And if personality is the person's identity, they can't discuss anything as human beings – in the sense I mean 'human being'. When I meet a person, I see both – their personality and their human identity – but I choose to answer out of the common human identity, waiting to see whether the other person is catching the idea that we are alike. In the personality, we are unlike. The difficulty is that people usually listen to me as a stranger, as someone unlike, and they want to understand *me*. And they are blind to the fact that I don't want to explain myself: I want a dialogue on the basis of the natural identity.

Whom can we have exchange with?

What about relationships in general with other people? How do you think about the possibility of exchange with other people? You have a feeling about the different people you have exchange with, and what kind of exchange is possible with the different people. Some people you find it impossible to have an exchange with. What do you measure that by?

P: Why is it different, you mean?

S: Sure, why is it different? Why, for example, have the two traditions – the theological and the pantheist – also been divided geographically from each other, throughout history? Why were they forced to live in isolation from each other? It was because they had different basic ideas about reality: the one had belief in one God, the other had belief in gods. Or even if people believed in the same God, they believed in him in different ways: the one was Catholic, the other was Protestant. In fact there have been many, many more differences within Christianity: I think about three and hundred and twenty different Christian sects – that was a figure I heard. They live divided – why? It's only because they have a different idea about reality.

P: And that affects the way they see each other?

S: Yes. If a Jew becomes a Christian, immediately there is the possibility of exchange with other Christians. Our view of whom it is possible to have exchange with is very, very limited. That's why we are struck by the absence and death of those with whom we can have exchange. Of course, as regards people with whom we like to have exchange and with whom we have regular exchange, it is a great sorrow if they are absent. But how would you experience it if you could have exchange with everybody you meet? There are always a lot of people you meet on a practical basis, but how would it be if you had the experience of being able to talk to everyone in the same way – that is, from the beginning as likes, without some identification with some unlikeness?

P: Yes, I can see that it would be very different.

The bondage of love

S: We experience only difficulties if we seek to bind people's consciousness to ourselves. How would it be if we considered that we do not need to bind people to us, because they are bound to Nature in the same way that we are? We don't recognize this mystical bondage, which is love. We are clear about the common bondage to all our bodily needs, which we can see, but we tend not to recognize and reckon with our connection to human beings by the similar type of bondage that love represents. You can reckon with the fact that you are hungry, you can reckon with the fact that a dog is hungry, you can reckon with the fact that every species needs light, warmth, air, and so on. So we reckon with animals, plants, everything that has life, because we know about their bondage to these needs, to which we ourselves are bound. We can reckon with them, know about them, trust in them, because we have the same bondage. We experience in daily life that these needs are binding. But can you describe how they are binding? There is no thread that binds, there is no power.

P: It is just clear that if you don't respect the bondage, you die.

S: Yes, gradually, but not immediately. If you don't breathe, you can live for three minutes. If you don't drink, you can live for three or four days – or perhaps more, I don't know. If you don't eat, you can live for perhaps thirty days. Perhaps sixty days. But if you don't love…

P: You can live your whole life. So science does not take account of this bondage to reality through love?

S: …this mystical bondage – which is not mystical, because we know it. Every living body is bound in principle to the same things: light, warmth, air, food, the Earth – in the Earth's case through gravitation – reproduction and movement. But we do not reckon with the bondage of love, the basic bondage. That's why I sometimes talk about it being like gravitation. It is a power that does not have any manifestation. That is why it is impossible to give love, and why it is impossible to take love. When people have that idea, they work themselves to death to realize love, without any success – in fact, only with the opposite result. They become more and more confused about what love is.

Identity

M: I am still struggling with your view of our identity and would like to go back to that. Would you say there is something separate, something detachable that can move – when this body we are now connected to dies – between the Being and creation and wherever it is we 'go to' – what is sometimes called, I think, 'the other side' of creation?

S: Try to bear in mind your original existence in the Being. In the Being your original existence can't move, can't be active, except for the movement or activity you experience as your consciousness, your ability to experience. And in creation you can't remember that it is your identity in the Being. It is only through creation that God makes it possible for us to have the illusion that we can move and remember. Through creation you can become connected to this body that you have now and experience movement through this body. But by connecting to a created body you don't lose your connection to your original existence. When you die, you have that connection to use – and you probably retire to every night without knowing about it – and you also possibly have what tradition calls the soul*.

P: You mentioned the Christian idea of soul briefly earlier, but this is the first time you have used the word 'soul' as part of your view. How do you see the soul?

S: We have a certain relation to it during our dreams at night and, in the daytime, as our personal states of judgement and understanding. It is constituted by Nature as a personal causal system of rememberable evaluations and conclusions that we have previously reached through thinking.

P: …which follows along with our ability to experience after we die?

S: Yes, according to many traditional statements, and that's also what I suppose. But these are things that we do not have to deal with or understand in this life. We have to understand this life here as self-evident, perfect for its purpose. Therefore, the first human problem is to agree on the creator's meaning with the whole creation. That is why philosophy was called by some traditions 'the science of sciences'. Life on 'the other side' of creation must be self-evident in the same way, so we don't need to worry about it now. It's only our anxiety about death and our lack of belief in God – that is, our lack of a proper understanding of the original cause and meaning of creation – that makes us want to know. We are born to this life without any previous knowledge. This life explains itself to us adequately – if we don't confuse each other by using language to develop infinite power, in an agreement, never discussed, that the whole creation, including life on Earth, is basically meaningless. If this life explains itself to us adequately, why shouldn't the next?

M: Well, coming back to your hypothesis, Stefan: am I a separate entity in the Being?

S: Yes, only not separate. You are something, an entity in itself, without parts that belong to you – but you are an inseparable part of the Being. Therefore, you can't experience anything in the Being or have any power there. And both in the Being and in creation, you can only ever *feel* that you are an entity, an individual. You can never *formally**, *objectively experience* yourself as an entity, because you can never be outside yourself.

P: What about people who talk about themselves as if they are outside themselves, such as when they say 'I want to know myself' or 'I want to find myself'?

S: This is because our created body gives the illusion of a wholeness with its own, inseparable parts. The feeling of having distance from everything, of being outside, separate from everything, can give us the idea that we are outside ourselves, that we don't belong to, or are separate from, ourselves. If we were to think that we belonged to the non-created Being, then we would understand that we *are* outside our own created body, in the same way that we are outside every other created body. It is simply that our connection to our own body via a nervous system is different from our connection via perception to all other bodies. But all bodies belong to creation, and every attempt to discover ourselves, that is, to have the same 'objective' connection to our own ability to experience that we have through the senses to our own body and all other bodies, is irrational.

P: And the idea of an objective connection to our mind?

S: It's the same irrational idea, because our consciousness has the same immediate connection to its own mind as it has to the body to which it is connected. In both cases, the idea of an objective connection can be appealing, because it fits with our wish to control and impose our own order on our minds and on our bodies – just as we want to do the same with creation – rather than allowing the order of Nature to control them and order them.

P: The general view is that we are a mind connected to a body. Is it your view then that we are a consciousness connected to a mind and a body?

S: Yes.

P: So how are 'soul' and 'mind' different, in your view?

S: They are essentially the same, inseparable thing. But there are two aspects. I interpret the mind as the mental aspect, the thinking we do to understand causality. The soul I interpret as the emotional aspect, our evaluation system – generally based on a mixture of Nature's impression on us and of memory and language – on which our understanding of causality is based.

P: So the soul is primary?

S: Yes. It's our evaluation system that gives rise to our need to think about and understand causality.

P: What do you mean by 'evaluation system'? What is it that we evaluate?

S: Basically all values are offered to us by Nature, but every living being has to make choices, personal evaluations, all the time, among the values that Nature offers. Other species make these evaluations, but because they don't have an everything-covering language, they can't make a common, theoretical problem out of it and, as humans generally do, let this theoretical problem overshadow their practical relation to reality.

M: Some people have an idea that the consciousness that we are is somewhat like a drop of water that disappears in a big pool of water, as it were, when we die, losing its separateness in the process.

S: But why water? Why a pool? Why a process? These are pantheistic ideas of Being. The pantheistic notion of drops of water and a pool stems from their experience of introspective science, where the surroundings are experienced as a fluent medium, without the experience of distance that gives the feeling of being outside things. Instead of 'water', 'drop' and 'a pool', I use the terms 'the common ability to experience', 'a part of the Being' and 'the whole Being', and I say that in this life, too, we are never cut off from, and never can be cut off from, our connection to the original Being.

In my view, there exists only the real, unchangeable object – God and the conscious parts – which together make an indivisible one. And then there is activity expressed by this object. Originally this is expressed only by the whole object, God, because the parts have no power in the original Being. But then activity is also expressed by the parts, though only within creation, through the power they acquire there.

P: Let me just check if I understand you: the parts can't create in the Being, because they don't have power over the Being. Only God has the power to create in the Being. But the parts can 'create' in creation. They can create activity, because they become connected to a body in creation.

S: Yes, and it is only possible, both for God and for the parts, to create activity. What makes for human confusion is that humans think that they can create something original, like a cup or a table. But the cup and the table are only activity – arranged and constantly rearranged by creation as what we experience as the matter of which the cup and the table are made.

P: But the non-created object – in the philosophical sense – that God and the parts is can't be compared with the relative objects or matter of creation?

S: No. The non-created object that God and the parts is can never be experienced in an objective way, from the outside, either by the parts or even by God. And that non-created object is the same all the time; it can never change. It can become active, can continue to be active and can cease to be active, but it can't create other objects of its kind, only activity.

What is confusing is that God makes in creation what appear to us to be objects. He does that because thinking needs objects as a basis. It is impossible to base thinking on the absence of objects, that is, on 'nothing': understanding requires that we are able to trace an activity back to some object. If we hear a birdsong, or any sound, we have to go back to a bird, or to something that makes the sound. So God has to give seeming objects. But at the same time, God solves the confusion that arises from our experience of seeming objects, by allowing us the insight that what we experience in creation as objects are not really objects – because they are endlessly changeable, that is, destroyable. And if they are destroyable, they can't be real objects.

P: And would you say that we have the experience of seeking to understand an activity by tracing it back to an object because God wants us to do the same in the case of the whole activity that is God's creation: he wants us to trace that whole activity back to its original cause, the original whole, himself, so that in that way we will come to understand that he exists?

S: Yes...that he exists as the whole Being, and that each of us exists as a part of his existence – so neither the whole nor the parts can be destroyed.

P: So this is another way in which creation is perfect for God's aim?

S: Yes.

P: Pantheists also understand that real objects don't exist in creation, don't they?

S: Yes, but they draw the conclusion that there is only activity, a flow. And that's where they stop. For them, basically there is nothing that is existent. For them, everything is flowing. But they don't say *what* is flowing, and that is irrational. They say there is no unchangeable existence, no unchangeable Being, only one ever-changing, creative flow, a changeable, random order regulated only by impersonal physical and moral laws.

In my view, the activity that is creation is also one order, but it starts from the whole Being, from God. And it obviously takes place within God, if God is the whole. That's why the activity also obviously cannot be shown to us as starting from the whole Being. Rather it appears to start from seeming objects. It appears to start as the activities that go out from each object as an interacting closed system, as one active order.

The parts of the Being

M: Is there a limited number of consciousnesses?

S: You mean 'parts of the Being with the quality of consciousness'?

M: Yes.

S: There must be, otherwise, given that the parts are existent, we would have to accept that something can come out of nothing, that is, we would have to accept the opposite of the axiom that no thing can arise, originate from nothing – and that would make consistent thinking impossible. But I don't think it is relevant how many parts there are. You know that however many parts you meet, each part manifests basically the same consciousness, the same ability to experience. And if you think of God, you have to think of God also as like, as manifesting the same ability to experience. The only difference is that God experiences his own existence, which includes us, the parts. But no part can experience the whole existence, God. Our relation to God in the Being can never be changed: we can never be God, the whole, and God can never be a part. But how many parts there are is of no interest.

M: But in theory is it possible that a cow, for example, could have a permanent consciousness?

S: In theory, everything is possible! But from the point of view of my hypothesis, the answer is 'no', because the cow is a form. It's only an apparent object in creation. A cow does not *have* a consciousness. As I said earlier, consciousness is never *in* anything in creation. A permanent consciousness, a permanent conscious part, is *behind* the cow. Think of it as being the same as it is with humans. Cows, horses, humans don't really exist – they are just activity. In the Being there exist just parts, with the same quality, consciousness. A particular conscious part is connected to a cow in creation, and what that particular conscious part is able to do is determined by the fact that it is connected to a cow's body. But the conscious part is not a cow. It can only act as a cow. As a human being, you have to take into account God's need, which leads to the idea that the whole creation is made because God wants to be understood. And if you have the desire to understand God, then you want to become connected to a human body, because only as human beings can we talk about God and his need.

P: Would you say that God himself is 'incarnated' in the whole of creation?

S: Yes, because he is originally the whole reality. But he shows himself in creation, as the manifold, through all the celestial bodies, that is, including the Earth. He can't show himself as a whole, in the way that he is able to show the parts indirectly to each other as wholes. But in our minds we can connect God to the whole creation – in the same way that in my mind I can connect the conscious part that you are to your body, and you can connect the conscious part that I am to my body. But it doesn't make sense to try to find my consciousness *in* my body, or yours *in* yours. We can think of consciousness as only fully 'incarnated' in human beings, because the human species is the only species we can talk with about the whole reality. We can therefore understand another person's interpretation, and can become conscious of whether the other person is interested in the original cause and meaning of creation or not.

P: And if I find that they are not interested?

S: Then I don't get their attention. If they say, for example: 'I'm not interested in all this philosophy, I am only interested in flowers', then I don't meet the human being. I meet someone who is identified with flowers. In a way, I effectively meet only a flower – because the other person refuses to talk about anything but flowers. Maybe the next time I speak with them it won't be the same. But in general I have no interest in meeting again those who are identified with different details of reality. I am only interested in meeting human beings. But I know that everyone on the Earth *could* be interested in the whole creation. So if they are not interested, I think to myself: 'They are not interested *now*'. So I try and awaken their interest every time I meet them.

M: If a cow dies, does its consciousness go over to the other side of creation?

S: The cow's consciousness is not in the cow's body. It is only connected to it. The connection can change, but the consciousness remains the same.

M: But does the place of the consciousness change?

S: You mean 'the place of the conscious part'?

M: Yes.

S: You too are also now in the Being. If you dream, you are connected to your dreams on the level of the so-called transcendental or 'abstract' creation, and if you are in deep sleep – that is, sleeping but not dreaming – you remain in the Being, without experiencing any connection to creation. If you are disappointed with creation, you may just remain in the Being and have no interest in having a link to creation – until you have the interest again. In the Being there is no time, so the time-scale is unimportant. You can't remember how long you have been in deep sleep.

M: But there are no parts in creation? The parts are in the Being?

S: That's right. Within creation there are only participants in creation. We give relative names to the different objective manifestations of God's and the original parts' consciousness that exist within the unitary order of creation.

M: So 'parts' is not equivalent to 'humans'?

Consciousness and creation

S: No. The relevant idea is 'conscious part' – of the Being – without it referring to the created body of a human, of an animal, of a plant or of an object. The part has basically the same consciousness as the whole. Consciousness is a single quality: the ability to experience. God experiences the whole Being, whereas, in the Being, the parts, though they have the ability to experience, experience nothing – except, as I've said, perhaps themselves and an immediate feeling of a resistant, surrounding reality. More experience for the parts is offered only by creation. Within creation, what the parts experience varies according to what created body they become connected to. The words 'humans' and 'animals' relate only to creation. All human consciousnesses – or, to be more precise, all the conscious parts that are connected to human bodies – are parts of the Being, but we shouldn't be thinking in terms of different forms of consciousness.

P: So your idea of consciousness is quite different from that of the development theories of the pantheists?

S: Yes. For them, consciousness is developable. They have the idea of having different incarnations in order to develop an infinite understanding of causality within creation. For me, memory-based thinking can be developed, but not consciousness, the ability to experience. The thinking process, in my view, has to serve the needs of the consciousness, and that requires us to understand the original cause and meaning of creation. And the needs of the consciousness are, primarily, the need for love, and then the needs of the particular created body to which the conscious part becomes connected. This latter requires a particular understanding of causality in creation.

P: And it is how your idea of consciousness relates to human beings that is important, and not how it relates to plants and animals?

S: I am only interested in plants and animals in relation to the second problem of causality – that of causality in creation – because they are an inseparable part of the whole creation. But it is irrelevant to think too much about consciousness in relation to them. Some interpretation of the Indian tradition has the idea that one non-incarnated human consciousness not on the Earth is responsible for every species that is not a human species, and that that particular human consciousness rules the species it is responsible for from another level of creation. This could be true, but it makes no difference to us how it is. What is relevant to us is that consciousness must also be manifested objectively by the whole creation – that is, including the celestial bodies and life on our own celestial body, which express an absolute, indivisible order – and that the different levels of the whole creation can never be separated, either from the original cause, or from each other, either in their beginning or at their realized end, which we experience on the Earth via our created senses. All separation is a meaningful illusion made by the created senses.

P: And an order is an indication of consciousness?

S: Yes, because only a conscious being can have the need, and an associated purpose, for an order. We always assume that there is consciousness behind anything that expresses and maintains an order. We see it readily behind the order that is a plant or animal or human being. But a microorganism or a molecule or an atom or an elementary particle is also an order, though one that isn't generally obvious until such things combine to construct a larger order, such as a plant or animal or human body. But God expresses and maintains the order of the whole creation, which includes the celestial bodies. And the consciousness of the parts can come into this order, on the Earth's surface, as what we call 'life'. In human beings the consciousness of the parts manifests, through everything-covering language, as a responsible subject, as the reasoning, subjective background to the objective appearance of our own and other human bodies.

P: So we have to be led to the idea that consciousness is behind the order of the whole creation, otherwise we won't come to the idea of God?

S: Yes. That's why belief in God is natural. If, on the other hand, people don't believe properly in one non-created creator behind the whole creation, then people generally make a distinction, from what they suppose to be their position as outsiders on the Earth's surface, between 'not conscious' – that is, 'dead', 'mechanically interacting' – and two interpretations of the idea 'alive'. From this general viewpoint, the first relates to animals and biology on the Earth, and the second refers to human beings, when it means 'alive *and* conscious' – as I have said already.

In my hypothesis, I don't make such a distinction. God's creative consciousness is behind the whole creation, and consciousness must come into creation indirectly in the way that it does: basically, from the direction of the invisible whole – represented in creation by the impression of space – and relatively, through the largest objects, that is, the celestial bodies – stars, suns and planets – as light. It comes in more directly on the Earth's surface, as the chemical affinity represented by the generally invisible, smallest objects, which create, in an endless process of reproduction, the meaningful cooperation of all species.

P: Do you mean that the fact that elements have 'preferences' when it comes to organizing themselves with other elements is indirect evidence of consciousness behind them?

S: Yes, because these 'preferences' are obviously as meaningful as the fact that different species 'prefer' different types of food – and just as the light and heat of our sun or other celestial bodies is obviously meaningful.

P: Because all life needs the light and heat of the sun?

S: Yes, and because for humans the light of the stars gives us in addition an impression of the whole. As we said before, every impression of meaning is indirect evidence of there being a consciousness at work behind it. The problem is that no tradition – neither science, nor pantheism, nor theology – accepts the idea of only one, non-created consciousness behind the whole creation, as I do. That's why they talk about chance, randomness and chaos and evil – that is, about originally unorganized relations, which humans can change and organize according to their own meanings, bearing in mind only the mechanical impersonal laws, along with, in the case of pantheists, impersonal moral laws, and in the case of theology, God's commandments, which rule or should rule the unorganized relations.

P: And atheists who don't have such laws or commandments...?

S: They can't avoid confused discussions about ethics and various systems and rules for organizing relations, such as anarchy and democracy.

The problem with dualism* in theology – God and Evil – is that it doesn't have the idea of a non-created whole with parts. This means that God is not present in an understandable way in creation, which leads to the idea that either God does not control creation – the theory of deism – or that he controls it as we do socially through commandments and punishments. So in this view, too, humans have free will, bound only by the mechanical laws that rule creation, and they must therefore blindly follow God's authoritarian commandments in order to avoid Evil or punishment.

P: When you said a moment ago that the sun's light is meaningful, you don't mean that the sun is conscious?

S: No. No body in creation is conscious. So – going back to the way consciousness comes into creation – chemical affinity organizes larger orders, such as microorganisms or visible plants and animals, which give a so-called 'concrete' impression of consciousness. And consciousness comes most directly into creation in relation to human bodies, where consciousness can avail itself of an everything-covering language. Other species can only communicate their evaluations and their understanding of causality through their behaviour – so-called body-language – based on their existential needs. All they can do is accept the whole present creation as the only truth, without any possibility of being interested in its or their own body's background, or in a non-created, or past and future, reality. To have such an interest requires an everything-covering language, which can then be used in two basically different ways: either starting philosophical considerations about the background from the hypothesis of the existence, behind the created, illusorily existent creation, of a non-created reality – God, as a whole, in the way I propose – or, refusing that, accepting as the start for philosophical thinking only our objective and subjective, that is, mechanical or biological, or transcendental, experience of the created reality and people's interpretations of it. The consequence of this last is an authoritarian belief in one mystical God or pantheism or polytheism. These three types of tradition confused each other: in the case of theology, by only conceiving of God – the hypothesis of a non-created reality – as the creator of parts; or, in the case of pantheism, as the reproducer of himself in a mystical, transcendental way; or, in the case of polytheism, by being born and killed in a mystical succession. All of them are in contrast to my conception.

What I say is that only the consciousness of the parts – that is, not the parts themselves, but only their ability to receive and express – comes, through created but invisible possibilities and connections, to the surface of the Earth. There it becomes – at its other end, as it were – connected to the ongoing creation of one 'concrete' body, beginning with fertilization, gradually developing, being born and continuing to develop. From a certain state of its creation – birth – we can use the body, as a free, created whole, for receiving and expressing, in a similar way to how nowadays we use the invisible connections of the latest cordless telephones as a whole, without being a part of them.

So with human beings this unlimited consciousness – which is not predetermined by existential needs as it is with animals – becomes communicable between human beings. You can't use human language in relation to animals, plants or minerals.

P: Why did you say a few minutes ago that consciousness 'must' come into creation in the way it does?

S: Because the creator, the whole, who can't come into creation in a visible way, wants to be understood by his parts. So for this purpose, living bodies have to be built up gradually on the Earth, in order to produce human bodies to which the conscious parts can connect. Human bodies couldn't survive without the whole system that produced them.

P: And the conscious parts have to come into creation in order to understand the creator? They can't understand the creator from their position in the Being?

S: That's right. So God has to give us the idea that there is a consciousness behind the whole creation. So the whole creation has in our experience to act by itself, that is, to manifest consciousness – just as living bodies on Earth do.

P: And we take something acting by itself, moving by itself, as being conscious?

S: Yes.

P: Summarizing then: so far in our dialogues we have come across three arguments – all of them in themselves axioms – for the existence of God as you conceive him: (1) the original cause must be a conscious subject, because only a conscious subject can be a cause; (2) an order – in this case, creation – must be evidence of consciousness; and now this third one, (3), that something – again, in this case, creation – that moves by itself, that acts by itself, must have consciousness behind it. Is that right?

S: Yes, though those aren't the only ones. I have also referred to the axioms that (4) no thing can arise, originate from nothing; (5) that which exists, is existent, can never change, become some other thing, or cease to exist, that is, become nothing; and (6) it is impossible to create anything other than activity.

P: In your hypothesis, the objective impression of consciousness starts with objects. Generally, people regard consciousness as starting with animals, or perhaps with plants.

S: Yes, but we can remember axiom (6), which says that all objects in creation must be an illusion of the senses, that the boundary between objects in creation, which seemingly cannot act by themselves, and living or conscious bodies, which can obviously act by themselves, has to be made only for practical reasons. Viewed philosophically, chemistry too acts by itself, and the whole reality acts by itself – which is why we have to make the hypothesis that there must be a consciousness at work behind the whole creation.

M: I am still preoccupied with this question of consciousness and things in creation: could a conscious part of the Being be attached to a tree?

S: The basic need of the parts is to meet other conscious beings, which we can't do in the original Being. Why should a part attach itself to a tree? What can a tree experience, compared with the experience that a human body and human language allow? We have to discuss these questions until we have some mental clarity on them. But it has nothing to do with the question of God-consciousness*.

God-consciousness

P: What do you mean by 'God-consciousness'? To me it sounds a pantheist phrase, but I imagine you don't mean it that way.

S: God must be conscious of humans, or more precisely, the parts of his Being. Just as God lives in consciousness of us, who are conscious parts of him, we should live in consciousness of God as the whole to which we originally belong. That is what I mean by God-consciousness: being conscious of God as the whole Being behind creation.

As things generally stand, humans identify themselves simply as human beings. As children they learn to call that identity first by a personal name and then, some years later, by 'I' – which has become known as the Latin 'ego' or as 'the self'. If we don't become – by the same language-based education that gives us this other identification – conscious of God, we experience ourselves, in the face of changeable creation, as if we ourselves are original creators, that is, gods. That is the choice that only humans can have, and it is a choice that, because of language, they cannot avoid. Whatever I choose to be conscious of, that I become conscious of: either the creator – God – or myself and other people as creators, that is, as gods. The difference is that, if I choose God, I can do so only by considering things philosophically. If I don't choose God, I can't avoid choosing my own or other people's interpretations of their objective and subjective – that is, mechanical and biological – or transcendental experience of creation as a starting-point for philosophical considerations – simply because God is not present in creation in the form of an illusory object, whereas human beings are. But it is for me to choose what I want to be conscious of. At the same time, we can't avoid the consequences in our philosophical discussions of the fact that we are related to creation and to each other, because nobody can deny being subjectively conscious of their own created body as a part of the whole surrounding creation…

P: ...so it doesn't make sense to see oneself as an outsider in creation?

S: Yes... and nobody can deny being objectively aware of that whole reality as only an ongoing activity, a creation – because it changes in every detail, so it can't be an original reality. Knowledge of these two things is common to everybody, and is therefore the basis of common sense.

P: So the choice of the second identification – choosing humans as creators – goes against common sense?

S: Yes, because it forces people to deny that this reality is originally a meaningful creation, otherwise they can't deny the creator. They have to maintain that this reality came about by chance, and that it is ruled only by mechanical laws and by moral laws – in the case of the pantheists, impersonal moral laws, in the case of the theologians, moral commandments given by God – but not by a conscious meaning. But that goes against common sense, because we experience creation in all its details as perfectly purposeful in a way that we cannot copy, that we cannot reproduce as our creation.

God: the original object, including his parts

P: You talked earlier about God being the original object. But it's your view, isn't it, that the parts also exist as objects?

S: Yes, of course.

P: So God is not the only object?

S: God is the whole, real, non-illusory object, and then there are the parts, which are also real, non-illusory objects. The quality of both – consciousness, as the ability to experience – is the same. These conscious objects, the parts, are inside the whole conscious object. Everything is three-dimensional. And every object has the ability to experience.

M: That makes me think of objects with space around them.

S: That is the problem with our experience of only dissectable, illusory objects. There cannot be space between the parts, if it is a whole. 'Whole', in reference to a living organism, means an immediate, distanceless relation between parts. And, as I've said, the word 'part' implies 'part of a whole' – otherwise we wouldn't use the word 'part'. Just as we wouldn't talk about a whole, unless we were thinking that it had parts that belonged to it.

P: So we as objects always exist in the original reality, the Being?

S: An object can exist only in the original reality, because object means 'something which exists'. It is an axiom that something that exists can't come out of nothing, nor can it end, become nothing, cease to exist. Nor can it change.

This axiom leads to the further axiom that only activity can be created – which I have already referred to many times. And – another axiom just referred to – only if an object is conscious, what we call a subject, a conscious being who is conscious of its own existence as a living whole, can it have a relation to itself, and so be an original cause of activity. Within creation we call something an object even when it is not conscious – on practical grounds, to help us to distinguish between things that move by themselves and things that don't move by themselves, so that we know to treat them differently. But such 'objects' are not relevant in philosophy. From the philosophical point of view, an object can exist only in the original reality and has there the one common quality of consciousness, and, in the case of the whole, can vibrate, move in itself, and thereby express, realize creation.

As a conscious part of the original Being, you are an object. You can't experience the object you are – neither in the Being nor in creation. In creation, you can just imagine that you are a part in the whole. Isn't it a matter of indifference how you imagine your object? Isn't it only your quality that matters? 'Object' just means that it is indestructible, as unchangeable as God's existence.

M: So it's not just a quality?

Object/quantity and quality

S: No. That is the pantheist view. My view is that you can't have a quality separate from an object.

M: Can you give an example?

S: 'Walking' is one quality of a leg, 'standing' is another, 'kneeling' is another. So every activity that an object can demonstrate is a quality. But we can't separate the quality from the object that demonstrates the quality: we can't separate walking or standing or kneeling from the leg. There is only confusion if you separate them and talk, for example, about qualities as something in themselves. That's what is generally done with consciousness when it is replaced by words denoting quantity such as 'I', Self, personality, spirit, and so on.

It's also what is done when people talk about a feeling without referring to the cause of the actual feeling – that is, to the object or subject that gives rise to the feeling. Then feelings become mystical. If we know the cause of a feeling that we have, but don't refer to that cause in language, then that feeling will be mystical for other people. If we don't know, or if we have forgotten, or if we are not ourselves aware of the cause of our feeling, then it will also be mystical for us.

M: Can you be a subject and an object at the same time?

S: Yes. It is always at the same time, only we can't experience our consciousness as an object, separate from creation. We can only experience it as participating invisibly in creation.

M: Because God is an object, but also a subject?

S: Yes, in the same invisible way that you are a real object and subject behind the visible, illusory object that in creation is your body. God is the whole unchangeable Being with the quality of consciousness. And you can't separate the quality – consciousness – from the quantity, the existence, the object – the unchangeable Being. You can't separate either God's consciousness, or your own consciousness, which is basically the same quality as God's – though not the same quantity, but only a part of it.

P: We have used the word 'quality' a lot, and I realize I am not clear what is meant by it…

S: You experience, you feel your consciousness, your ability to experience, as your basic quality throughout your life – in the same way that every living being does – altering daily between the awake state, dreams and deep sleep. But language can only *remind* us of our immediate experience of a quality – for example, consciousness, red, hunger, running, excitement. It is impossible to create through language a mental understanding of what qualities are: words can never adequately convey the experience of a quality. We can, however, discuss qualities – but only by tracing them back to their objective origin. In the case of feeling conscious, this is to the hypothesized Being. If we don't make this hypothesis, we trace it back spontaneously to our own created body, or, when we observe the effects of consciousness in the surroundings, to other living bodies, interpreting it there as 'life'. In the case of our other feelings of qualities, we trace them back to the illusory objects in creation. For example, 'tomato' refers to both quality and quantity, but we can't describe or explain the taste of it, its quality. We can only refer to its quantity, the tomato itself.

P: What is the difference between quality and quantity?

S: Let's use the example of a tomato again. If you relate to it objectively, if you think of it outside you, it is a quantity, something that exists – in creation, that is. If you relate to it subjectively by eating it, and you then think of your experience of a tomato, then the tomato is a quality: you remember its taste or smell or texture, for example. But in fact the quantity that the tomato is and the quality of the tomato belong together. They are two aspects of the same thing. It's not possible to separate them. It is only language that makes us think they can be separated and discussed separately as quality and quantity. Other species, which don't have the human, language-based interest in causality, can't make this separation. The enjoyment of the quality, the taste – which is always experienced as activity, of which the quantity is the formal, objectively existing cause – can be separated in our mind from our interest in the construction of the quantity itself.

P: It sounds strange to say that taste is an activity.

S: All experience is of activity – creation's activity. But all thinking about causality in creation requires a single, relatively existent starting-point, and then, if we are to continue to think – in order to be able to understand cause and effect – other relatively existent points as causes. In this thinking, we break creation's activity down in our minds into quantities and qualities – physical qualities and, on the living surface of the Earth, biological or psychological qualities.

The quantity and quality of consciousness

P: You have repeatedly talked about consciousness as a quality. How does the relationship between quantity and quality apply to consciousness?

S: When it comes to the quality of consciousness, we don't have in our experience a quantity to which it corresponds. We tend to think of the corresponding quantity as our whole body. But the body is also the source of many other qualities – seeing, hearing, thinking, eating, digesting, and so on – so it can't be exclusively the source of consciousness. If we persist in thinking that the corresponding quantity for consciousness is our whole body, we are forced to decide which particular aspect of our body it corresponds to – hence science's search for the quantity and construction of consciousness in the human body.

P: But seeing, hearing, thinking, and so on, have parts of the body to which they correspond. Why couldn't we say that consciousness shares the brain with thinking?

S: The brain is the scientifically localized place of memory, and thinking is impossible without a memory of our earlier experiences. But what experiences is our consciousness. Similarly it is consciousness that sees and hears, not the ears and the eyes or the brain. And consciousness also rules thinking. Science knows a lot about thinking, but nothing about consciousness, and it tries to investigate consciousness as something, a quantity, in itself.

This search for consciousness is futile, in my view – as futile as science's search for the origin of life. My solution is to suggest that the corresponding quantity of consciousness is our non-created object as a part of the Being, and, in the case of the consciousness behind the whole of creation, God's invisible object – including the parts, our objects – as the whole of the Being. This gives us, and also our children, a rational understanding of theology's authoritarian statements about God's almighty, constant presence, and also an understanding of God's purpose with his otherwise mystical, autonomous creation.

P: What other differences does your view of consciousness – this idea of it as a quality of our object in the Being and of the object that God is – make?

S: Without the idea of a non-created quantity to which consciousness corresponds as its quality, our natural experience of consciousness of the ever-present, whole creation becomes confused by our thinking, which then becomes memory- and language-based, rather than anchored in reality, that is, in the Being. We become interested solely in how everything in creation is constructed and in our experience of everything as absolutely changeable. As a result, we lose our interest in the background to our consciousness. Instead of identifying ourselves with the hypothesis of a Being, we become identified with our memory- and language-based conception of infinitely running time. We then live only in relation to all the ongoing, running activities in creation, totally preoccupied with changeability and with human creativity based on the changeability of all objects, which reveal only a basically mystical, and never a real, background.

If we don't think of ourselves as a conscious part of God and if we don't think of God's consciousness as being behind creation, we become identified with our thinking, which in practice means our memory-based knowledge of creation and our ability both to destroy living and non-living objects and to construct non-living objects, in a generally accepted illusion that we can change the original reality and create a new reality, through our individual or collective power, solely by ourselves, that is, without Nature's help.

P: Then we will essentially be adopting the modern scientific view?

S: Yes, but with the difference that scientists and those people to whom we delegate responsibility for human cooperation in societies – what we call the authorities or politicians – generally have more regard for Nature's creativity than those who don't have this delegated responsibility and are completely identified with all the possibilities for human creativity.

Science and consciousness

P: Could you characterize then how your view is basically different on this question of consciousness?

S: At the basis of thinking, according to the modern scientific view, is the idea that non-living objects, with no consciousness behind them, are acting in accordance with impersonal mechanical laws, that is, mechanical necessities that have no meaning. All living bodies then come mysteriously into this picture of the universe on the Earth's surface. These living bodies, too, are considered to be without consciousness behind their activities and to be acting mechanically, that is, without consciousness of a meaning – with the exception of human bodies. Human bodies are generally regarded as the only conscious bodies, because humans can not only follow meanings – as objects and animals do, via mechanical and biological necessities – but can also create their 'own' original meanings, and can follow and realize those.

P: So animals, within this view, are regarded as not being conscious?

S: That's right. They are thought of as acting primarily in accordance with meaningful biological necessities and secondarily, in relation to their surroundings, in accordance with meaningless mechanical necessities.

P: But then the biological necessities, though meaningful – that is, though determined by needs – are regarded as operating mechanically, as we have said before?

S: Yes. Because human beings have an everything-covering language that enables them to communicate their experiences, predilections, memories, considerations about causality, meanings, motivations and activities, humans are considered the only conscious beings. That means, only humans are regarded as capable of acting meaningfully. But this interpretation is blind to the distinction between, on the one hand, natural needs and meanings and the enjoyment in satisfying those, and on the other, human-made meanings and the enjoyment of the need to satisfy those.

P: So the view is that only humans can determine their own behaviour? Animals act meaningfully, but their behaviour, in this view, is determined entirely by their needs and external circumstances?

S: Yes. That is more precise. So humans – in this view of reality as having basically no meaning in itself – are considered absolute strangers to each other, because, unless they ask each other, they can't know what the meaning is behind each other's creative activities. They can only understand each other when they are satisfying their existential needs, because then it is obvious to everyone what the purpose of their behaviour is. But they can't know what human nature is, that is, true human nature – as I see it: the ability to experience and the need to be understood as likes – which lies behind the way of thinking and the evaluation system that humans have. The modern way of thinking and the modern evaluation system – which are separated from Nature and are based only on a global, mechanical investigation of Nature's changeability – emphasizes human creativity and technology. And this technology is expressed alongside Nature's permanently ongoing creativity, but with the latter interpreted as absolutely 'meaningless' and mechanical.

So today, on the basis of the view of modern science, we consider the visible objects in creation – that is, quantities – to be the original causes of the activity in the whole reality. This activity is regarded as expressed by a basically 'dead' Nature – in itself an irrational idea, because something that is dead can't act by itself. Since creation is not seen as having a conscious meaning behind it, it cannot then be loved as a whole. It can only be regarded, either with enjoyment or with anxiety, as changeable in every detail.

P: But it cannot be loved as a whole because love can only be experienced in relation to a conscious being?

S: Yes. Viewed in the modern scientific way, this activity is then regarded as having three basic qualities: enjoyable, that is, good; not enjoyable, that is, neutral; and causing suffering, that is, bad. The goal then becomes to create enjoyable things, and to fight against everything that causes suffering.

A precondition for becoming free of identification with the ego and of identification with time as history, and thereby free of a constant lack of love, a constantly unsatisfied need for love – which we experience as anxiety – is to remember that objects can't interact by themselves, can't be the cause of their own interaction. A conscious meaning behind the whole creation is required in order to bring about their interaction.

P: That's a long answer to my original question! But you think it all follows from a failure to view consciousness the way you do?

S: Yes. I think it is crucial. And I know that it can be difficult to grasp what I am saying, because nobody these days sees consciousness in this way. No historical tradition presents consciousness as the non-created, non-developable, unchangeable, basic quality as the cause of knowledge, but not the same as knowledge.

As I have said before, consciousness, as I use the word – and nobody now uses it in the way I am trying to introduce it into human language – has two aspects. The first aspect is the ability to experience, to receive impressions. This allows us to be able to experience, via the nervous system, the needs of our own body, which have to be satisfied. We are also able to receive, via our senses, impressions of the whole creation. In this way, both our bodily needs and our need for love can be satisfied.

P: So we want to experience love in relation to everything that we experience?

S: Yes, we don't want our need for love to be disturbed by anything that we experience. If it is disturbed by any element of creation, we make efforts to avoid or alter that element.

The second aspect of consciousness is the ability, having received, to give out, to express, to be meaningfully active in relation to what we receive. This second aspect of consciousness relates to our need for the technology with which to satisfy all our bodily needs in the surroundings. In the case of our existential needs, we have to adopt the position of outsiders and, treating creation mechanically and practically, we have to cooperate purposefully with our surroundings to satisfy those needs. In the case of the need for love – which relates to our encounters with other conscious beings – we have to use the technology of everything-covering language to satisfy it, both in relation to humans and in relation to the whole creation. We love other species spontaneously, because we understand them. They are not mystical to us. The fact that we can't understand and love our own species equally spontaneously is due to the fact that humans can't love the whole creation in the same spontaneous, unconsidered way that other species do. We have to agree in language upon an understandable relation to the whole creation, as a precondition for an agreement about our own identity. Otherwise both creation and humans remain mystical to us. We have the need to make these agreements because it is impossible to feel undisturbed love in the face of something that is mystical, unknown.

The need to understand and be understood

P: And by 'in relation to the whole creation', you mean that we need human language in order to understand and love the original cause?

S: Yes.

M: Is all this true only of consciousness in creation?

S: Yes. In the Being, the parts can't satisfy their need for understanding. Only God has the ability first to experience, take in the whole Being, and then, in doing that, to recognize his need to be known and understood by his parts, as the precondition for two-sided love. It is self-evident that God loves his own existence, the whole Being, and it is self-evident that one-sided love is not satisfying. So it is self-evident that God has the need to be understood and loved by the parts of his existence, which is the only possibility God has for being loved.

P: Do you mean by 'self-evident' that God simply experiences it and has no reason to question it?

S: Yes, but this is so not only for God. We experience the same need for two-sided love as self-evident in relation to conscious beings. Consciousness of this need in God's case is the cause of creation, of activity, of giving out, expressed by the power of the whole Being. God gives creation as pure activity, not as a thing. He doesn't form or make 'something'. We, in order to communicate, give out meaningful sound – which, too, is pure activity. If our talk is in accord with the meaning of creation, then we understand God and enjoy love when this communication by sound takes place. If we don't understand creation, we want to create. We then use language for realizing our own creations, for satisfying our own artificial needs, rather than for understanding each other. Therefore, we have responsibility for human language, and God has responsibility for creation – which is God's language to us. Creation is pure activity, and language is pure activity. We give nothing when we talk – just communication, just vibration.

M: It seems confusing to me, because if God made creation so that we could understand the whole, the way he made it also makes it hard for us to understand the whole.

S: But if you imagine now that you are God, the whole, and you want to give your parts the possibility to understand their situation – which includes under-standing you – then you can start to think, from your situation, what God *must* do in order to realize this need that he has. He must show us, the parts, a reality that is not unified, if we are to have a perspective on the whole and the parts. There is no way that we can see the whole, because we are inside it, so God has to give us experiences that can lead us to conclude that the whole exists.

P: Do you think that this is more difficult for us adults because we are brought up to think out of ourselves, and not out of the whole, this unity? I know you think that a child has that sense of the unity, of living in a whole, quite naturally, so that it isn't so difficult for the child. But it is difficult for us as adults, having lost that view, to get back to it – though it would be a much easier starting point for our thinking.

S: Yes, I think that is so. But doesn't the image of the manifold, with the stars around us, give us an idea of the whole? Yet we fail to interpret it as an indirect, created image of the whole, and we fail to interpret human bodies as a more direct, but still indirect, created image of parts within the whole. And so we don't interpret the image of the manifold as a connection to God, a connection that is similar to the connection we have to each other and to every other living body that God has created.

Every part of the Being has to become connected to a body in creation in order to be able to experience company, through their body. And God creates this image of the manifold, which gives us the idea of the whole as the creator,

God. God always has the same identity, always shows himself through his creation to everybody. We, by contrast, have to change bodies in creation – when our present one gets worn out and dies – but we don't change our identity as conscious parts of the whole. God doesn't change creation. It is a human idea that creation can be changed. Creation is changeable only on the surface. It also seems to be changeable fundamentally, because it is only activity – as we now at last know also from modern science.

P: 'At last', because the original aim of modern science was to find the existent start behind creation?

S: That's right. But creation is a complete, meaningful order, which we cannot change. We can change the surface of creation only up to a certain given limit, but we can't change creation fundamentally. We can never change the cause of creation, nor its meaning, which gives it its order. We can change some details of creation, for example, by eating these sandwiches we have here. Everything changes in the details on the surface. Generations come and go. But the whole creation does not change. It is always being expressed for the same practical purpose. And if it were not being expressed, we would not be able to experience anything. The meaning of creation is that we should be able to experience God – indirectly through his activity – and each other, and in this way be aware of what the need of consciousness is, this need being the same for God as for every living individual: to be loved. That means to be understood, because it is impossible to love without understanding.

P: What do you mean by 'understanding' in this case?

S: Understanding is more than just knowledge. It presumes understanding the whole causality – the cause and meaning – of all these activities that we know about. Understanding of causality must for humans, in my view, involve making the hypothesis that the same single identity is behind the active diversity that exists on the surface of creation, and that this identity gives the meaning to this diversity, this interaction, that is, it expresses it so that we know about its purpose – because he has the same basic need that we have.

First there is experience – what we call 'knowledge' when we remember, recognize, what we experience. And then there is understanding of the mechanical causality in what we experience, in what we know about. You have to experience creation, and so know about it. You have no choice about that, do you?

P: No, I can't refuse to experience creation.

S: And you have to understand the mechanical causality in what you experience, don't you?

P: Yes, otherwise I wouldn't be able to survive: I wouldn't be able to meet my existential needs, or some accident would befall me through the lack of some technical understanding.

S: Isn't it quite another form of understanding if, instead of only knowing about, recognizing an activity and understanding the mechanical causality in it, you understand its meaning: that is, the need behind it and its purpose?

P: Yes, it is.

S: What is the difference?

P: In the first case, I only know about and recognize an ongoing activity and understand it mechanically. In the second, I must also know about the need of a living being and recognize the purpose of this need in its activity.

S: Yes. Creation is shown to every living being, so every living being *has* to experience it, *has* to know about it, has to understand it mechanically to some extent. But only human beings, because of human language, can be interested in understanding the *whole* causality. But the whole causality is not the whole mechanical causality in creation. It is primarily the original cause and meaning of the whole creation. We need to understand that as a precondition for understanding the creator's need and purpose in creating the whole creation. Animals' understanding of creation-based, objective causality is limited to the causality they need to understand in order to satisfy their existential needs. Humans, on the other hand, have the language-based capacity for unlimited understanding.

P: 'Unlimited' in the sense of 'not limited to their existential needs'?

S: Yes. Animals have no choice but to use their capacity for limited understanding: their needs force them to it. Humans, on the other hand, once they discover their language-based capacity for unlimited understanding, can choose how to use it. They can choose to use it to understand the original cause and meaning of the whole creation and to recognize the creator's need and purpose in it, and then to relate to creation accordingly. Or they can be influenced by the anxiety generated by mistaken, language-based ideas about reality – such as the ideas of the existence of a dead reality, or the existence of 'nothing' – to concentrate their capacity for unlimited understanding on understanding solely the objective causality that is within creation, with the aim of using this causality for their own individual or collective benefit. They then act without any regard for the creator's purpose with creation, that is, without the idea of an original cause and meaning to the whole creation. This exclusive concentration on benefiting human beings makes it impossible for humans to experience undivided love for the whole creation.

P: ...whereas animals, because they don't have the language-based capacity for unlimited understanding that humans have, can't be misinformed about creation and its cause and meaning?

S: That's right. So their need for undivided love of the ever-present creation can never be disturbed: they spontaneously use creation in the way that God means them to use it. That's why we can understand other species, but not our own species – unless, that is, we agree about creation and God's meaning with creation and with human language.

Animals, love and understanding

P: But how can animals love creation if they don't understand it – because you have just said 'it is impossible to love without understanding'?

S: But understanding for animals means knowledge by experiencing. Animals experience creation and love creation without any problem, through experiencing it basically as life, without having any idea about its opposite. So they can only experience 'alive' and 'not alive': that is, they can only experience things as active, moving by themselves, showing the ability to experience; or as no longer showing this ability, becoming passive, not moving by themselves. Animals can't have the idea of 'absent', nor the idea of 'absent' transferred to the idea of time: so they can't have the idea of the past or the future. They love life without the possibility of becoming, like humans, interested in their bodies from outside, or in themselves as something separate from what they love: the whole. They love their own body because they love the whole, and they defend it because they don't like to suffer.

P: So you wouldn't say it was 'survival instinct' that made them defend themselves?

S: That is a human interpretation of animals' behaviour. But if animals can't have the idea of death, then they can't have the idea of survival either. They either flee or defend themselves because they don't like to be forced or hurt, not because they want to survive.

And animals love not just their bodies, but also the surrounding reality in the same way, because it satisfies their existential needs. They can't have the language-based idea of 'distance', interpreted as 'nothing', that would separate them from it. They can't have the feeling of being an outsider that is characteristic of humans when they become identified with the word 'I'.

M: Do animals need love?

S: Yes, they need the company of likes – which is what we call 'love' – and they get it too. We also understand their need for love, company – that's why we go up to animals and pat them and stroke them. And they also feel comforted by us when we give them food and other things they need.

P: Do they *understand* their need for love?

S: No, they can't reflect in a language-based way on any of their needs. They experience them when they become actual, and then they satisfy them, without reflecting any further about them. The only difference between their need for love and their existential needs is that undivided love for the whole creation is present all the time for them, along with love of their own life. And they don't lose it when they suffer, as humans do. They can never think of killing themselves, because they can't think of death, as an alternative to life. Nor can they become identified with time – the language-based memory of past reality – which creates for humans anxiety about the future.

P: So in terms of everyday life, animals understand everything they need to?

S: Yes, of course, otherwise they wouldn't be able to survive. But they can only communicate it by body-language and sounds. Animals understand Nature, because they live with their needs. All these needs guide animals' thinking, and so they understand without realizing that they understand. 'Not understanding' for them means 'failing to satisfy a need'. If that happens, they then try to satisfy that need in another way, until they are successful. They don't have a problem loving life, because all their needs give them enjoyment – because every time a need is satisfied, enjoyment is felt, with animals as much as with humans.

Humans can have a problem loving their life, because we have a problem understanding life. We have language to enable us to understand life, and we could understand life if we used language to understand the original cause and meaning of creation, and thereby the proper common meaning of our lives. Traditionally, as I have said, we use language out of our desire for power, to create meanings or purposes and to realize them all in order to escape anxiety – which is what humans suffer when they don't understand something – and to avoid physical suffering.

M: Why can't all the understanding that we need be given to us, just as all the understanding that animals need is given to them?

S: The understanding of what our body needs and how to satisfy our bodily needs *is* given to us. And we are also conscious of our need for love. But the understanding of how to satisfy the need for love is not given to us unconditionally, as it is given to animals.

P: By 'not given to us unconditionally', do you mean that for us there is a precondition for undivided love of creation?

S: Yes, and that is that humans have to understand the creator as the invisible, conscious whole – God – behind the visible creation. So the need for love can't be satisfied in humans in the same way that it can be with animals, who are not conscious of God. Generally, our need for love doesn't get satisfied, because we don't understand the creator's meaning with creation. All that we are generally conscious of is our lack of understanding – and without understanding, it is impossible to love what we experience, what we know about.

M: Why can't this whole question be automatic with human beings?

S: Because the cause – the non-created whole – can't be made visible from outside, which is what we mean by automatic, or self-evident, knowledge. Human beings are interested in the whole reality, and therefore have a responsibility to understand the invisible original cause, and thus the whole causality. Animals have neither this interest nor this responsibility. But they also understand causality, traced back to subjects and objects in creation, but only as much as they need to for their survival. Only humans can dream about being able to complete their understanding of causality one day and then be original creators.

P: So animals don't have responsibility to the creator? They don't have to understand the original cause of creation as humans do?

S: That's right.

M: But you said animals love automatically.

S: I didn't say 'automatically'. I said animals have no problem with their need for love. They have one feeling for themselves and the surrounding reality. They can't hate or have all these alternative feelings – such as anxiety and alienation – which we humans experience towards reality.

M: So love isn't automatic with them?

S: 'Automatic' is a typically human idea, referring to a 'dead' relation between 'dead' parts. Such so-called 'dead' parts exist only in things or functional orders – machines – that humans construct and power by energy. Such functional orders are not to be found naturally in reality. That's because creation is one order, originally powered by consciousness – basically, by the consciousness of the whole, and relatively, by the consciousness of the parts of the whole – and it is impossible to separate anything out from it as not cooperating, not interacting. 'Dead' parts are not to be found in it.

Animals don't break reality theoretically into pieces, as we do when we learn language and as scientists do practically in their investigations. They love reality as an undivided whole, not in its separate parts. They love unconsciously because they can't start and stop loving – because they never stop loving to be alive. Therefore, they can't experience a lack of love. They don't consciously experience their need for love, and they don't consciously experience satisfaction of that need. They simply give their offspring the care they need. It is only we who interpret this as a decision on their part to 'give love'.

Because humans are made conscious through language of the idea of love and of ideas about what love and the lack of love are, we become confused about love. We believe we can possess it, be rich in it or poor in it – that is, we can believe we have received a lot of it, or that we have received little of it and so still need a lot of it, and that we have a lot or little to give. So we become aware that either we or others don't love and only try to give or take love, and then we get the idea that whatever we do, we have to do it 'with love' – and not because of a natural response to a common natural need to be understood as likes.

M: You say that animals love unconsciously. How can you have unconscious love?

S: Because unconscious love is the natural state of every conscious being. It is impossible to desire anything other than love – nobody ever wants to be hated. And it is impossible ever to experience enough love – in which respect love is different from our existential needs, which can be temporarily not satisfied or temporarily satisfied. Love, as with everything else in creation, only becomes conscious in humans, through their learning of everything-covering language. This makes it possible for humans to communicate their memory and so to have a conscious idea about every thing and every need – both the need for love and all the bodily and artificial needs – and conscious ideas about what counts as satisfaction, and theories about how to achieve satisfaction.

With animals it is different. They experience their whole surroundings, but they have no concept 'the whole', because they aren't interested in the original cause of creation. They understand all the causality that they need to understand, and they can't have the idea of developing knowledge about causality as an end in itself. So animals are never conscious of not understanding, and so they can never experience lack of love.

P: And because they never experience lack of love, they are never conscious of love either – because they would need to miss it to know what it is they are missing, as we have said.

S: Yes. But because humans can become confused, through language, about Nature's purpose for human language, they then can't avoid consciousness of lack of understanding and of lack of love.

M: But doesn't being unconscious about something mean 'automatic'?

S: Okay, we can say it is 'automatic' in a way, if we mean 'spontaneous', 'unconsidered'.

M: So animals' love is automatic in a way?

S: …because it is unconsidered. Animals don't try to express love as an end in itself, because they don't have a language-based idea of love. They have no experience of lack of love – in the way they can experience lack of light, heat, air, water, food and so on – so they have no problem with love. Love is only a problem for human beings because they generally live completely in language, interpreted as something independent of reality, rather than in reality!

You can only understand love, in my view, if you start from God as the invisible, non-created whole. You have to have God's purpose in creation clear, then you can understand why it is that we need to love all that we experience and why love is undivided and cannot be divided, measured or compared. But you can't forget God, creation and God's purpose in creation, and then try to understand how love functions. Because love functions in humans spontaneously, too – or 'automatically', if you want this word – otherwise we wouldn't be able to feel lack of love. But God doesn't want it to function automatically. He wants his parts to love him consciously, for his creation, in a common understanding that it is perfect for its purpose, and that it can't be changed and made better by its participants on the basis of the language-based idea of 'perfect' – 'perfect' being imagined as without any relation to some purpose.

P: And because God is invisible, he can only be loved consciously? That is, you have to have the idea of God first, and that idea you can only have in a language-based way. You can't have this idea of the whole unconsciously. Experience doesn't give it to you. You have to reflect philosophically on your experience to come to the idea of the whole – which you can see expressed as the absolute interaction of everything, what we call Nature. And animals can't do that kind of reflection. Humans on the other hand can't avoid creating an idea of the whole – this interaction or oneness of Nature – but then they can come to two different, mutually exclusive, ideas about it: that it is meaningful or meaningless. If they decide it is meaningless, then the questions arise: *How is it constructed?* and *How can we give it meaning?* If they decide that it is meaningful, the question arises: *What is its meaning?*

Love and power

S: That's right. So God has to give humans this problem with love. He has to give them the choice between love and its opposite: power, force, mechanical relation, what we call manipulation when it relates to human beings. We can manipulate other species only physically and with loud sounds, whereas with humans we can also use language.

It might also be said that generally humans love, live and function unconsciously, too, just as we breathe unconsciously. If we don't think what we are doing when we breathe, we can think that we are breathing on our own terms, by our own nature, and not on the terms of the whole Nature. In the same way, if we love, we think we are loving on our own terms, by our own nature, and not on the terms of the whole Nature. Human beings do love 'unconsciously', in my view, in many situations – just not in those situations in which they consciously *believe* they love!

P: …because, as we said earlier, we make so many ideas about what love is, through our memory-based thinking, so humans think that in this situation or that situation they ought to feel love, and can even imagine that they do when they in fact don't?

S: Yes. Love is only possible when we are in our original identity, where love is a natural state. This state we lose when we identify with our thinking. Everyone knows when they experience love – if they are not confused in their thinking about love, that is. Everyone recognizes the feeling of love, of not feeling any fear or reservation when meeting living beings. But love can't be deliberately expressed, that is, it is not in our power – nor even in God's power – to express love, either in language or in anything else that we might think of as an expression of love. Love is spontaneous; it's the original state of being alive.

P: So all our efforts to demonstrate love are pointless?

S: Absolutely. Of course, it is much nicer if people try to demonstrate love rather than try to demonstrate hatred or indifference. But unless people are confused by their thinking, they can easily feel the difference between a 'demonstration of love' and the feeling of being loved itself.

P: So would you say that God experiences conscious love to his whole existence and that he wants conscious love back? But though humans may spontaneously or unconsciously love in certain situations, they can't love God spontaneously or unconsciously?

S: Yes, of course.

M: So the love animals have for creation doesn't satisfy God's need?

S: No. At the same time, God knows about his creation, and he knows how creation is built up from the Earth's surface – through minerals, plants, animals, and human beings – so God doesn't have the idea of trying to experience conscious love from animals.

M: And animals can't love God, because they can't know about God?

S: That's right. They can enjoy life in peace and harmony, with the feeling of belonging together to all species and to the whole reality – and that is the principle of love.

M: What is love?

S: If you mean 'What does love feel like?', that question can never be answered. It is as impossible a question as 'What does coffee taste like?' You can experience the taste of coffee when you drink coffee, but however much I try, I can't describe or convey to you what the actual taste of coffee is. You have to experience it. So I can only say what the precondition for experiencing love is. I can't say what love itself is.

M: Can you say more again about what you see as the precondition for love?

S: God, from his position as the unchangeable reality, understands us, as the parts of his existence, and thus he understands our need for love. But in this original situation, we can't as parts understand the whole, God. He has to give us the conditions to be able to understand and love him, which he does through creation. So we have to understand God's reason for his creation – that he has the same basic need that we have – as a precondition for understanding creation and thereby loving him, for his creation, a creation that suits his reason perfectly. Then we have the same background and have no problem understanding and loving each other, having the same feeling for other people's lives as we have for our own life. It's the same undivided love that animals have for the whole creation. But humans can't enjoy this undivided love without consciousness of God as our like, which implies satisfying God's need at the same time.

If we don't want to know about God, it's because we want to understand the original cause in the same rememberable way that we try to understand everything in creation: as mechanical causality – rather than in the way I am talking about. By attempting to trace things back to the creator on the basis of how creation is made – instead of starting with the problem of 'why?' – confusion is created about what undivided love is. We are failing to remember that we basically love all species in the same way, because they belong to the same reality as we do and because we have the same sorts of need as they have. And we are failing to remember that all our problems with our own species relate to the fact that humans live more in their own history than in the ever-present reality. Then they identify themselves, bind their identity to, voluntarily chosen predilections, which we cannot immediately know about. And we also can't immediately know which system of social order, that is, which man-made rules for behaviour, they are following as a substitute for, as they see it, Nature's anonymous 'disorder'.

P: In other words, we can't understand our own species spontaneously because their behaviour is determined by a mystical mixture of natural and voluntary needs?

S: Yes, and also mixed in are their consciousness of the ever-present reality, what they have learnt about history, and their identification with their own personal history, which is unknown to other people. When that is the case, all that is noticed is the destructive side of Nature: the suffering, death and human evil in creation. The result is that we become interested in power – in order to be able to make creation and humans better, more enjoyable. And as long as humans want to have power, they are totally closed for conscious love – that is, they make the conditions for conscious love completely impossible. Power is the opposite idea to the idea of love. We can demand and force obedience, and perhaps admiration, but not love, because it is impossible to love on demand, command or from force. But when we lack the experience of mutual love, we can regard admiration as if it were the only possibility for love. But admiration is only possible between unlikes, whereas love is only possible between likes.

P: What about the problem of suffering and evil in creation? How do you see it? The existence of suffering and evil puts a lot of people off the idea of God.

S: The problem of suffering and evil is due to the fact that creation is forced to destroy everything it creates, because it is not the original reality, that is, it is not existent. If it kept on creating without destroying, the axiom that something can never come from nothing would not be valid. There would also then be more and more of everything, endlessly!

Creation can only exist as a closed system of simultaneous construction and destruction, which is why everything in creation is destroyable. Our problem with creation is that we can't create anything that Nature constructs, not even a so-called elementary particle. We have to use creation as the material, with its natural properties, for our own creations, and whatever we create is foreign to creation, and creation has to destroy it, too. If people are identified with their thinking, they identify primarily with the destructive side of creation. That gives the irrational belief that we can change the whole reality, and build up a new, better one.

In reality, only Nature creates and destroys. Life 'forces' every living being – through enjoyable needs – to understand and love Nature's activity as one, as indivisible. It does this via our meaningful participation in both the constructive and destructive side of the same Nature – and the two can't be separated: the same Nature creates and destroys. Humans can only understand the creator's purpose. If they don't, they complain in the naive belief that Nature could only be constructive. The complaint is that God allows humans to be destructive.

P: So people don't complain about creation or Nature?

S: No. People never complain about Nature, because everybody knows that we cannot alter Nature and because Nature is not seen as the creator. They only complain about people's bad creativity and about God, that he didn't make a good enough creation and perfect humans – which becomes *their* aim. The complaint only has any force because of the Church's irrational idea that God is almighty and arbitrary, that is, not bound by anything in his creating.

P: ...which gives doubting believers the idea that God has a completely free hand in relation to creation, so he could have made a better job of it, particularly of human beings?

S: Yes. And we take over the idea of this supposed freedom for ourselves. It is what attracts and binds human beings to the idea of development. They want to develop power as an end in itself, so as to be able to realize whatever meaning they choose – whether that meaning is in harmony with creation's purpose or not. Unless we understand the meaning of creation, we can only have an unclear feeling – 'deeply' in what we call 'the conscience' – about what is in harmony with the meaning of creation and what not. But we can never be clear about it and communicate and agree about it; we can only predict its opposite and talk about disharmony and catastrophe. Our basic feeling is then anxiety, rather than undivided love. We seek to escape this anxiety and our consciousness of what we interpret as our transiency in the ever-present reality through identifying solely with our memory-based thinking. The purpose of that thinking is to learn to control everything that we need to control. But we want to develop power infinitely, in an effort to control everything.

P: And as part of that, we don't understand the place of ageing and illness, for example. It just seems pointless suffering.

S: Yes. The biggest source of suffering is the idea that we must die – even if people say that they are not anxious about death, but only about suffering as they die.

Use of language: to cover reality or to express oneself?

P: Stefan, I would like to go back to the subject of language. Your view is that language is given to us so that we can use it to arrive at a conscious love of God?

S: Yes, by understanding the meaning of creation. Humans, unlike animals, have the ability to reflect on life using language that covers the whole reality. Language gives humans the possibility of choosing: either 'I use language to cover the whole reality', or 'I use language to express my self to other people as an anonymous, unique being'. But if I adopt the latter view, I can never experience humans as likes. I can't experience others as likes if I think they won't understand me unless I explain my self to them. If people are 'unlike', then I want to discover, get to know, overcome resistance, acquire knowledge of – and this is something different from love. Love can only function when we don't try to discover, but when we take each other as known, on the basis of the same quality – consciousness, the ability to experience – that we have fundamentally in common. Otherwise, I have to give people my version of the human being, my unique version, my personality – there cannot be another one like it. That is to present myself as a god, since God by definition is the only one of his kind.

Only the whole, the oneness – God – can be one of his kind. The parts of the whole are many. And even though, in creation, we are in the whole and are interacting with it all the time, we can never *experience* ourselves as a part of it, because we can't experience the whole – we can't see or touch the whole. We can only come to the belief that we are a part of it through reflection. But, because of the freedom of thought that we have, we can believe the opposite: that we do not belong to it. In the very moment that we do that, we become like a god. We stop feeling that we are a part. We feel ourselves instead to be a unique entity, independent of our surroundings, an independent whole among other whole bodies, separated by empty space.

And if I don't think of myself as belonging to the whole, I take the whole to be the diversity. I take it to be a totality, the sum of its parts, rather than a whole. Then I think I can change it, I can do what I want with it – at least on the Earth's surface. I can have the idea that by changing the parts, I am changing the totality. But then I can't understand and love it as a whole – though perhaps I can admire certain parts of it. And I can't feel that things belong to one another, because even the parts that appear to belong to one another as parts of the totality are not real parts: they themselves can be broken into parts, endlessly. So we can never find a real part as such, that is, one that is indestructible, unchangeable or not transitory.

P: The emphasis on language is very strong in your ideas.

S: Yes. I think we should consider this idea: how would it be if, instead of using language to express ourselves, we started using language to express the purpose of reality and to understand each other in relation to the whole purposeful reality, that is, in relation to what life means seen from the point of view of the creator? Then the question, *What is the meaning of my life?*...

P: ...becomes a general question, *What is the meaning of life?*

S: No, it becomes: *What is the meaning of life from the point of view of the creator?* Then the question as to what is the meaning of life for everybody is answered. And then the question, *What is the meaning of my life?* never arises, because then we are in agreement about what the meaning of life is.

'Who am I?'

P: In the same way the question *Who am I?* can be put as a general question, *What is a human being?*, and needn't be put as a question that each person has to answer for themselves in a different way?

S: Yes, and the answer is self-evident if we think of ourselves as conscious parts of the same reality. The question is natural for a human being, because a human being can't avoid learning everything-covering language – so we want to understand what a human being is.

P: You mean, only because we have language and are given the term 'human being'?

S: Yes. Animals can't ask the question *What is a human being?* or even *What is an animal?* But if language is not used properly – that is, to understand the whole – we won't be able to understand the parts.

P: But does the child not ask, even when quite young, *Where do I come from?* or *Where do people come from?* But I suppose that's a different question.

S: Yes, yes, it's a different question, but related – because they are asking after their origins. If they get a correct answer as to where they come from…

P: By which you mean, that they are a conscious part of God's Being, and not 'from Mummy's tummy'?

S: That's right. The body comes from 'Mummy's tummy', and the consciousness, the ability to experience, becomes connected to that body. The parents can say that they wanted the child's company, and so they helped to provide a body for it, and the child wanted their company, so it became connected to that body. But there is no hurry to say this. Parents should wait for the child to put questions and for the child to have developed language enough to be able to understand and ask more.

But if children were given a correct answer to this question – starting with where creation comes from – then they would ask quite different questions, and not the question that children, and also grown-ups, ask nowadays, *Who am I?* They would ask philosophical questions based on their experience of the ever-present whole creation and its purpose. And when the philosophical questions about the cause and meaning of creation are clearly answered, what else would they ask? They would then need to ask only questions about practical things, based on what people sense commonly – in other words, based on common sense. That means that their questions would be based on a consciousness of the ever-present reality, and not solely on memory- and language-based thinking.

Children's questions and child-rearing

Grown-ups would then only need to give answers to practical questions, and only until the children are grown up, that is, until the children can manage life for themselves. We have to answer children's practical questions, because there are practical things they don't know about which the grown-ups do know about.

This form of understanding they have to develop, for as long as it is necessary and meaningful. But as a grown-up, I am not God for them. I was just born before them, and so I must teach them. When the children are grown up, that is the end of their absolute need of their parents. But if we don't give the necessary philosophical answers to basic questions, then we get question after question after question about causality – because nobody answers the questions in a satisfactory way, which means, tracing them back to the question of meaning, so that everybody can find the answer confirmed by our impression of the ever-present whole.

P: So would you say that children ask 'why?' out of a natural wish to understand the whole creation?

S: Not just the whole creation, but every activity they come across – because we can only understand an activity if we understand its purpose, its 'why?' But if children don't ever hear any talk about the purpose of the whole creation, or don't get a satisfactory answer to their questions about it, then all our answers to their other questions fail to satisfy them, because they can't place them within one logical system. If the original cause and meaning is not agreed, the whole problem of causality is open, and then the plurality, the diversity, is regarded as the sole origin of our experience of causality, and so also of our questions. This is what has happened in science, which says that every new solution, every answer to a question, raises more questions.

P: I don't quite understand that.

S: Because science dissects and dissects thing, it keeps coming upon new cause after new cause, with every new cause always requiring further dissection in search of further parts of this new cause. Children, too, keep coming up with question after question, so long as the grown-ups reflect this scientific view in their answers – because the child's need for philosophical understanding of the total connection between all causes, with a beginning from the original cause, is not satisfied by such answers. Such answers only reflect an interest in more and more new causes. So science has to tolerate a growing gap between its various branches as its knowledge increases – in the case of science itself, in its hurry to understand more, and in the case of the technocrats and industrialists who apply science's new findings, in their hurry to create meanings, and thereby new creativity, to enhance life's qualities. And all the time both are blind to 'dead', 'meaningless', 'chaotic' Nature's creativity and destructiveness. Against this background, children come to see grown-ups as not like them, in that the grown-ups can't give answers to, or are simply not interested in, the philosophical questions that seem natural to the child. So children come to see the grown-ups as unknown, alien, mystical, and also as ridiculous, because grown-ups want to control everything, without showing any interest in the whole. It's the result of an authoritarian approach to children, whereby we try to make them believe things about meanings that are just not logical, that don't make sense to them.

P: Would you agree that if we grown-ups all agreed about the philosophical question, we too would discuss only practical questions, rather than all these individual 'points of view' that tend to characterize discussions among grown-ups?

S: Yes. In this respect we are no different from animals. Young animals also need answers to practical problems arising out of their need to satisfy their existential needs. And practical problems can be solved and the practical task of rearing offspring can be achieved even without the help of human language. With animals it is done via body-language – with each species imitating only its own, so that there is no confusion. Other species don't have this unlimited language that we have, but they can still solve the practical problems of survival.

P: And by 'unlimited language' – as with the phrase 'unlimited understanding' earlier – you mean not limited to dealing with the existential needs?

S: That's right. Humans can use language in relation to any meaning they choose. Nature forces humans to think about causality. But it doesn't force us to think on the basis of a particular meaning. We are free to choose the meaning. Animals are forced to think about causality, but only on the basis of the meanings determined by their existential needs.

P: So – going back a little – the question 'Who am I?' – put psychologically, as when people talk of trying to 'find themselves' – arises from a failure to give children early in life clear answers to their philosophical questions?

S: Yes, and it also arises through language, and through learning grown-ups' general identification with the grammatical word 'I'. That we have to understand. In fact, the question – 'Who am I?' – is not actually voiced out loud.

P: Because it is not seen as something we need to agree about, but as a personal thing?

S: Yes, and nobody can answer it in a satisfactory way. It remains a silent, personal question, along with the question 'What is the meaning of my life?' If anyone was to ask, they would be told: 'You must find it yourself, because you are free.'

P: So you would talk to children, even young children, in simple terms about these ideas?

S: Yes. For children it is easy to understand things philosophically, for the sole reason that they think of themselves as belonging to Nature. They feel they belong to Nature one hundred per cent. They haven't questioned this feeling, whereas grown-ups, who see themselves as free from Nature, have. And for children, the grown-ups are not an authority. Grown-ups are the same as themselves. In their own eyes, children are born into the same species as the grown-ups, and nobody is an authority. Children think: 'The grown-ups know more things than I do', and they accept without any problem that the grown-ups can do many things they themselves can't do. But the child thinks: 'But I can learn, I learn easily. I just need to have communication with grown-ups so that I can learn.'

But in the child's eyes the grown-ups are always seen as likes. It is we who teach children alienation. And we develop alienation as far as it is possible to develop it, by emphasizing this 'I' identity.

'The god within'

P: What about the idea in some psychology of 'the god within', the idea that somehow there is a bit of God in each of us?

S: Compare it with my idea that we are parts of God in the Being, but that in the Being we lack perspective – we can't move, we can't see anything, we can't experience anything. That's why God gives creation, which allows us to have a perspective on everything and on each other. How would one then see this other, pantheistic explanation, 'God is within us'?

From the pantheistic viewpoint, God doesn't exist, and pantheists don't think of themselves as parts of him. They see the whole merely as an eternally ongoing, continually new, active interaction, ruled by impersonal laws and not by one creator's consciousness. It is not existent, but abstract. Like every activity, it is absolutely changeable. They talk about this activity as 'divine nature' or 'the Godhead', but both are impersonal. Then pantheists talk about 'divine sparks', which can develop into gods.

If we don't have the hypothesis of the conscious, existent Being, then, rather than thinking of ourselves as parts of the Being, we experience ourselves as parts of ongoing creation That can lead to the idea that God is within us, in a developable form. But because the thought of many gods interacting, independently of each other, is impossible, the idea of hierarchy can't be avoided, with some of the gods being higher gods, some lower gods, and others even lower 'gods in the making'.

This is reflected in the organization of society. The idea of a pantheistic society is not modern, it doesn't belong solely to New Age thinking. It's just that New Age tries to unify the old pantheistic theories. These had a renaissance when science declared publicly in the 1950s that it couldn't continue its search for the original cause in the direction of the details of creation. So pantheism is as old an idea as history – I don't want to say 'as humanity', because I think it is very probable that humanity at one time or another believed in God in a logical, non-authoritarian way.

P: Some people might say, Stefan, that in your hypothesis there is hierarchy, too: a hierarchy between us and God.

S: There is no hierarchy, in my view, either between human beings, or between God – the whole – and human beings. It is not a hierarchy. That's the whole point. We can never be God, because we can never be the whole. And God can never be less than God, because God can never be a part. Therefore the position of God and the position of the parts are definite, and not changeable. But every part can live in consciousness of one and the same God or in its opposite.

P: But could you not say that there is a fixed hierarchy, with God above and us all below him?

S: If people don't want to know about God in a logical, self-evident way – that is, to recognize God's need to be understood as being expressed in his creation – then they have to live in a hierarchy, as authorities for one another, unified by the task of having to organize a peaceful collaboration between humans who see in their own species only unlikes, strangers – because, in accordance with modern education, everyone wants to be unique and not like.

If people believe in God in the way I am suggesting, they will still need to form some organization whenever they undertake a task that requires cooperation. If it is creating a society together, or if it is cooperating to build a house together, or whatever, organization is required. But then the organization is set up in a common agreement about its purpose and for a specific period of time, until its aim is achieved. And then there is no difference, for example, between those who have responsibility for the whole house, those who bring the bricks, those who bring the cement, and so on. The people are not different qualities. It is the same quality, whether you choose one role or the other. And you adopt the expression of one role for a while, until the house is built. We have to take these roles, but these roles are not our identity. Human identity is not threatened, endangered, if I take a little role in a corporation; it is not enhanced, increased, if I take the role of the leader in the corporation. I take it because there must be a leader, and because there must be all these roles in the corporation.

P: Okay, but couldn't somebody say that simply to have the idea of God introduces hierarchy?

S: Yes, but only if we introduce an irrational idea of God: as a part, and not as a whole. I know that some people say that, because they don't see God as the whole. In that case, they can only see God as a superior part, and so they must say that there is a hierarchy, between parts. If there is a superior part, there have to be inferior parts, and that is the basis of the idea of hierarchy. But if they interpret God as the whole and the whole creation as starting in the whole, it is impossible to talk about God as someone superior in a hierarchy.

P: Why?

S: God is the whole and we are the parts. Can you change that? In a hierarchy there is always a constant changing of roles and positions. People are always struggling to get a better role.

P: So if God is the whole, he can't change his role, and if we are the parts, we can't change our role.

S: No, we can't change our role. We are parts in God's creation and God's existence.

P: But can't we say that God starts above us?

S: ...as the whole and then gradually becomes a part?!

P: Oh, I see, he can't lose his role as superordinate.

S: That's right. And apart from the role of the superordinate 'whole', the only other role that exists is that of the subordinate 'part'. And all parts must be subordinate in the same way. That's why there is the saying that the sun rises equally on the evil and the good [Matthew 5:45 '...for he maketh his sun to rise on the evil and on the good, and sendeth rain on the just and on the unjust'], because there is no reason for a hierarchy.

P: So to talk about a 'fixed hierarchy' as regards God and us doesn't make sense?

S: No. Because there is no hierarchy. Hierarchy is where one person has the highest role, and there is a gradual reduction of position as you go down the hierarchy. But in relation to the whole, there are only two roles: either the role of the whole or the role of the parts.

P: And just as there is no hierarchy as regards God and us, would you say that there is no hierarchy within creation, between us and animals, for example? – even though you have used the phrase 'the highest species' in these dialogues to describe the human species.

S: The whole universe is shown by Nature to our eyes as one closed system, one order. Life on Earth is also shown as the same. If we don't reflect logically on the creator and his meaning with these orders, and if we don't understand that the precondition for a meaningful creation is to create senses to which the original distanceless whole is not shown, then we don't see the two orders – that of the universe and that of life on Earth – as one meaningful, understandable order, but as two mystical orders. In the universe we see no sign of hierarchy, because we see neither the creator – the whole – nor conscious parts. It is only on the Earth's surface that we have an unavoidable problem deciding who is creator – God or human beings – because we still don't see the whole, but we meet conscious parts. In meeting conscious parts, we can get confused by the idea of hierarchy if we don't have the idea of an original whole with original parts – and then the experience of mutual and undivided love will be rendered impossible.

P: And if it's a fixed hierarchy within creation...?

S: There is no hierarchy in creation either. Creation is one closed, interacting system, in which all the roles are allocated and no species can change its role. The closed system requires that all these roles develop from the Earth's chemically active surface. It needs micro-organisms, plants, animals, and what we see as the highest species – but nothing beyond that. This idea of one closed system – involving both the universe and life on Earth – is what Darwin missed with his theory of evolution. The idea of hierarchy and unlikeness always stems from theories of development – invariably endless development towards some undefined end-point imagined as perfection – whether they be ancient pantheistic ones, theological ones, or modern, Darwinistic ones.

P: So as regards us and animals, for example, our roles are fixed. I can't become a cow; a cow can't become a human. Humans are the 'highest' species only in the sense that they have a particular responsibility.

S: Yes...based on their unavoidable need, created via human language, to understand the original cause, that is, the creator's meaning with the obviously created reality.

So the parts in creation are forced to cooperate within the closed system, in order to satisfy their existential needs. Fixed roles are required because all the needs are different. But at the same time all the needs are in absolute accordance with one need, which the whole system serves: God's need to create and, at the same time, to destroy everything he creates, as a precondition for being understood by humans, rather than being misunderstood or neglected.

Because humans have to cooperate – and it's not a matter of whether they want to or not, because the closed system requires their interaction – they can develop unlikeness in their survival skills and can create hierarchy among themselves. If they want to, they can mark their cooperation formally in some way – for example, by issuing uniforms denoting different ranks – and can make their different roles in a cooperation their identity. In this sense, we can talk about a more or less 'fixed hierarchy'. But we shouldn't build up such fixed hierarchies. Undivided love requires that any cooperation that humans construct should not be fixed by identification with innumerable traditional or temporarily allocated roles. A fixed hierarchy is what you have in authoritarian societies. But if a society were not authoritarian, people would spontaneously create forms of cooperation. But it would be for each particular task, always with changeable roles, always for a limited time, and without being identified with the roles they have in such cooperation. Identification with all these different roles based on the skills that survival requires – that is, making them into identities, beginning with the roles that reproduction requires according to Nature...

P: ...so not seeing ourselves as basically men and women?

S: Yes... identification with such roles can only create confusion about our basic, real identity. This confusion then gets transferred to every child via language.

Dialogue 4

PHILOSOPHICAL LOGIC AND ITS BASIS: THE SELF-EVIDENT

Our relationship to reality

Philip: I want to go back to the feeling we can have that we are not a part of reality. Are you saying that distance, and therefore separateness, is an illusion of this created reality?

Stefan: Yes. If we take distance to be real and focus solely on our experience of everything from a distance, from outside, from an objective perspective, we don't experience ourselves as a real part of reality. It is necessary to distinguish between experience that is influenced by memory- and language-based thought and experience that is direct, via the senses. In the new scientific, objective thinking, we experience only the relation to reality that our senses give us. That's also what happens when we don't think philosophically, but only technically, mechanically. Philosophically, we should take into account our first subjective relationship to our own body, established through our nervous system, before our experience of everything outside our body that is mediated to our ability to experience by the body's senses. And that first relationship to our body is without distance. That is, it is not technical or mechanical, it is not based on resistance, power or force, as our relationship to things outside us is. It is based on our experience of needs and on our enjoyment in satisfying them with the help of our bodily capacities, which we learn to rule with the help of our nervous system.

And relation is not one-sided: relation is not just from us to each thing outside us. It is two-sided, many-sided, and all-sided. It is also mediated by impressions from outside – light, sound, resistance, and so on.

P: So the relationship of every thing to every thing?

S: Yes, the interacting relationship between every created thing – first established in our experience by light, which makes it possible for us to see every thing separated by what we experience as distance or empty space. It is obvious that the whole universe is an interaction, that every thing is always related to every thing, even if we break things up into their smallest parts. Nothing is free from this interaction. And it is going on all the time. Our whole visible reality is one indivisible interaction…

P: Including the activity that goes on beneath the surface of bodies, and not just the activity we experience between bodies?

A separate life or a common life?

S: Yes. The whole creation is just one activity, which provokes the thought that an origin of the whole interaction must exist, an origin that is not present in an apparent way within creation. That is why the hypothesis of a non-created whole is necessary. But generally people don't want to think of relation as already established by Nature and as all-sided, because that would actualize the idea that everything belongs absolutely together, that everything is an absolute unity. Nowadays everybody wants a separate life rather than a common life, because it is the generally accepted view that we should develop power rather than cooperation. This makes us blind to the fact that a separate life exists only at the start.

P: You mean in our invisible origin, as a separate, but inseparable, conscious part of the Being?

S: Yes. But this we can only agree about as a logical belief on the basis of philosophical considerations. But even without such an agreement, we find that every living being has a separate ability to experience, a separate feeling that they exist. And we also find that the moment we come into creation, the moment we are born, our life is a common one, not a separate one.

Agape vs eros

If we were to remember that we can only have this common life that is established by Nature, then the idea of undivided love – or, as it has also been called, *agape*, God's love or Christian love – would also be actualized, that is, the idea of a common love for the whole indivisible Nature. This idea and the idea that relation is already established by Nature are impossible to combine with the idea of 'free', independent thinking – which originates in the idea of being outside. Nor can they be combined with *eros*, interpreted as the historical alternative to undivided love or *agape*. Eros is called 'love' because it necessarily actualizes a relation to another human being and not to another species. But *eros* is simply a temporary, practical relation between two necessarily human beings based on predilection, special fondness, 'falling in love', starting to love – in the absence of an agreement about the necessity for an undivided love for the creator of the whole established Nature.

P: And as such, *eros* is just one of the practical relations that demand choice – a more or less durable choice – based on predilection?

S: Yes... durable problems of predilection such as the practical relation between parents, children and parents, employers and employees, authorities and subjects, and so on – which require a choice on one or two or several occasions. Other non-durable problems of predilection require decisions all the time, also based, like all predilections, on likes and dislikes: what to eat on different occasions, what tasks to do about the home or at work, and so on. The difficulty is that people don't make a clear distinction in language between undivided love and predilection. They say they 'love', 'love more', 'don't love', 'hate', in the same comparative sense in which they say they 'like', 'like better', 'dislike', 'hate'. Predilections, which are unavoidable, and undivided love do not exclude each other, but they should be distinguished from one another – both mentally, that is, in language, and in our daily experience of them, that is, emotionally – as two different qualities.

P: So *eros* regulates the practical relation required to satisfy the need of reproduction?

S: Yes, for every species. And it is only in the absence of the feeling of undivided love that *eros* itself is interpreted as love.

P: I would like to come back to this, but I still want to understand the significance of what you are saying about relationship.

Subjective relation and objective experience

S: We have to make clear the difference between subjective relation and objective experience, because the terms 'subjective' and 'objective' got confused early in the seventeenth century by rationalist philosophers who, following Descartes' proposal – *cogito ergo sum* – began seeing human identity in doubting and thinking. Objective experience – that is, the experience of objects outside us – is always one-sided, because objects cannot experience, cannot have relation. Subjective relation is always two-sided. That's what relation is; that's what relation starts with. So love is two-sided. But, in my view, we can't understand the conditions laid down by God in creation for the Nature-based* start for relation – permanent undivided love – until we make this hypothesis about the non-created, unchangeable existence, the conscious Being, conceived of as the original subjective relation between the original whole and its original parts. This Nature-based start for relation is originally only one-sided: it is experienced originally only by the whole, and is therefore unsatisfying for both the whole and the parts in the original Being. If we take this view, then we start to experience love not only as a relation between two, but as a relation between three: between two parts who consciously experience and love their relation to the omnipresent whole. Ignorance of the natural conditions for our meeting each other creates the confused idea that we are forced by Nature to have two different sorts of thinking: subjectively logical – that is, biologically consistent – thinking, and thinking that is only objectively consistent. The first is bound by unavoidable natural meanings; the other – and this is what makes for the confusion – is not bound by any meanings, but is bound only by mechanical necessities, interacting powers. In other words, this second is thinking without love in the picture.

Only a subject, a living being, who can be conscious of the purpose of its activity, can be logical. But a subject can still be objectively inconsistent by misjudging the activities of objects or of other subjects. So we can say that animals are always logical, but that by Nature they have, meaningfully, differing capacities for being objectively consistent.

P: Whereas human beings...?

S: Human beings were always very keen to develop objectively consistent, or scientific, thinking, in as many areas of the total creation as possible, without any commonly agreed regard for creation's purpose. The knowledge gained in this way was also always used as a superior power to conquer people who didn't have it to the same level. But from 1600 onwards the development of such thinking was given an historically new impetus, and in the eighteenth and nineteenth centuries the new science was also put to the same use, that is, not just to benefit humanity, but also to conquer the whole globe from Europe.

After Einstein's discovery of the relativity of the object, the idea of a new, mystical, objective form of thinking – in contrast to the well-defined, non-mystical, matter-based, objective or rational thinking – was introduced. This new mystical objective thinking was interpreted as a direct continuation of the old scientific objectivity. This was relativism: the idea that there are no principles, no exact definitions. All thinking is regarded as relative, because energy – the new idea of the absolute – is also relative, because it can appear in different forms. Such thinking based on this idea of energy was still seen as the same as the earlier exact, objective thinking because science neglected the principal difference between 'matter' and 'energy'. It simply changed the idea of matter to the idea of mass – in Latin, *quantum* – and introduced the ambivalent idea of 'quanta' – in Einstein's formula, M combined with c – as measurable units of energy.

The development of this thinking was accompanied by two world wars and the gradual loss of colonies through the global spread of objective knowledge, including the knowledge that can be used for conquering by force and the new energy-based idea of a free, human creativity. This led to the establishment after the first war of the League of Nations, replaced after the second by the United Nations, in order to try to avoid the use of force between nations and with the new idea of developing infinite, free human creativity as the alternative – both philosophically, that is, theoretically, using language, and practically, through the development of modern industry and technology.

P: Are you saying that this relativism led to such things as the declaration of human rights – to protect the practical freedoms that people saw themselves as now having – and experiments in such freedoms, as, for example, in education, with projects like A. S. Neill's at Summerhill, with its emphasis on personal freedom?

S: Yes. It led to the idea that human creativity is free, and this freedom should be respected in the organizing of societies, in the rearing of children, and in education. This new mystical form of objective thinking led to a new interpretation of subjective thinking. This is the new paradigm that was demanded as necessary by Thomas Kuhn in his book *The Structure of Scientific Revolutions* [University of Chicago Press, Chicago & London, 1962]. In contrast to the original meaning of 'subjective thinking' – that is, biological logic* based on the natural existential needs – and in contrast to the meaning to which 'subjective thinking' was transferred in the seventeenth century – that is, non-exact and also irrational, tradition-bound, superstitious thinking – the new interpretation regarded 'subjective thinking' as the rational – interpreted as 'natural' – source of human creativity. This creativity was viewed as an end in itself, as independent of natural meanings. It was motivated by what it saw as Nature's basically meaningless creativity – this view being represented in a modern way by chaos theory. This new 'subjective thinking' was thus seen as the source of artificial meanings not developed by Nature and as the means by which they could be realized. The idea was that each person had to work out for themselves how to be happy in life.

It really flowered in the sixties, and has gained force since then. In the seventies this occurred via the idea of the New Age, which was responsible for a renaissance of the ancient idea of human creativity based on introspective, so-called transcendental, science. Since 1989 it has occurred through the globally established market economy, with its idea of each person becoming individually and infinitely rich through the exploitation of every possibility for human creativity, driven on by the spirit of competition. Since then the surface of the Earth has no longer been seen as the platform for life and for what we need for our lives, but has been seen only as the platform for human creativity. The absence of any feeling of responsibility or ethics towards Nature has created, in place of the old moral rules, a new idea for responsibility and righteousness. This is based on different monetary systems, as all the unlimitable artificial needs, evaluations and products of human creativity, together with all the needs, biological values and biological products that are provided and limited by Nature, have become translated into money-based mathematics related to current supply and demand. This takes place in increasingly international money-based markets, which no one can have an overview of or supervise. So there is an enormously complicated economic responsibility – and, in fact, a growing necessity to regulate economic criminality. 'Egocentricity' and competition are now no longer seen as things that need to be avoided and as the major problems that need to be dealt with if we are to live in cooperation. They are seen instead as positive things that advance the development of general human creativity.

P: So we can say that humans today are much more confused – or almost totally confused – by the emphasis on this new 'subjective' thinking?

S: Yes... 'subjective' interpreted as free, unbound, original. It is much more confusing than the earlier interpretation of 'subjective' as 'inexact' or 'irrational', because everybody is at the same time fascinated by its products. In my view, life is cooperation, so subjective thinking should mean meaningful, ethical thinking, on the basis of the question 'why?' – that is, for what purpose the whole creation is made, not how it is made and how it can be changed and developed to suit individual human purposes. That is how this new subjective thinking about free human creativity is in fact applied: in relation to global information and education on the sole basis of the scientific question 'how?' and in relation to human creativity based on a science that doesn't deal with the meaning of Nature's creativity. The problem is that it is impossible to take objective science away from people by burning books, or to control education or do anything else to eliminate this subjective confusion – which is what authoritarian traditions vainly tried to do in earlier times. The only way forward I can see is to start a global commitment to reach a global agreement about the original cause and its meaning – before the global confusion about our objective knowledge has such consequences that Nature itself takes this knowledge away from humans in its own destructive way.

P: This has taken us some way away from what you were saying about experiencing love as a relation between three. I would like to come back to this, because I think it is a very important point. As I think you have put it once, together two – or more – people can enjoy the common whole creation. It's not a question of enjoying just each other as separate from the whole creation, as outsiders in it.

S: That's right. That's possible for everybody who understands that we belong absolutely together, living the same life that God offers everybody through creation. That is the original idea of the Trinity: the oneness of the parts within the whole. Before creation, this original relationship is conscious only for the whole, as one-sided love: God loves his own existence. But it can become conscious for the parts, too, through creation. Considered in this way, creation is perfect for this aim.

But it depends on the will of the parts whether or not they want to test, adopt and live by the hypothesis of this original, inseparable relationship, the fact of belonging absolutely together, both to the creator and to each other. If we don't make this hypothesis, our knowledge of creation is regarded as imperfect, and therefore developable. In my view, objective thinking – that is, understanding of the causality manifested by the separated manifold – is developable. But objective thinking is just something we get in creation to enable us to understand objective causality in creation, so that we can satisfy our existential needs. It is senseless to develop objective knowledge of this causality as an end in itself, because it can't lead to the discovery of the original cause. And there is no point, while being blind to creation's purpose, in trying to make creation better than it is, since it is made perfectly for its purpose, by the original cause.

P: And it was hoped by science that it would discover the original cause?

S: Yes. In olden times, it was said – in introspective science – that the 'concrete' creation could be ruled using the knowledge gained from the transcendental experience of creation – which, as we've said, they thought of as experience of an 'abstract', original reality.

Modern extraspective science, on the other hand, introduced the hope of being able to find the original parts of creation – using the atom theory – so that creation could be ruled by controlling it starting from its smallest 'concrete' form.

Philosophical reflection vs thinking

P: You said that we need thinking in order to understand causality in creation, but don't we need thinking also to understand God?

S: Yes, but not what I have just called objective thinking, that is, the kind of thinking that is based on objective causality in creation. You don't need that to understand God, because you can never investigate God's activity from its invisible, objective origin in the direction of the whole. Nor can you investigate the original parts' activity in the direction of the invisible parts that are behind what we experience as the activities of the living and non-living manifold. That's why you can't objectively prove that the activity you experience as creation is God's or the parts' activity. That it is, as I have said before, is self-evident, axiomatic – that is, it can neither be proved nor falsified; it is something that we can only agree together or not.

The basic, first agreement has then to be that only a subject, and not an object, can be an original cause of activity, anywhere. It doesn't matter whether it's God or somebody else. If a cup or a table moves, nobody takes the cup or the table as the cause of that activity, that movement. The question is only whether there can also be behind the whole an active subject that experiences relation, or whether this is the case only behind the created objects that we experience as subjects experiencing relation.

P: But I thought that your view was that we were given thinking in order to come to an understanding of God.

S: We are given everything-covering language and philosophical thinking for that purpose. We should distinguish between thinking in relation to causality in creation – of which even animals are capable – and language-based, communicated, philosophical thinking or reflection in relation to the invisible original cause and meaning of the whole visible reality. In the absence of everything-covering language, animals are unable to communicate either their experiences and memories of reality, or their conclusions about causality – other than by body-language and a restricted number of sound-combinations particular to each species. That is why they cannot have any interest in invisible, so-called abstract things, or in the abstract or theoretical thinking characteristic of humans.

Philosophical reflection is not thinking in the way that we generally interpret thinking. Philosophical reflection is only actual in relation to the invisible original cause. And that is for the very reason that the original cause is invisible: we don't have an objective experience of the original non-created cause, only of created parts that have a mystical origin. It's also because creation, our impression of reality, which we experience as absolute changeability, appears to be contradictory in all its aspects – because we don't reckon with the fact that it is necessary for everything that is created also to be destroyed. By contrast, the non-created original cause and the purpose with creation must remain unchangeable.

P: What do you mean by 'creation appears to be contradictory in all its aspects'?

S: Nothing in creation seems to be intended to stay. Everything changes, gets constructed and destroyed, comes and goes, including the generations. All this happens without the source being revealed – because the source is neither the visible, non-conscious details of creation nor the visible, conscious participants in creation. The source is the invisible whole, which we have to consider as living, as conscious, if we want to understand the origin of creation.

P: So in relation to the original non-created cause, we can't use the thinking that we use in relation to the objective causality in creation?

S: That's right. Philosophical reflection is what is involved in checking whether creation can be understood without contradictions, that is, without contradicting our subjective and our objective experience of reality – for example, on the basis of my hypothesis about the original cause and meaning of the whole creation. If it can't be understood on the basis of my hypothesis, then we have to choose another hypothesis and check that one, until we find a hypothesis that does not contradict our experience of the whole of Nature.

Resolving creation's apparent contradictions

P: I still don't understand what you mean by creation appearing 'to be contradictory in all its aspects'.

S: Everything in creation is changeable: between a beginning, a start, a coming into existence, and a mystical end, a dissolving into a mystical nothing or some mystical 'energy'. Modern science tells us that even suns begin to exist and cease to exist. This gives us the impression that the whole creation is contradictory through and through. Since we experience creation as the whole reality, the questions arise: *Does reality exist or does it not exist? What is the meaning of a creation that destroys everything it creates?* The fact that creation does this gives us the impression that creation is meaningless. It seems senseless to produce and at the same time to destroy what is produced.

The philosophical question of the original cause actualizes creation as a whole. It emphasizes what creation produces, rather than what it destroys, and from the point of view of what the meaning is of both its production and its destruction.

In generally held philosophical interpretations, both the constructive and destructive sides of creation are emphasized separately. That is why there are only conflicting theories and no logical agreement about the original cause. Every such theory has the idea of *two original causes*: one cause for construction – which is interpreted as the good side – and a second, separate cause for destruction – which is interpreted as the original cause of evil. In my view, there is just one original cause of both the construction and destruction in creation, for the practical reasons given earlier [see p.108]. In my view, evil comes in through human language, when people act according to confused ideas about these two sides, based on their ignorance of the reason for these contradictory forces – that is, based on their failure to question tradition and to understand that the construction and the destruction do not have to be judged as a mystical contradiction, but as an evident necessity.

P: What you said a moment ago – and you have said it before, too – about philosophy relating solely to the question of the original cause could be said to be rather arrogant. It could be said that you are just choosing to call 'philosophy' what *you* think 'philosophy' is, as a way of disqualifying what everyone generally understands as 'philosophy'.

S: Well, that is how I define philosophy. Other people use the word in relation to authoritarian assertions by different people: either the founders of religions or so-called gurus, or other interpreters of creation and life's mystery. People cannot avoid hearing about the problem of the original cause. So humans have to deal with philosophy as long as there is no agreement about the original cause. And even if they find a non-contradictory, logical answer on which they can theoretically agree, they still have to continue checking it, in order to find out how to relate to it.

P: You mean, in order to understand how to think and behave according to it?

S: Yes. That is what I mean by establishing an ethical relation to the creator and creation – that is, becoming orientated to the meaning, instead of being disorientated about it.

P: …that is, rather than relating according to rules and commandments based on other people's understanding?

A common, concrete start for thinking

S: Yes, which is a moral relation, rather than an ethical relation. My view is that without the philosophical hypothesis I am putting forward, it is impossible for us to have a common starting-point for our thinking. If we don't have the objectively unprovable hypothesis of an unchangeable, non-created, original, objective Being, we can only start our thinking from the objects that creation offers us. That is what the Greeks, for example, did, when they took different abstract elements – ether, fire, air, water and earth – as the original, objective cause. But nothing in creation can be understood as the original cause, because nothing in creation is unchangeable or indestructible. And even if there was such a thing as an indestructible part of creation – such as the atom that Democritus proposed – a part or all the parts together can never be the cause of the whole.

P: But your theory is not the only historical theory based on the hypothesis of a non-created, conscious reality. Theology has such a theory too.

S: Yes. But theology couldn't argue its belief in a non-created, unchangeable existence – God – philosophically, because it didn't think of God as an objective whole with objective parts. On the basis of 'mystical', introspective science where everything appears abstract and is experienced as abstract – because it doesn't offer any resistance – it said that God is abstract. And they thought of God as a whole without parts. But a whole without parts is what a part is without a whole – whether we think of it is as something abstract and intangible, as basically we should think of creation, or whether we think of it as something concrete and tangible, as we should think of the Being.

P: ...because a real part is something that cannot be further divided?

S: Yes. That forced theology to say that God creates parts as his likes in order to have company. But the idea of something abstract – interpreted as something mystical, as something different from concrete – can't be a common start for thinking.

What can be confusing for humans is language. Everything that is put forward in language can be interpreted, 'experienced' as an objective reality and be a start for human thinking, even if it has nothing to do with reality. But a common start for thinking has to be something concrete, and it has to be something that can be the conscious origin of meaningful activity – otherwise logical understanding can't start. Only an activity that is meaningful can be understood, as opposed to merely ascertained or stated. And only a conscious being can be a cause of meaningful activity.

P: This mention of 'concrete' and 'abstract' takes us right back to the beginning of these dialogues.

S: Yes. We should remember that in our *experience* 'concrete' is a relative term not only for a more or less solid something but also for liquids and gases. That's why we have to make the hypothesis of one concrete – in the real, absolute meaning of concrete – whole: an indestructible something with indestructible parts.

P: Would you say your hypothesis is a scientific hypothesis?

S: Yes, I would say so: because it gives us a start for real, objectively-based thinking. But it doesn't exclude the subjective behind the objective, that is, the ability to experience relation, relation experienced in an original or axiomatic way as only love, undisturbed by the problem of predilection.

P: And that start is the non-created reality, God's and our invisible Being?

S: Yes. And such an objective, concrete start is what science wants, but cannot realize, because it can't find in creation an indestructible object – such as it was hoped an atom or an elementary particle would be – on which to base its thinking about the whole causality. Everybody can imagine the existence of a non-created reality and also understand that it must be impossible to prove it scientifically. That is because scientific proof means 'objective proof', which means experiencing something from outside. Not even God can experience the non-created reality, himself, from outside in the way that we, thanks to created light, are able to see everything that is created.

Checking Hlatky's hypothesis

P: If your hypothesis can't be objectively proved, can it be checked in any way?

S: The only way you can check my hypothesis that God establishes a separate relation between the parts and himself, the whole, through creation, because he needs to be understood by his parts, is by asking yourself the following questions. First, is the hypothesis of the indivisible non-created Being – interpreted as a conscious relation between a whole and its parts – logical, that is, can it be compared with our experience of every living being? Or is it more logical to see it as a non-conscious object, or as a sum of endless activity?

Second, is it logical to have the idea of a need to be understood, common to God and the parts – the only difference being that, as I have said before, in the Being – God already understands the parts, in a one-sided way – that is, from his side – but the parts can't understand either God or each other?

Third, is creation starting from God a necessity if God's need is to be satisfied? Or is it more logical that God should do it with perfect power, without any need or purpose? Or is it more logical to believe that basically there is chaos, so that human creation is necessary?

And lastly, we have to check whether we can understand creation on the basis of this overall hypothesis – that is, we have to check whether creation is perfect for the purpose of satisfying God's need, and at the same time our basic need, to be understood.

P: How can we check whether creation is perfect for this purpose?

S: If you imagine what technical problem God has if he wants to make creation with this purpose in mind – to establish relation between himself, the whole, and his parts – then you can check it by theoretically taking away from creation anything you like or changing anything in it you like. Having done that, you can ask whether creation would or would not still be perfect for this aim. In other words, can creation only be the way it is, or could it be different? The foremost question then is whether God as the whole could create for every part a direct relation to the whole similar to the direct relation that the parts have to each other through a created, unitary body.

P: And you don't think God could, because our experience of creation must replace our lack of experience in the original Being, otherwise we would have no perspective on the whole – or on each other either?

S: Yes. If we were to have an objective relation to the whole similar to our objective relation to each other in creation, the creation of a body representing the whole – a body that could be seen from the outside as we can see each other's created bodies from the outside – would be necessary. That is impossible.

P: But what could we theoretically take away from creation to check your hypothesis?

S: Try taking anything away. Take the stars and the whole sky away, for example. If you do that, there is no impression of the whole and no impression of light. It is through the light-giving stars that God shows us indirectly that we belong to a whole.

P: How so?

S: Doesn't the surrounding darkness between the stars – what has always been known as 'the cosmos' – or the surrounding blue or cloudy sky create for every child and every living being the impression of a surrounding whole? – until, that is, this impression is taken away from humans through teaching them that there is a not-existent empty space behind the manifold.

P: I see what you mean.

S: We can continue this process – of theoretically taking things away from creation or changing things in creation – until we become convinced that everything in creation is organized in such a way as to point us indirectly towards the need to make this hypothesis. I think that without this hypothesis of the original cause, we can never reach a satisfactory understanding of the whole causality – as I've said before.

P: In which case, we will be doomed, as science is, to endlessly exploring causality in creation?

S: Yes. How many libraries are there full of books devoted to causality in creation? Yet in spite of all these investigations, we have got no closer to the original cause of the whole creation. And that is because this one cause of the whole creation is not, when the matter is considered philosophically, accessible to scientific investigation. But it could be accessible to every child as a satisfactory belief on the basis of philosophical considerations, if everything-covering human language were used to communicate it rather than to defend authoritarian theories.

Is creation perfect for its purpose?

P: I am still not clear about this process of 'checking whether creation is perfect for its purpose'?

S: Let's take an example of something humans create. How do you check if a car is perfect for its purpose?

P: You drive it.

S: Yes, but in order to drive it, you must first know its purpose: that is, you must know that it is meant to be driven. Once you know the car's purpose, you can check whether the car is perfect for its purpose: by using the steering wheel, the pedals and all the different parts to drive it, and seeing if everything is necessary for its purpose. That's how we can also check if creation is really made to meet God's need to be understood – and our need to be understood, too.

P: And, again, by 'being understood', you mean being understood by another conscious being as like, which means belonging in the same way to the same reality?

S: Yes. Now we can't understand a car unless we presuppose a creator and a user, and unless the user understands what the creator has created the car for. It is impossible to understand a car as something in itself. The same is true of creation. In the case of creation, God is the creator and we are the user. His purpose in creating creation is not that we should use creation, as animals do, without consciousness of its creator, him, and of his purpose with creation. God's purpose is that, using everything-covering language, we should understand the creator and his purpose with the whole creation. The car is creation, if you like, and we should be conscious of the creator's purpose when we use it.

So we can understand God as like in his need to be understood by his parts – even though he has a unique role as the only creator of the visible reality, 'the car' – by checking every detail of creation to see if creation serves God's purpose, God's need, perfectly. And we can understand every living being as basically like, in their roles as users of the same, common creation – having language in the case of humans, or not having language, in the case of animals.

P: So when you say 'check', you don't mean 'check empirically'?

S: No, if by 'empirically' you mean 'objectively'. The basic hypothesis of the original cause can't be checked objectively – because, as I have said several times now, we cannot experience the non-created Being from outside: neither the whole Being, God, nor the conscious parts of the Being, ourselves. I mean 'theoretical checking' through philosophical reflection based on axioms and bearing in mind the obvious fact that we have not only a distance-based, objective experience of surrounding creation, but also an immediate, subjective experience of it through our own, obviously biologically created body. This subjective relation relates primarily to our existential needs, which are the needs of the body, including the need for reproduction. It relates only secondarily, through the bodily senses, to our objective experience of creation, through which all our needs have to be satisfied. Subjective relation also includes for humans, who are dependent on language, the problem of satisfying not only our need for company – to be understood by likes – but at the same time also God's need to be understood as like, rather than as a mystical, perfect magician who has no need or purpose.

P: Do you emphasize this idea of our immediate, subjective experience of creation to distinguish it from modern science?

S: Yes, because the modern scientific interpretation is that our distance-based, objective view on surrounding reality is primary and is what is characteristic of humans. I think this is as misguided as the pantheistic interpretation, which talks about the distanceless transcendental experience of reality as primary. The pantheists call it absolute or cosmic consciousness.

P: So your way of thinking about this checking is very different from other people's way of thinking.

S: Yes, and that is because we don't make a proper distinction between checking the logic of an activity bearing in mind its purpose, which is what I argue we should do, and following or tracking an activity solely with the aim of learning to control, reproduce or change it according to our own purposes, which is what science does. This is the big problem. The hypothesis of the original cause requires a different sort of conviction from that required for scientific hypotheses, which relate only to causality in creation. It needs the hypothesis of the creator's objective existence and of the subjective purpose behind his creative activity, bearing in mind that we can only recognize the flow of creation. Recognizing the flow of an activity – how it starts, goes on and stops – is not a real understanding of causality. Real understanding starts when we know both the cause and the purpose of an activity. Then we can check if an activity is in accordance with its purpose – that means 'logical' – or not.

I have been doing this checking since I first made this hypothesis, in the early sixties, and I have been doing it for you all the time while we have been talking. I have tried to show you how everything is built up in creation with a particular meaning in mind: that God wants to 'show' himself indirectly to us, the parts, so that we can understand the original relationship between him and us and the logical reason for his creation. If you don't lose sight of this point, you can check my hypothesis and everything I have said from this point of view: that of God's technical problem in making the original situation understood. And if you checked and did become convinced by this view, you would not then regard your own need to be understood just as your own individual problem, since God has to solve this problem too. And at the same time that God potentially solves his own need to be understood, he also potentially solves the problem for us – by forcing human beings to learn and use everything-covering human language.

P: ...with which we should arrive at an understanding of God?

S: Of God first, then of each other – because, if we understand God, then we have no problem understanding each other. If we refuse to understand God, the original cause, the creator, first, then it is impossible to understand each other, because it is impossible to understand the activity that we represent for each other without knowing the origin of human life and its *common* need and purpose.

P: You mean understand that we originate as parts of the original Being where we cannot experience anything?

S: Yes, so our original desire is to experience, and this is made possible for us by creation. In creation we experience other conscious parts, and that actualizes the experience of love. We generally have no problem in loving living Nature on the Earth, that is, other species, because in them we meet our likes, since we know that they also have the ability to experience and that animals have the same needs that we have. But if we don't understand that human beings have their origin in the Being, as parts of God, we become confused about our own and other human beings' identity. The basic motivation for our activity must then become to develop ourselves as free, independent, original and unique creators, and to understand each other as such: that is, as having the same identity as original creators.

P: ...but not as likes?

S: That's right.

P: So, going back to the issue of checking and its relation to axioms: you said that our checking should be through philosophical reflection based on axioms.

S: Yes, those axioms we have referred to already and which we generally fail to bear in mind – and which are actually basic for all thinking.

P: Do you mean for thinking about objective causality as well as for philosophy?

S: Yes. Even an animal's thinking, for example, is guided by the axiom that an object cannot be the original cause of its activity.

P: Yes, it is interesting to see a dog, for example, dealing with an unfamiliar, man-made, moving object, like a small clockwork toy.

S: In relation to subjects and objects, animals act and react appropriately – in accordance with Nature's purpose for their lives. But without language, animals can't have a language-based idea such as 'life'. Nor can they have other ideas separate from their experience, about their life and the things which they experience as self-evident, things mediated for them only by Nature without verbal explanations. So they can neither feel absent nor have the idea of absence. When something is absent, they can't think 'How is it that it is absent?', 'Why is it absent?', or 'I am sorry it is absent'. Or when something is back, although they are glad, they can't think 'I am glad it is back'. What is absent does not exist for animals. They can't think historically; they can't have the concept of time.

And all axioms – precisely because they don't need any verbal explanations, but can only either be agreed upon or denied, in which case the absence of the experience they refer to is taken as the truth – can be checked only by you yourself against your own experience. But by that I mean against your total current experience. And your total current experience starts with your ability to experience: primarily your own body, and then everything – living and non-living – in the surrounding manifold.

So in philosophy, we have to check for ourselves and come to an agreement as to whether, for example, it is the primary need of a living being to have company with likes. Or is the opposite the case: do living beings not need the company of likes? Generally the need for company is not seen as an existential need, but in fact we couldn't even be born and brought up without this general need. In fact, unless this need existed, we could not be manipulated through the misuse of language by other people – in just the same way that, if our general existential needs did not exist, power could not be used in society to manipulate us.

P: So if we did not need things in order to survive in our everyday lives, we would not be open to being manipulated by those people that provide those things? Individuals have much less access to those things now than they used to, so the possibilities for manipulation in that respect are much greater nowadays.

S: Yes.

P: So you can check these contradictory ideas against your experience and find out which of the two possibilities corresponds with your experience and which, therefore, is the one that is a valid conclusion – that is, which one is the axiom?

Philosophical logic

S: Yes. You check axioms on the basis of your Nature-based, original experience of your own life – that is, on the basis of the information given to you by Nature. So it is your own experience that determines philosophical logic, quite independently of the information and language-based ideas that you get through human language.

P: I find that an unfamiliar usage of the word 'logic'. Can you explain it more?

S: It is a totally unfamiliar usage! The word 'logic' has never been used in history in relation to the common need of consciousness to be understood as like – because we never talk about this need, and we never talk about basic likeness as the precondition for love. We never reckon with the fact that the need to be understood as like is the basic need of every living being.

Historically, the word 'logic' has been used in relation only to our existential needs or to our artificial needs: if an activity fulfils such a need, we say it is 'logical'. The word 'logic' has never been used in relation to the question of the original cause and meaning of the whole creation, that is, in relation to God and the purpose of his activity, derived from his need to be understood – which is the way I use it. It was not used in this way in history because, without a general agreement about the need of consciousness, the hypothesis of God's need was not made. So all answers to the question of the original cause were given only in an irrational, therefore authoritarian way, and not in a logical, understandable way. It was said that God cannot have any needs. So creation was never supposed to be logical. No tradition talks about there being a logical reason behind creation that would make it understandable.

P: To make it clearer what you mean by 'philosophical logic', can you say more about the way the word 'logic' is generally used?

S: In order for any need to be satisfied, activity in relation to the surroundings is required. If the activity fulfils the need, we generally use the word 'logical' to describe that activity.

P: So if I am hungry and have a need for food, it is 'logical' that I should eat something?

S: Yes. And it is easy to judge if an activity is 'logical' or not if you take an example of existential needs, as you have done. Where it is more difficult is in the case of the artificial needs of human beings.

P: And by 'artificial', you mean in your terms a need that is not associated either with an existential need or with the basic need of consciousness to be understood?

S: Yes. Now in our surroundings we meet, alongside mechanical activity, biological activity that is driven by common, and therefore known, existential needs. We also meet human beings, who can be driven both by their biological needs and by numerous artificial needs. These artificial needs can vary from person to person, and so are not common to everyone.

P: And they will not always be declared by the person.

S: Yes, so we will not always know what they are. So we will only be able to judge whether the activity of a human being derived from an artificial need is 'logical' or not if we know what that artificial need is – that is, if we know what the person's 'individual philosophy', their 'individual logic', is. That's why, if our species is generally guided, beyond our existential needs, by numerous, differing artificial needs, we can't spontaneously know, we can't spontaneously understand our own species.

P: Can you give an example of this contrast between natural and artificial needs?

S: We can find it logical that everyone needs a flat or house to live in. This relates to a common, existential need, and so is 'legal' according to Nature. But what the individual chooses to put in their flat – by way of special fittings, appliances and furniture – is a different matter. We can find the choice a particular person makes in this respect 'logical' if it is in line with what the particular person feels they need. But that logic – which relates to an artificial need created by that person – has nothing to do with the common need, which Nature 'legalizes', to have somewhere to keep warm in and feel protected.

P: I see. But isn't unlikeness – as here between artificial needs – necessary if we are to feel that we are an individual?

S: Yes, of course, it is necessary and natural. That is precisely the main point about identity! Everything in creation has to be different on the surface. Not even two leaves on the same tree are exactly alike. It is the speciality of humans to produce uniforms!

So – going back to my overall point – 'logic' in this sense is related to living beings' behaviour in relation to their environment, as only living beings can have a meaning to their activities.

There is another reference for 'logic' in the generally accepted sense of the word, and that is the activity represented by the use of human language. In the eyes of other people, we can use human language 'logically' or 'illogically'. This is what is known as Aristotelian logic. Essentially, we shouldn't contradict ourselves.

If in philosophy – that is, in discussions about the original truth – what is 'logical' is restricted to what is consistent with this Aristotelian notion of logic based on Nature's construction and destruction, rather than to biological, meaning-based logic, then discussions become bound to the traditions of language – which take this view of logic – rather than to our present experience of the whole creation, which we basically experience through our own body as living, biological, and only with the senses as acting mechanically.

P: And you make the contrast between the idea of each person having their 'individual philosophy' or 'individual logic' and the idea of a 'logic' inherent in creation that is equally valid for everyone?

S: That's right. Generally, the word 'philosophy' relates to what is regarded as the *mystery* of creation – 'mystery' because the need for creation and the purpose of creation is not understood. If creation is regarded as a mystery in this way, then either authoritarian rules of conduct have to be imposed, or it is left to each individual to work out for themselves the particular meaning of their own life.

Each such philosophy can be logical in relation to its basic idea, but not in a general sense, that is, not logical if we relate it to our common experience of the whole creation.

I, however, connect the word 'philosophy' with the *meaning* of creation. So the word 'philosophy' and the problem of philosophical logic, in my view, is only actualized by the problem of the original cause and meaning of the whole creation. We have to make an objective hypothesis about what the original cause and purpose behind creation is.

Because we can't control the original cause itself, we can't check the objective origin of the creator's behaviour in the way we can check activities in creation, which is by tracing them from their obvious causes to their obvious effects or from their obvious effects to their obvious causes. So we can't apply what is the generally accepted, scientific method. It is true that in the case of biology and in the case of the technology created by humans, the scientific method takes the purpose of an activity into account. But it doesn't do that in the case of the technology, the mechanical science called physics, and not therefore in the case of the universe – or, as I would call it, creation – as a whole.

In order first to make the hypothesis about the original cause and its purpose, and then in order to check our hypothesis about its purpose, all we need to do – as I have said before – is to reflect on our common total experience of reality. And by 'total' I mean our ability to experience, our experience of our own body – with its needs and its capacities to satisfy those needs – and our experience of everything in the manifold. Our hypothesis is 'logical' if it corresponds to that total experience, 'illogical' if it doesn't.

P: So in that sense the 'logic' by which we arrive at our hypothesis of the original cause and its purpose, and by which we check its purpose, derives from the experiences of creation as a whole that we all have in common?

Agreeing on axioms

S: Yes. And these common, Nature-based experiences are what axioms are. They are the original truth given to everybody, in the same way, by Nature. They are not different people's relative interpretations of these experiences mediated by human language.

Because axioms are common, we can discuss them. If we are to use them as a basis for further discussion, we have to agree about them as axioms. That means we have to agree to let them be valid, and not let their opposites – which are bound to different traditions of language – be valid or also valid.

P: So we should reject their opposites, which means also not letting an axiom and its opposite both be valid at the same time?

S: That's right, otherwise we will be left with unsolvable contradictions.

P: So an example of an axiom would be: only a living being, that is, the presence of life – the ability to experience – can be the cause of activity?

S: Yes. We have an unsolvable contradiction if we take the opposite view – which science takes – that non-living matter, that is, matter alone without life, can also be a cause. Another example would be the axiom that only something concrete, a really existent thing, can be the objective cause of activity. There would be an unsolvable contradiction if we also allowed that 'nothing' – the absence of everything, the idea of 'abstract' interpreted as the existent opposite of 'concrete' – were regarded as a basis for causality. We talked about this earlier.

P: What does it matter if we are left with contradictions?

S: Unless we can agree about the original cause and meaning of creation, we will live in confusion about the cause and meaning of our earthly existence. This creates anxiety and alienation. And because in practice it is impossible to live without meaning, we are forced to create our own meanings. This leads to contradiction and conflicts over these individual, created meanings, as much between human beings as in the relationship between human beings and Nature. That's why, unless we agree about creation's original cause and meaning, it will be impossible to get rid of war, which is waged on two fronts: one front between groups of human beings, because of their different philosophies or ideologies, and the other front between humanity and Nature, because of the lack among humans of a common philosophy.

P: What if a central tenet of one's philosophy was that one should have tolerance for the viewpoint of others? Wouldn't that avoid war?

S: If we discuss the basic need of common Nature – as God's nature, which is also common for us: the ability to experience and the need to be understood as like – then we have a common viewpoint and a common logic from which to start. Communication of this viewpoint to everyone is then seen as a precondition for its being understood and for an agreement about it being reached. The viewpoint is then seen as common, and not as one's own. 'Tolerance' – in place of force or war – only comes into play when compromise is necessary. But compromise in philosophy is only necessary when contradictions are accepted at the outset.

In everyday life compromise is only necessary when there is a need to agree about conflicting predilections. These are only problematical in the absence of the experience of undivided love. Any compromise by one party or the other is then experienced as 'giving in' or as only being made on some expectation of a tit-for-tat at some later date.

P: By contrast, I remember you giving the example of dogs fighting over a piece of meat. Once the last morsel is eaten, the fighting stops and there are no 'hard feelings'!

S: Yes... because animals, not having an everything-covering language, don't first have to break the whole reality into pieces and then try to work out how to put the pieces back together again as an understandable whole. That means that they can only love reality unconsciously as an indivisible whole.

Authoritarian traditions or Nature-based logic?

P: So the philosophical hypothesis can be checked on the basis of axioms?

S: Yes. And that is an important aspect in which I think my hypothesis is different. Traditional theories of the original cause were not presented as hypotheses based on axioms that everybody could check in this philosophical way. They were presented as authoritarian statements: that is, not as understandable by logical thinking, but as knowledge ascertainable by defined methods.

P: ...such as by developing a perfect life through following God's commandments – in place of understanding God?

S: Yes... commandments given and overseen by priests, but traced back to God.

P: ...and in the case of pantheism, by developing perfect knowledge and power?

S: Yes... and applying this so that you can develop a perfect life and a perfect society, that is, a perfect life together. Philosophy in my sense has never been implemented traditionally – though it has been continuously represented by each new generation of children when they first learn language. On the basis of their Nature-based experience, children question what grown-ups say – until they, the children, become confused about what of their experience is Nature-based and what language-based. So children's use of Nature-based, philosophical logic never gets a proper response. The traditions tell them that it is possible to know, that is, to experience or to meet, the original cause – and 'knowing' involves 'controlling' rather than 'checking'. Modern science, on the other hand, lets them believe that the original cause can be, but has not yet been, discovered. At the same time, modern science tells them that there is no original meaning, and that therefore the ever-present original order should be of no interest to them. 'The question of meaning is free', children are told. So then there is no chance for children to apply philosophical logic to any defined hypothesized meaning.

P: You've said earlier that children's – in other words, every person's – total, current experience from inside the whole reality is what gives rise to the philosophical question about the original cause and meaning?

S: Yes, which is why it is only possible for us to discuss and agree upon this question in the light of our common, total, current experience. The philosophical question in fact contains two inseparable questions. One is the question of the original cause. The other is the question of the purpose of the original cause's activity, that is, creation. To answer the first question alone is not enough, because it doesn't say anything about the nature of the cause. Just saying that God is the original cause means only that the original cause is a living being with the ability to experience. But it says nothing about what God is experiencing, and what, based on his experience, the need and purpose of his activity is. And the pantheistic theory refers to existent laws, but not to an existent being who could be the cause or creator of the laws. And laws can only interfere in an ongoing activity. They can't explain the start of that activity.

P: And the pantheists say that there is no original given meaning?

S: That's right. The meaning is the development of the participants in order to make and maintain a meaningful order, which requires cooperation between the participants.

My view is that we have to understand both the original cause and its meaning with creation. And I presuppose that my life is meaningfully established by Nature – by God's Nature – in the same way as are all other lives and the whole creation, to serve the purpose of this understanding, that is, to make it possible for us to understand the original cause and meaning of creation. If we don't have philosophy, we remain unconscious of these. With philosophical understanding, we are conscious of them.

P: So I have to assume that my own total current experience of reality is basically the same as that of all other humans, and that my life has the same natural meaning as theirs?

S: Yes, and we have to assume that this natural meaning is to understand and agree about the cause and meaning of our current experience of the common whole reality, as a precondition for being able to love it and love each other. We can only understand creation if we presuppose the timeless, never-changing Being behind creation and so presuppose the fact that we belong absolutely together as conscious beings within this whole...

P: ...which gives a feeling that we are generally used to having only in families, or, to a lesser extent perhaps, in relation to our country or some other group we belong to, rather than in relation to the whole.

S: Yes, that's right. The alternative to this feeling of belonging absolutely together within the whole stems from our being confused by our experience into thinking that we are outside reality and into regarding ourselves as separate from everything, and, from this temporary position as humans, into regarding ourselves as having a free will to create and realize any meaning we wish. And all this we do – in this alternative view – in the face of a meaningless, dead reality, and, on the Earth's surface, in the face of an equally meaningless, destroyable, cruel life full of fighting and killing.

Consciousness vs thinking

So to choose understanding and love – that is, the insight that we belong absolutely together with the same identity – we need only to identify the faculty of consciousness, our ability to experience, as fundamental, and not the faculty of thinking. Consciousness is the ability to experience. Can you experience anything in your surroundings, including your body, without this ability?

P: No.

S: Could you think about your experiences if you were unable to remember them?

P: No.

S: Nature makes it possible for us to remember our earlier experiences – by providing us with a brain and a nervous system. So the ability to experience, then our experience of our own body and of the surroundings, and then memory – these are the preconditions for thinking. You can't experience without the ability to experience, though you can experience your body and your surroundings without memory. But then you can't think without memory. So which comes first: the ability to experience, experience itself, memory or thinking?

P: It must be the ability to experience.

S: Of course. Now all these assertions I have just made, which you have agreed with, are axioms. They reflect our immediate experience of being conscious, and, through our nervous system, our immediate experience of our distanceless relation to our own body. That body represents not only our existential needs and the ability to satisfy those needs, but also our memory and the rememberable evaluations and conclusions that we have previously reached through thinking, which together constitute what we call the psyche* or soul. They can't be proved or argued. They can only be agreed upon or not agreed upon. If you had not agreed with them, I could not have proceeded with my questions and we could have not proceeded to the conclusion that we reached and agreed upon. That's why philosophical understanding must be based on dialogue, and not on authoritarian statements and objective explanations.

P: What if I had chosen to deny these particular axioms?

S: Then you would have been in contradiction with me, and also, I suggest, with your own experience of Nature, and I would have asked you to argue for your denial. But we are free to assert whatever we want – though not without consequences.

So if you agree with me, on the basis of these axioms, that the ability to experience precedes thinking, you must agree that Descartes, the founder of rationalism – who said that humans were essentially doubting and thinking beings – is mistaken. We have to regard consciousness, considered as the ability to experience, as fundamental. We experience something, and it is then Nature – not you, not we, but Nature – that arranges for us to remember for a time what we have experienced – if, that is, you don't lose your memory, your ability to remember. You can lose that, of course. All you have to do is drive badly and have an accident and suffer brain damage. Then you may lose your memory. But you don't lose your ability to experience. You can never lose it, even when you die. You can believe you lose it when you die, because if somebody dies, from the point of view of other people all their abilities to act and to express themselves disappear when their ability to experience loses its contact with their body. The idea that there is nothing after this life was only introduced by modern atheism.

Philosophical reflection

P: So how would you characterize philosophical reflection succinctly?

S: Philosophical reflection is the work of the brain aimed at understanding any hypothesis put forward about the original cause and meaning. These hypotheses can't be tested objectively – as scientific hypotheses about causes and effects can be. They can be tested only subjectively, against our own experience of the whole creation – including our immediate experience of our own body – as it is shown to everybody, and relatively against other people's interpretations through language of their own experience of being situated in creation in the same way. All interpretations – both our own and other people's – should take account of the fact that creation is self-evident, axiomatic, that it is not arbitrary but absolutely meaningful, and that it is self-explanatory in relation to its original cause and the meaning of the fact that we are all, in common, faced with it – creation, that is.

P: By 'self-explanatory', do you mean that creation explains itself to us – or rather God explains himself to us through creation? In other words, our experiences in creation leads us to the idea of the original cause?

S: Yes, indirectly, through the philosophical reflections that creation provokes us to make – and only as an idea, a belief, because the original whole reality can't be shown from the outside to our senses. So we should interpret creation itself as self-evident. We should not interpret it on the basis of people's interpretations of creation – which is what we do if we believe in authoritarian interpretations. And that means we should have the same attitude towards creation in our philosophical considerations – that is, as regards understanding the original cause – that science has towards creation as regards mechanical understanding.

For science, the ever-present reality is the truth, and not what people say about it. The difference is that the mechanical understanding that science is interested in is based on details of what we experience in creation as non-conscious matter. This is the belief in original parts and in the possibility of discovering and controlling these original parts. There is no regard for an original whole and for the purpose of creation. My hypothesis starts from the idea of an original whole considered as conscious matter, the creative Being – which is both God and his parts – with the idea of the creator's purpose in mind. This excludes any notion that the parts of the creative Being can develop an original authority to express independent, original creativity – that is, to change chaos or Nature's 'unsatisfactory' order into a better or perfect order, as other views would hold. This last idea is the only alternative to a meaningless obedience to present, but meaninglessly existing, conditions – in other words, to what is called fatalism or belief in destiny.

And as I have said, my hypothesis cannot be objectively proved because it relates to an unchangeable, timeless existence that can never be experienced at a distance, from outside. It is not even possible for God to see himself from outside, as we can see our body, mediated by light, in a mirror!

P: And modern science, as you've said, treats reality as if we are outside it, as a result of not taking our total current experience of creation into account.

S: That's right. It takes into account only our experience of the objective surrounding reality, based solely on the typically human ability for theoretical thinking, in which humans regard themselves as outsiders with only a mechanical relation to creation.

We should regard our purely memory- and language-based understanding of reality as relative – that is, not as valid in itself, but valid only if we can check it against our total current experience in the ever-present reality.

P: So science tries to understand reality without taking into account our experience of being conscious and our immediate experience of our own body?

S: Yes. It judges everything – our own ability to experience, our own body and our experience of the manifold – from the point of view of an outsider.

P: ...rather than seeing humans as part of reality?

Creation is self-explanatory

S: Yes. But we can't, on the other hand, simply decide to see ourselves as part of reality. We can't escape experiencing ourselves as outsiders unless we have a self-evident hypothesis – that is, one based on axioms – about the original cause of the visible reality considered as a creation, a purposefully given order and meaning.

I think this view should replace the efforts we have traditionally made to explain reality for each other and for our children as an historical, ongoing, changeable event – which is the view that our memory-based, that is, time-based, science of creation puts forward.

P: Do you mean that we don't need science in order to understand reality? We can understand it on the basis of our own experience?

S: I mean that we can understand the original cause and meaning of the whole creation by philosophical reflection based on our everyday common experience of creation, without any special science of the underlying details of creation. By 'special' I mean 'not common to everybody's everyday subjective and objective experience of the whole'. Science discovers more and more of the invisible details of our everyday experience and traces them back to the Big Bang. But these 'invisible' details can't explain the whole reality. In them we can find only the same axiomatic knowledge of creation – of its absolute changeability, which is the characteristic of all activities – that is visibly shown to us in our everyday experience of creation through an illusorily concrete background, the manifold. Today scientists know this.

P: So an atom is what it is – axiomatically – in exactly the same way as a tree or a stone is what it is? It's just that you have access to an experience of a tree or a stone in your everyday life and not of an atom. But don't scientists claim that the normally invisible thing – the atom or whatever – explains the bigger thing, the one that we have experience of in our everyday life?

S: Atoms, trees, stones, the whole manifold, are separately enjoyable, meaningful illusions produced by the overall activity of creation, Nature. Therefore it is impossible to understand any of them separately, scientifically, as things in themselves. Nowadays scientists know that the bigger parts of the visible reality are built up as a sum of smaller parts only formally, but that it is impossible to add Nature up, that is, to treat it as a mathematical sum of independent, separated units. You can't understand the nature of an atom on the basis of the nature of its elementary particles, the nature of a molecule as the sum of the nature of its atoms, and so on. If you ask a scientist whether science explains reality, they say, consistently, 'No, science only explores and describes reality'. That's why they don't talk about 'creation'. 'Creation' is the original reality for them.

P: But people generally believe that science *explains* reality.

S: Yes, I know. And scientists make little effort to disabuse people of this idea.

P: Do you think that your hypothesis explains reality then?

S: No. Reality is self-explanatory. My hypothesis provides only the precondition for understanding what creation indirectly reveals: our original situation as parts of the non-created whole where we are unable to use practically our common identity, the ability to experience.

The axioms

P: If we choose to take this approach to the question of the original cause and meaning of creation, what are the axioms that we need to agree to allow to be valid?

S: …without allowing their opposites to be valid or also valid, as I said before. [See p.136.] Most axioms we allow to be valid in our thinking without allowing their opposites to be valid or also valid. But if we are identified with our memory-based thinking, rather than with our common experience of the entire reality, then we allow certain opposites to be valid or also valid and start thinking out of them.

P: I find this difficult to follow, but perhaps it will become clear when you give the axioms.

S: Yes, let me give the basic axioms and their opposites briefly, then we can go into each of them in more detail:

The first basic axiom – which relates to all thinking, even to that of animals – is connected to the basic contradiction in our experience: the experience of 'something' on the one hand and the 'experience' of nothing on the other.

P: And the inverted commas around 'experience' are because we cannot, of course, have an experience of nothing?

S: Yes. This last, as I have said before, is the language-based interpretation of distance as three-dimensional space or emptiness. But everybody knows, by simply reflecting on the fact, that it is impossible to start a thinking process from – that is, to make an evaluation of or to draw conclusions from – 'nothing', the absence of 'everything'. So for anyone who bears in mind the clear difference between Nature-based thinking and language-based thinking, the first and basic axiom will, I believe, be understood as valid:

Axiom 1: *No thing can arise, originate from nothing. Not even activity can arise out of nothing.*

Its opposite is that something can arise out of nothing – which is what some scientists maintain, particularly cosmologists. And Christianity maintains it, too, when it says that God created out of nothing.

From this basic axiom follows the next:

Axiom 2: *That which exists, that which is a real, existent, permanent, concrete, and not illusory, something, can never change, become some other thing, or cease to exist – that is, become nothing. Nor can it be reduced to only an abstract potentiality, or to a potentiality to become something, akin to the language-based idea of energy.*

One opposite to the belief in an unchangeable existence is the belief in nothing. The other opposite is the pantheistic view: that activity is something in itself, without there being anything that expresses that activity. This is just another belief in non-existence, the absence of existence.

Axiom 2 means that something, what is existent, also can't start to be. It can't even change, because that would mean it would stop being what it was and would start being something else. What can easily confuse our thinking is the fact that everything we experience in creation as existent is changeable and can start to be and can cease to be. That's why nothing that we experience in creation as existent can be understood as an original cause.

P: …because, according to Axioms 1 and 2, activity has to be created by some thing, some existent thing, so the original cause of the activity that is creation has to be some existent thing?

S: Yes. This is self-evident, which is why humanity has always either tried to understand the original cause philosophically, or, the alternative, has tried to discover it, as in modern science; or has even claimed that it is possible for each person to discover it, that is, experience it – as in the older introspective science – as activity, energy, abstract power, and, in some Christian views, as God.

From these first two axioms follows the next:

Axiom 3: *It is impossible, even for God, to create anything other than activity.*

The opposite of this axiom is the idea that something existent can be created. But if it were possible to create something existent, then something would be able to come out of nothing. So the idea in theology of God creating something, such as conscious beings and existent things, and the general idea that humans can create existent things, are irrational.

Pantheism takes activity as the original cause, and interprets the meaning of this activity as the development of consciousness – from no consciousness to perfect consciousness – interpreting consciousness as something abstract and yet as in some way existent, but changeable and developable, like everything in creation.

Science, since Einstein, has taken energy as the original cause, acting through non-living objects that have been created by energy. And it sees energy as in some way existent too. And then both science and pantheism regard consciousness as developable, which means that consciousness can't be the quality of the original cause.

P: ...because the quality of something existent must be existent too – which means it can't change, so it can't develop?

S: Yes. That's the problem with the term 'energy', too, both for science and for pantheism. It can be interpreted only as the source of all the developable qualities in creation, but not as one and the same original quality of an original cause.

And finally theology: although it takes consciousness as the quality of the original cause, it makes the mistake of talking about God as a perfect, almighty, abstract consciousness who has no need – which makes it impossible to find a logical reason for creation – but who creates humans in his likeness. This also introduces the idea of development for humans: to become like God.

P: You mean humans have to strive to become as perfectly 'good' as God?

S: Yes, which means to have the perfect purpose – love – behind their activities in relation to God's creation, on the basis of moral rules given by God but mediated by humans. This is the basis of so-called righteousness.

Those who take the pantheistic view want to develop more and more knowledge of, and power to control, what they consider to be the 'abstract', original reality – knowledge and power of that being how they interpret consciousness – and in this way become perfect. Of course, they also have the conception of undivided love. However, it is not interpreted as righteousness in relation to a given order, but as a basic concept for the organization of cooperation in society.

Those who take the scientific view also want to develop more and more knowledge and power, with the aim of controlling creation – which, as with the pantheists, they see as not having a given order, but as being randomness or chaos formed only by meaningless laws. But even science has to recognize the need and the necessity for love as basic to the successful organization of society – as did all earlier traditions.

In all these interpretations, the idea of consciousness as developable is misleading, because no tradition makes the distinction between the ability to experience and that which is experienced. It is thinking, reflection and understanding which is developable. The ability to experience is a precondition for thinking and understanding, and not a rememberable consequence of understanding. It is misleading if we don't distinguish the ability to experience and what we experience. The first remains the same; the second goes on functioning, is constantly changing, progressing and regressing, building a memory of objects, evaluations and causalities – which, taken together, are what I interpret understanding as.

P: But then you have also argued that we have to distinguish between understanding as it relates to the original reality and understanding as it relates to creation.

S: Yes, because God's experience and understanding – which encompasses the original reality as his own existence, the understanding of which is the basis for his activity – must be different from our experience, which encompasses only the created reality. That is why a scientific understanding, which is only of creation, is not satisfactory. We have the need to understand the origin of creation, but it is impossible to do that by developing more knowledge of creation. We have to use philosophical understanding, which means to take the right stance in relation to all the contradictions that creation presents us with.

P: You mean not to take the absence of things – the idea of 'nothing', and so on – as the basis for our understanding?

S: Yes...or the absence of life – death – or the absence of love – evil. That includes taking the correct stance in relation to Axiom 4 – to bring us back to the Axioms – which relates to the idea of consciousness:

Axiom 4: *Only a conscious, living being who is conscious of its own existence can be active out of itself and thus be an original cause of its activity.*

The opposite to this axiom is to imagine that a non-conscious being – what in creation we call an object – can be a cause. This axiom means that, as regards the original reality, it can be active as a whole only if it is a conscious, living whole – otherwise it would be a non-living object. No part of this original, conscious, living whole can act as the whole, therefore only the whole can be the cause of creation.

Only a conscious being is able to have experience and, as a result of its experience, a need for purposeful activity. My idea, following from Axiom 1, is that the activity that we experience as the whole purposeful creation is regulated by the need and the purpose of the creator, God, arising out of his experience of his own existence, which gives him his need to be understood by his parts and thus creates a personal need for purposeful activity. An activity can only be understood if it is purposeful – otherwise we can only register the activity as ruled by mechanical laws. To understand a purposeful activity, you have to know its purpose, and then you can check whether the activity is consistent with its purpose or not. An activity can only be purposeful if it follows the need of a conscious being logically, that is, consistently.

P: Going back a little: can the ideas in science of chance and chaos be seen as related to the idea of nothing?

S: Yes, these ideas are in place of the idea of a meaningful cause, which only conscious beings can have behind their activity. 'Nothing' means having neither existence nor meaning. 'Chance' and 'chaos' mean activity that has no purpose or meaning. Science – and pantheism too – accepts the lawfulness of creation, but denies that it represents a single, overriding order.

Axiom 5 follows from Axiom 4:

Axiom 5: *Only an object conscious of itself and which exists unchangeably can be the unchangeable – that is, recognizable as one and the same – original, mechanical cause of activity.*

This corresponds to my idea of God's objective, concrete existence. Generally, God's existence is interpreted as 'abstract' – and then with 'abstract' not seen as the opposite of 'concrete', but rather, as I have said before, on the basis of our experience of solid, liquid and gaseous matter. 'Abstract' then is seen as a sort of more subtle matter, and so as something in itself.

P: Whereas for you, 'concrete' relates to the original reality, and 'abstract' to Axiom 3, that only activity can be created. In your view, all activity in itself – theoretically separate from what is being active – is abstract?

S: Yes, 'separated from its context' – from the Latin, *abstraho, abstraxi, abstractum*, meaning to separate, remove. In fact, this separation is achieved by thinking, and is expressed for humans in language. But such separation cannot occur in reality, and to think that it does occur leads to confusion and to a distorted picture of reality. Axiom 3 means that it is impossible to find the original reality in creation. An object interpreted as existent can never change, be something else or become nothing.

P: So what are examples of opposites to Axiom 5?

S: As I've said, 'nothing' is one opposite of this axiom of a conscious object, the opposite that science adopts.

The idea of changeability is another, the one that pantheism adopts. Changeability corresponds to my idea of abstract, because all activity is in itself just movement, and therefore abstract – that is, not existent. Activity is what gives us the impression of changeability. Activity can start, it can go on in different ways, and it can stop. But it cannot do all that by itself.

The cause of all activity must be something existent. A cause – something that expresses activity – and its ongoing activity are inseparable. If you separate the two in your mind, and start to interpret activity as existent in itself and, whether it is resting – that is, potential – or ongoingly active, interpret it as being without a cause, this leads to the pantheistic idea of activity as the original cause. The pantheists then relate that activity to abstract, impersonal laws, that is, laws that are not bound to an existent, conscious object who expresses the laws as a precondition for a meaningful order. My view is that the laws that we experience are intended to produce a meaningful order – in the same way that humans create laws with a particular order in mind.

The pantheist view misguidedly transfers the idea of 'abstract' or 'changeable' to 'object', that is, to something existent, something unchangeable. This misunderstanding relates to the fact that our experience of objects in creation is that they are changeable. The misunderstanding follows from our ignorance of Axiom 3, *It is impossible to create anything other than activity.*

The opposite of an axiom

P: I want to be clear at this point: the opposite of an axiom is not itself an axiom?

S: No, the opposite is simply the experience of the absence of something that we have previously experienced as present.

P: For example, death in relation to life, nothing in relation to something, darkness in relation to light, and so on?

S: Yes. Both the presence of something and the absence – that is, the negation – of something, can't be valid. But we can choose to take the negation as valid, as if it were an axiom, because we are free to choose where to start our thinking from.

P: But like the axiom itself – that is, the presence, though variable presence, of something – the opposite of the axiom – that is, the absence of that something – is also based on our experience of creation, isn't it?

S: Yes, but can you experience something that is absent? And bear in mind that 'absent' can have two interpretations: 'present in another place' and 'not existing'. That is our problem with the words 'life' and 'death'. 'Death' is a state that is not variable in the same life: you can't die and come back to life. Whereas other things you can experience, then no longer experience and then return to experiencing. Because the word 'death' means the absence of any experience – whereas 'life' means the ability to experience – we can make all sorts of ideas about 'death' and even think of it as a state of non-existence, of non-life. But the idea of a non-living state is absurd. What could it be like? No quality, no activity, nothing – what is that? A situation without experience is what in my hypothesis is the situation for the parts in the Being. But that is not 'death'. Life is generally seen as an absolute starting-point, rather than as a continuation.

P: All right, I agree then that you can't experience something that is absent, but isn't it possible to experience that something is absent?

S: Not experience, but remember. That is, we can experience something and then realize that what we have experienced is no longer experienceable right now, even though we can remember how it was. But we can't experience something that is not there now. We don't generally distinguish between these two. We take them to be the same. That is what makes us confused about what reality is: experiencing or remembering. That's why we can live, practically speaking, in history, theoretically excluding our experience of the ever-present reality.

Both the axioms themselves and their memory-based negations are based on our experience of creation – because creation has to be expressed as basically contradictory: that is, as simultaneously present/existent *and* not present/ not existent; simultaneously becoming present/seemingly existent *and* disappearing/becoming absent. That means we experience it as unrestingly changeable. If it were unchangeable, ever-present in the same form, we would then, quite logically, regard creation as the original reality.

The only experience of the original reality that we have is its basic quality, the ability to experience – what is generally called 'consciousness'. But even this experience can be confusing, because we don't experience its objective form, its mass or quantity: the non-created unchangeable object, our original reality, our identity, that which is conscious. And this is what science tries in vain to discover. So we have as an axiom to interpret our impression that creation is existent as a meaningful illusion, made for our senses. We should take neither its presence nor its absence as an axiom, but take creation as we are able to understand it on the basis of Axiom 3: as activity. This is what makes it necessary to have the hypothesis of a real existence behind both the illusory absence of the whole, God, and the illusory presence of the parts, human beings. All this is because it's impossible to experience the original reality itself – either in its whole or in its parts – because we can't have distance to what we originally are and also not to what we originally belong inseparably to. That has to be impossible for God, too. So in relation to every living being, even God, we have to take into account the original existence with the same quality – the ability to experience. But we have to assume that God has an immediate one-sided relation to the total Being and can rule over it – though not, of course, in the same way that we can rule over our own created body through our created nervous system, but in some similar way.

P: And generally we spontaneously take into account only the quality…

S: Yes, on the basis of our experience of the quality.

P: …and not the original existence, the original object?

S: Yes. The whole non-created Being, in my view, is the mechanical cause of God's creation, and the part that we are in the Being is the mechanical cause of our activity within creation. As parts of the Being, we are also conscious, existent causes of our own activities – originally based on the same need that we have in common with God – and are therefore responsible for our activities. This need is unconscious in the Being, but becomes conscious via language in creation. But we are not original creators. Our inescapable need for love requires us to live together. When our consciousness of community is suppressed, we experience a mystical anxiety or stress. So our need for love forces us, in the way that biology forces, to understand the cause and meaning of creation – instead of playing creators, which makes it impossible for us to love creation. In this way, Nature's biological force is as efficient as Nature's mechanical forces. We are original parts of the original, non-created reality and can never be something else. But we can't in any comparable way be the mechanical cause of creation, because creation can't reveal to our senses its original, mechanical start. That's why all the new scientific theories and all the old pantheistic theories about the possibilities of humans ruling over creation are irrational. Discussions of these irrational theories have recently taken on a new dimension – after the unsuccessful attempts to discover the smallest parts of the object – through the discovery of genes.

P: So we can't rule over creation, even though we can interact with it – or 'interfere' with it, which is what we do, as we have said, when we disturb it?

S: That's right. If our potentially confusing experience of consciousness is misinterpreted as consciousness of the original reality, it can lead us to ignore the existence of consciousness as the ability to experience. It can then lead us to take our ability to think and act and 'create' in creation as primary, as our original identity. Consciousness is then interpreted as secondary, as a developable product of thinking. But then we can never get rid of confusion, because, in this interpretation of identity, we take changeable creation with its contradictions as the original reality, and start thinking on the basis of irrational ideas about the original cause. We then consider humans to be original creators confronted with a changeable, formable reality – with nowadays the general idea of empty space, that is, 'nothing', behind it, rather than a given order behind it.

P: Going back to the axioms: it seems to me that if we choose to allow these axioms to be valid, we are forced to live in the present reality.

S: But the present reality is frightening if it is not understood as coming from the original cause. If we don't understand it that way, we trace our origin back to our birth, and further to Adam and Eve – which is history. And history's unchangeability then becomes our only security. The present reality is then the future – the frightening, unsafe future. All confusion arises because creation is not shown in our experience as coming from its origin: the existent, non-created reality. This has led historically to three different ideas about the original cause of creation, and different combinations of these three ideas. The first is 'nothing' and the second is activity. The third is created matter, which is represented by the visible manifold in creation. This last is interpreted as the original cause because in our experience of creation, the manifold expresses all activity as an absolute interaction between everything.

P: And you have given reasons earlier for regarding all these three hypotheses as illogical.

S: Yes.

Creation's contradictions

P: I want to go back to the point that you made earlier about creation being contradictory. I suppose you are saying that the axioms help us to resolve the contradictions?

S: Yes. The confusion in our attitude towards axioms arises from the fact that, as a self-evident technical necessity, creation has concurrently to construct and destroy everything that it creates. To avoid being confused about creation, we have to agree about this technical necessity. But in doing that we have to remember our common consciousness of the whole creation – creation considered as one activity, one closed system. And we have to bear in mind that creation's purpose is to create for our created senses an impression of an existent reality, in which things – such as celestial bodies, that is, suns and planets, and living bodies on the surface of our planet – last for different lengths of time.

P: And, as we've discussed before [see p.60], you don't mean that the whole creation is just an illusion, as some traditions say?

S: No, the only illusion is the impression that it is existent and not just activity. In reality creation supports, makes possible, an intangible but real relation to each other – so long as we believe that we have a non-created real existence and we don't try to find ourselves and each other in our created bodies. It also supports, makes possible, a similar, real relation to the creator, God – so long as we believe that not only we, parts, but also the whole, have a real existence and we don't try to find the creator in his creation.

If creation were experienced only as activity, we couldn't have a useful impression of it. The illusion of existence gives us the impression of distance, separateness, which is the precondition for the parts of the whole to be able to meet and understand each other as conscious parts within the whole. Distance, given by the illusion of existence, also gives us an indirect impression of the whole. But because of distance, this impression of the whole is not a unified impression of one body. It is presented in such a way that we are forced to choose between two conflicting interpretations of it. The one is to interpret it, on the basis of philosophical considerations, as similar to us, that is, as also conscious – which gives the self-evident belief in one God. The other is to interpret it, on the basis of our impression of the Earth and the other created celestial bodies, as non-conscious, or, on the basis of our impression of distance – experienced in relation to the whole as an endless empty space – as not-existent.

P: And this last is just a variant of the idea that the whole is non-conscious?

S: Yes. And these other interpretations give the non-self-evident belief that, compared with each other, the parts are different, and also that they are not subordinate to the whole, but in some sense above it. This means that they treat it and alter it according to their own will.

The consequence of the choice of the first, the choice of the belief – axiomatic, and understandable for everyone, and not irrational or mystical – in one God considered as the existent, non-created conscious whole behind creation, is that we then know each other definitively as conscious parts of the the same non-created reality behind creation, and we know in the same definitive way the creator and his purpose and meaning with the whole creation. Our first practical problem is then not our lack of knowledge of everything, but rather the lack of a language-based, common agreement about this choice and the immediate consequences of that lack of agreement. What we don't know about the invisible details of creation – which we can, if we need to, always explore further – is, in this choice, a secondary problem.

If we are to make proper practical use of this reality, we have to establish such a language-based, common agreement. Without it, we spontaneously take what is illusion in creation – the impression of resistance, which gives us the idea that creation is existent – as knowledge of the original reality. This interpretation of the experience that our created senses offer us will then totally occupy our philosophical thinking, leading to an endless and vain search for *knowledge* of our own identity and of reality's identity, the original cause. The search will be endless and vain because this spontaneous mistake makes it impossible for us to understand either creation or the original reality.

P: So is it also an implication of what you are arguing that the whole modern environmental movement – which is concerned, as you put it, 'with a proper practical use of this reality' – will miss the point unless it has a solution to the problem of the original cause?

S: Yes. Reality is then interpreted as changeable, meaningless and passive, rather than as meaningfully active.

Types of whole

P: You said a moment ago that if we allow these basic axioms for thinking to be valid, without mixing them together with or confusing them with their opposites, then the question of the original cause is solved, as creation is self-explanatory. Do you mean that these axioms rule out the other hypotheses and suggest your hypothesis of the whole and the parts?

S: Yes. But I think that we need to be clear in more detail at this point how we understand the idea of whole and the idea of parts, as well as the relation between these two ideas, which is basic to all thinking. An agreement about this is necessary, because on the basis of creation, and in the absence of any experience of the original relation between them in the Being, we can only have inadequate experiences of what 'whole' and 'part' and the relation between them are.

It is necessary for us to have an impression of wholes and parts in creation, because thinking can only start from something that we experience as an existent whole that is in relation to its own parts and to other similarly existent wholes. The natural purpose of thinking, reflection, is the need to understand causality – both with regard to the immediate relation between one object and its parts, and with regard to the space-based relation between different objects. For typically human philosophical thinking, there is also the need to understand the original cause of the whole creation.

The inadequacy of our impression of wholes and parts in creation starts from the fact that we have no existent impression of the total whole. We have only the impression of an apparently existent manifold. And the difficulty is further compounded by the fact that we can't find in the apparently existent manifold a real, unchangeable whole, nor a real unchangeable part.

We experience the whole creation, which is our whole reality, as an interaction of the manifold, as the product of the inseparable cooperation of all visible, separate parts. Then we experience each part of the inseparable whole creation as a separate whole in itself: either as celestial bodies – which illuminate, in the case of suns, or which are illuminated, in the case of planets – or, on the Earth, our own illuminated celestial body, as various types of whole.

P: We have talked about this last point in passing before. [See p.27.]

S: Yes. On the Earth's surface, there are three types of whole. The first type is our experience of a living whole. This applies to living bodies. These we experience immediately – inseparably in the case of our own, and at a distance in the case of other bodies.

The second type of whole is interacting activities that can be interpreted as an abstract, functional whole – that is, in which the whole is considered in our minds as something in itself, as something separate from everything that is interacting. These can be naturally occurring, such as basically the whole creation interpreted as Nature, or as galaxies, or as the universe, or as our sun-system, or as ecology, that is, the entire system of life on Earth. Or they can be interactions produced by living beings that constitute a society or a community. Or they can be the artificial technical units created by living beings – such as bee-hives, ant-hills and houses – that become functional when operated or used by living beings or, in the case of such units as computers, cars and so on, when driven by energy controlled by humans.

The third type of whole is our experience of a non-living, so-called objective, whole. This applies to naturally existing objects, which we experience at a distance – such as a stone, a mountain, a heavenly body, and so on.

In order to get rid of all the confusing traditional and modern identifications with some of the many different, inadequate impressions of wholes and parts, we have to reach a global agreement about the fact that the most adequate presentation of the relation between a whole and its parts that creation shows us – and one that can't be compared with other impressions – is that of created living bodies on the Earth's surface.

This presentation can't be compared with the others because only a whole living body represents – as we said before – an experience of a meaningful relation to its parts. In all other presentations, parts are active by themselves, whereas the wholes they are parts of are not. In those cases the whole represents just a passive totality, just a sum of parts.

These contradictory experiences of wholes and parts then give rise to the philosophical question: *Is the whole active by itself?* That means: *Is the whole conscious, living? Or is it only the participants in creation that are active by themselves, that is, conscious, living?* And if that is the case, *Where does participation start?* This in turn leads to the two questions: *Where does life start?* and *Where does consciousness start?*

P: And the traditions were divided throughout history as to whether they considered the whole active by itself or only the participants in creation?

S: Yes. My view is that it is senseless to discuss the original cause of the changeable creation without having the idea of and belief in a conscious, non-created, unchangeable whole. In this view, only the whole, non-created Being is conscious – that is, has the ability to experience and to be active out of itself. It is our experience that nothing in creation – neither some living, illusorily existent whole, nor the not-existent, non-permanent parts of such a whole – can represent in an original way this ability to experience and to be active out of itself. All we can do is have an immediate experience of that ability, which belongs to the Being. That ability is our origin: our same, unchangeable identity. We can't discover, find or reproduce it, that is, make it relative.

P: You mean that the whole can't be represented within creation?

S: That's right. In creation either we can see and experience a whole or we can see and experience its parts. But we can't do both at the same time. That's why we have to dissect or destroy the whole, or make the whole invisible in some other way, if we want to study its parts. That's why every tradition that uses only creation-based ideas of wholes and parts is forced to agree that neither a living being, nor the whole reality can be understood as a sum, a totality of its parts – that is, as not having the ability to experience, considered as the original quality behind both the invisible whole and the visible parts.

P: But don't you use a creation-based idea of the whole?

S: No. My hypothesis refers to the relation between the whole and its parts as they exist in a created living being – in contrast to a sum or totality of parts, as is found in created objects – but it is not based on any other similarity between created living beings and the non-created Being.

P: Yes, I see. And the situation in the Being then…?

S: We will have already understood the Being if we suppose it to be conscious like us. But to reach this mutual understanding – between God and us – it is necessary to see the whole and its parts as opposites, but not as exclusive opposites. That is, we should see them not as an either/or, but rather as inclusive and, because of the same need of consciousness, as likes – as stated in Genesis 1:27 ['So God created man in his own image, in the image of God created he him...'], though it is not said there in what way we and God are like. In my hypothesis it is evident that only the whole can experience and rule over the Being as his own. We as parts cannot. The problem with the traditions is that they separate the whole and its parts. [See also pp.177-8.]

P: So they don't see them as inseparable as you do?

S: That's right. They make a confusing separation between the existence of the whole and the existence of the parts, seeing the whole as original and the parts as created. Instead of using philosophical reflection, they base their view on the relation between wholes and parts as this is experienced either transcendentally or in the visible 'concrete' reality.

P: So whereas your view is based on the absence of both the actual whole and the actual parts, their view is based on the absence of the whole and the presence of the parts?

S: Yes. Genesis makes the same mistake that all theology makes of separating them. No tradition talks about God and his parts or about gods and their parts. A conscious being is seen in every tradition as a whole without parts. This leads to the likeness between God and humans mentioned in Genesis by the serpent identified as Satan,[1] for example, being interpreted as relating to God's and the parts' ability to create, to develop the possibility of controlling creation, seen as good and evil, instead of relating to its meaning.

P: And for pantheism the whole is their transcendent experience of creation interpreted as the original reality, which is experienced as pure activity?

S: And then it is self-evident, in the absence of a single God, that humans must be developable gods – in which case the development of knowledge is perfectly 'legal' and 'natural'. That's why it is prescribed, not prohibited, in pantheism.

Equality and likeness

P: And a relation between 'equals' is not what you mean by a relation between 'likes'?

S: No. 'Equal' is a mathematical word for likeness. Two sums can be equal. 'Like' has to go back, in my view, to our ability to experience, which is what distinguishes every living being from objects and spontaneously actualizes, therefore, the feeling of love – because our basic desire is to meet reasonable living

---

[1] See Genesis 3:5 'For God doth know that in the day ye eat thereof [of the tree of knowledge of good and evil], then your eyes shall be opened, and ye shall be as gods, knowing good and evil'.

beings and not just non-reasoning objects that can only be manipulated. What we experience makes for differences between us, but those differences do not have to spoil the feeling of likeness, and therefore of spontaneous love, as long as we belong to the same reality. To say we are 'equal' is to refer to what we own, to what we have experienced, of the same reality.

P: What if I maintain that basically we are all equal?

S: That says nothing. You have to say in what way we are basically equal or like and in what way we are different on the surface, that is, not basically.

P: And if I say, as humanists say, that we are all equal in that we are all members of the human race?

S: Socialists say the same. But none of what they say is distinct unless we agree about whether the responsibility of humans is 'righteousness' in relation to God's purpose with creation, or whether human responsibility is in relationship to a basic randomness or chance ruled by impersonal laws. In the latter case, humans need to be creators of meanings – in accordance with Protagoras' *homomensura,* 'Man is the measure of all things'. Then there is no natural responsibility. Humans are only made responsible by other humans, for the meanings that humans create.

P: So to say we are all equal because we are members of the human race is to leave open the whole issue of the meaning of life?

S: Yes. That's why, if tradition doesn't talk about God and the purpose of God's creation, and if people don't question tradition on this point, but choose instead to create meanings in the common 'meaningless' reality, it will be in vain that they ask the question: *What is the meaning of my basically meaningless life?*

P: So going back to the idea of the different types of wholes, what is your point?

S: A real whole, in my view, is represented only by a living body. This is the kind of whole that exhibits a distanceless, inseparable, purposeful relation between the whole and its parts. In the other types, the word 'whole' is inade-quate, and is used in a confusing meaning transferred from the real meaning.

God – the only conscious, living whole

P: So your view is based on what we might call an organic whole?

S: Yes, where there is an inseparable relation between a whole and its parts – but not like our picture of a created living body transferred, with its details and organs, to the absolute whole.

P: So God doesn't have a head and a stomach and so on, and is certainly genderless?

S: That's right. He doesn't have our created bodily organs, so 'organic' is a little misleading. 'Living' or 'conscious' is better.

P: And your idea of whole you regard as more rational, since the original cause must be a living being?

S: Yes. God is the *only* conscious, living whole. We experience ourselves as conscious parts – that is, subjects – participating with a created body in an obviously created, purposeful interaction with other conscious parts that have living bodies and with objects that lack consciousness, that is, the ability to experience. If we don't have the idea of a given order created by a living whole, then our spontaneous belief will be that we are participating in the voluntary cooperation of a manifold – that is, in an abstract, cooperatively organized whole, a functional unit.

P: You say *voluntary* cooperation, because cooperation with God is not basically a choice?

S: That's right. It is an absolute necessity, but not an immediate, mechanical necessity. Rather it is a necessity that has consequences in time – just as our biological needs have consequences in time. The confusing thing about this basic necessity is that the consequences are collective, and can't be seen or followed in one individual life. We can continue, therefore, to educate our children to think that they are independent of all order, and dependent only on meaningless, mechanical laws and the temporary, changeable order of society. We can do this with any tradition until the collective negative consequences of a basically wrong choice become so obvious for that tradition that the participants in it change their minds and try to make another choice.

As I said before, if you choose not to breathe, you can do it for three minutes. If you choose not to drink, you can do it for three or four days; not to eat, one or two months; not to believe in God, *ad infinitum* – because the original living Being cannot die, either as a whole or in its parts. Something of this insight lies behind the German saying: 'Gottes Mühlen mahlen langsam aber sicher' ('God's mills grind slowly, but surely').

P: Why did you say a moment ago that if we don't have the idea of a given order, this other view will be our *spontaneous* belief?

S: Because the idea that we are participating in a voluntary cooperation is the only alternative to the idea of relating to a given order.

P: Yes, I see. So these five axioms underpin your view and suggest the kind of whole you are hypothesizing?

S: Yes. If we agree on these five basic axioms, and if we allow them to be valid – without allowing their opposites to be valid or also valid – then the question of the original cause is solved. Creation is then seen as meaningfully given, which means as self-evident, and is then self-explanatory as regards its cause and meaning.

P: I think that we have to constantly keep in mind that philosophy is concerned solely with the problem of the original cause, so that 'self-explanatory' here refers only to the original cause of creation and not to all the causality in creation – which is quite another issue...

S: ...for which we have memory-based thinking. The problem of the original cause has nothing to do with memory-based causality, because we can't explore any causality in the Being. Causality can be endlessly explored, because causality in creation can be endlessly explored – on the basis of different needs, or, in the case of human beings, also as an end in itself. The original cause – the single cause behind creation – requires only that we take the right stance in relation to the contradictions that creation presents us with. The original cause is self-explanatory and so does not require complicated intellectual work. The right stance in relation to the contradictions is always self-evident.

P: That means, we should allow only the axioms to be valid?

S: Yes. This only seems difficult if you have developed your thinking since childhood without regard for these axioms that are basic for all thinking, that is, if you have developed your thinking as an end in itself, with the aim of creating order – without regard for the order that is intended by the original cause.

So in my view, the whole has to exist as a non-created, original cause of the whole creation, which has to be regarded as a non-voluntary cooperation, through the illusion of distance, between the invisible whole and its invisible parts.

P: So we cannot avoid being involved in the cooperation itself, but whether it is satisfying or not depends on whether or not the parts have this, or some alternative, equally satisfying, hypothesis about the original cause?

The original cause is self-evident

S: Yes. The answer to the question of the original cause becomes self-evident if we let these axioms be true, instead of maintaining that their opposites are valid or also valid. It becomes evident too that not only the whole, but also its inseparable parts, must be inaccessible through creation. Practically, this means that the ego – interpreted as our ability to think – cannot help us to be more conscious about ourselves than we are before we start reflecting on, and then worrying about, our identity.

P: And the alternative view to this?

S: If reality is not traditionally regarded as self-evident, our experience of it leads spontaneously to a total identification with creation and our created, mortal body – which gives rise to a basic feeling of anxiety, instead of love. That's why the question of the original cause has to be separated from the question of causality in creation. Identification with creation and our created body makes philosophical understanding impossible, because we then take our situation in creation to be the original situation. Then, solely on the basis of our objective experience of our situation in creation, we try to understand the whole causality as objective knowledge – that is, we take the objects and subjects in creation as original causes, in place of the conception of the original conscious Being as the single original cause.

P: Would it be more precise to say that we regard the objects and subjects in creation as original causes, rather than, in the case of subjects in creation, their ability to experience – which has its origin in a part of the original Being – and in the case of the whole creation, God's ability to experience, which has its origin in the whole Being?

S: Yes.

P: And if we try to understand the whole causality as creation-based, objective knowledge, and leave aside the philosophical question of the original cause, we are not doing what we as human beings are capable of and responsible for?

S: That's right. We are not then using philosophy proper. Then we are doing no more than the same objective brain-work that every living being with a brain does – though only humans can do it as an endless end in itself.

Human vs animal thinking

P: Could you say a bit more about what distinguishes human brain-work?

S: What distinguishes the brain-work of humans from that of other species is human language. This allows us at any time to remember, communicate and discuss our understanding of causality in creation. This means that we can experience this pluralistic, manifold-based causality not only, like other species, in a meaningful, memory-based way, but also in a language-based, theoretical, that is, 'abstract', way. This has the potential to lead us to regard it as not having any overall meaning.

P: So we could see it just as concrete, mechanical causality?

S: Yes. If we do that, we are ignoring the subjective meanings that determine all biological activities and which make them understandable as logical or illogical, that is, as purposeful or mistaken. This opens the way for the human notion of purely mechanical, scientific thinking – what we also call objective thinking – that relates only to mechanical causality seen as a separate function in itself, without a conscious background. This theoretical, language-based, abstract thinking is generally, but misguidedly, regarded as the human being's special, conscious way of thinking, and as being different from the brain-work of animals and from the way in which animals, purposefully guided by their biological background, can understand causality. It is also regarded as the developable human identity.

P: You mean that we identify with our thinking about mechanical causality and because we can endlessly develop that thinking, we regard ourselves as developable?

S: Yes, this identity is generally called, in psychology, the ego or the self. In pantheistic theories, it is called the self. There it is distinguished from the ego, which relates to our experience of the 'concrete' creation through our senses and to the kind of identification with it which is called egocentricity – whereas the self relates in addition to experience of the 'abstract' reality and is therefore regarded as a creative, developable 'divine spark'.

P: So you are saying that this type of thinking – what we call scientific or objective thinking – is not what really distinguishes humans from animals? Animals think like this, too, except that they do it without language?

S: That's right – so they don't have the possibility of doing it as an end in itself. Therefore they never think theoretically, only practically, in relation to subjects and objects in their surroundings. Their thinking is always determined basically by their undivided love for the whole creation and by the actions that they need to take to satisfy their existential needs.

P: By animals' 'undivided love for the whole creation', you mean their enjoyment of creation, independently of their satisfying their existential needs?

S: Yes. They love and defend their life even if they suffer physically. And life means for them everything they experience. They can't divide reality up as we do when we learn language. Without human language they can't be identified with their bodies separately from their experience of consciousness. And they can't have the idea of death either, and so they can't feel anxiety.

What is our identity?

P: But if we misguidedly consider that scientific thinking distinguishes humans, this has important consequences for who we think we are, what we think our identity is?

S: If we identify with scientific, theoretical thinking – that is, if we identify with the thinking that we use to investigate the mechanical causality in creation, regarding that investigation as an end in itself...

P: And 'regarding that investigation as an end in itself' is an important caveat. We can't avoid being interested in investigating the mechanical causality in creation?

S: Yes, no species can avoid investigating it as a condition for survival, that is, to satisfy their existential needs. But we can avoid developing this knowledge as an end in itself – by which I mean independently of our existential needs or without any other regard for whether it is purposeful or not. That is the big problem with the development of knowledge about creation without a prior general agreement about creation's purpose. If we are blind to creation's biological logic, to the creator's need behind creation, we can't avoid becoming interested in the investigation and control of all causality in creation as an end in itself – that is, without any regard for whether it works for the creative or for the destructive side of creation. This holds not only for our concrete experience of creation, but also for our experience of it on the transcendental level.

P: Are you referring here to the development of so-called supernatural powers and the distinction between what are called 'white magic' and 'black magic'?

S: Yes. And of course the hope is that, through all this investigation and control – either at the transcendental or at the 'concrete' level – the meaning of creation will be understood and it will be possible to make creation more enjoyable, more lovable.

Neither the 'concrete' nor the 'abstract', transcendental attempts to control the constructive and destructive sides of creation can, however, avoid having to face the question of creation's purpose. In my view, we have to face it directly from the beginning of our participation in creation, from the moment as children that we are taught to use human language, and we should explicitly regard it as not comparable with mechanical causality. We should consider it as biologically self-explanatory, and as only understandable philosophically, on the basis of our common knowledge of the whole creation. This knowledge every child has to develop. And we should remember that it is Nature's information about Nature's conditions, communicated by Nature to everyone in the same way.

If we don't face the question of creation's purpose directly, we have to face it indirectly as the question of ethics.

P: ...because we can't avoid having to live together and therefore coordinating our different purposes in the light of some set of conditions or other?

S: Yes. But generally ethics is not discussed in the light of the conditions for cooperation established by Nature. It is discussed only from the point of view of the rules that humans must of necessity, if they are not orientated to Nature's conditions, establish: commandments, moral rules or other stipulations of social behaviour – which are changeable because they are created by humans. These run alongside the efforts of individuals to develop themselves, achieve their own purposes. So the major rule is generally to do not only what is good for oneself, but also what is good for everybody. But that still leaves unsolved the question 'What is good for everybody?'

P: But we began this by talking about the consequences of identifying with scientific, theoretical thinking.

S: Yes. If we identify with the mechanical causality in creation, this leads, through the human activity of dissecting and changing everything, to an identification with the impression of the absolute changeability of creation, and with human creativity: the ability to dissect and construct. The identification with changeability leads to an identification with time, which is then seen as two infinite, absent, never-present realities: history, the past, with its realized, defined, rememberable, unchangeable shape, and the future, which is non-realized, unknown, mystical and changeable. And while this future is fascinating for those who are identified with changeability and the ability to change, it is equally frightening.

P: And this idea of human creativity gives the illusory feeling of freedom that humans can have?

S: Yes, it gives the illusion of the human free will to change. But this contradicts the common, self-evident knowledge that Nature gives us of the whole ever-present reality and of our belonging absolutely to it. We can temporarily change many things on the surface if we need to – as animals do, too – but we can't change reality. But because we are identified with and fascinated by our ability to change and create, we want to change and create more and more. But everything we change and create we have to produce, reproduce and maintain by ourselves. Nature provides only the material and the energy for it. Nature would never take over from us and do it instead of us, nor would Nature ever support what we do. Nature only works against and destroys everything that we or other species create. That's why identification with changing as an end in itself always has unforeseen consequences: we can't learn to control the whole reality, because the original creativity and causality based on God's need and on the original, unchangeable Being is not comparable with the creativity and causality revealed by the transcendent and 'concrete' creation.

P: And, to reiterate, in your view, our identity is not the ego or the self, but our consciousness?

S: Yes. By that I mean our basic ability to experience, which is our primary ability. It gives us consciousness of our body and, through the senses, our active relation to the whole, ever-present reality.

P: What is the ego or self, then, in your terms?

S: The ego or self – as I interpret them – are only other names for what we generally call the 'soul' or the 'psyche'. The ego or self is built up on every living being's experience- and memory-based mental work – what we call reflection or thinking. It is the result of such mental work. It's what we need in order to be able to develop behaviour patterns, which we – and every other species, too – need in order to satisfy all our needs. The needs work as values. In humans the needs can also be evaluated, discussed and compared using language, and can become personal, individual values when they are associated with arbitrary predilections. It is these need-based values – which are an enormously complicated mixture of natural and artificial needs – that provide the logic to all our thinking and activity.

P: So in your view, animals must also have an ego or self?

S: They have to develop similar behaviour patterns through meaningful reflections, but they can't reflect on the fact that they have such behaviour patterns. So they don't have a problem with their 'soul'! And we would have less of a problem with our 'soul', our 'ego', if we thought about it as behaviour patterns with values and evaluations behind it – that is, as only a practical problem, and not an unsolvable theoretical problem of identity.

The 'soul' or 'psyche' or 'ego' or 'self' enables each living being to understand mechanical and biological cause and effect, and thereby to undertake all the purposeful activities that are needed in order to manage life in creation satisfactorily. For human beings, 'satisfactorily' also includes satisfying the need to understand and agree about the original cause of creation as being self-evident – and as therefore able to be understood by everyone in the same way – behind the illusory objective and subjective causes in creation.

P: Because the need of human beings for love can't be satisfied without this understanding?

Subjective and objective needs

S: Yes. Without a satisfactory understanding and agreement about the whole causality – in contrast to the development of knowledge of every causality – humans can't get rid of the basic anxiety they create for each other by confused language. This confused language is caused by our ignoring the question of meaning – that is, the subjective side of every causality – and by concentrating instead on the objective side.

The understanding of the invisible original cause as self-evident – that is, as based on these axioms or self-evident statements – requires the same Nature-organized, experience- and memory-based brain-work that the satisfaction of the other needs requires. No mystical or mathematical thinking is necessary, just special care for the nature and original purpose of human language – that is, an agreement as to whether it is everything-covering for the purpose of covering the whole causality, or for the purpose of covering only human creativity. And we should use language as it is intended by Nature that we should use it – that is, covering, for whatever purpose, in a transparent way – and not as it has been used in history, in an unclear, mystical, manipulative, authoritarian way.

P: Are you referring to the use of words that are not understandable by people on the basis of their own experience and reflection?

S: Yes, basic words with their opposites – such as something and nothing, life and death, concrete and abstract – and especially the opposite, but not contradictory, words, whole and parts, which, when used separately, lead to the basic confusion: the idea that participants are outsiders in creation.

So we should not use language in this way. Nor should we use it as an end in itself. That is what happened when the idea of objective thinking displaced the old, authoritarian explanations, which science regarded as mystical or subjective. The result is that today there is a global competition amongst individuals to 'cover themselves', present themselves, their own different, unique reality – which is the alternative to using language to cover our impression of the ever-present reality. People queue up, for example, to present their own reality on the Internet – instead of using the Internet as a means to achieve a global agreement about the meaning of creation. This latest and most efficient technological possibility for doing that, which has been misused along with radio and TV, has enormously speeded up the process whereby people can present themselves, their different knowledge and creativity. People have become fascinated by these possibilities and so find the idea of reaching an agreement about the ever-present, whole reality less and less interesting.

P: So philosophical reflection or thinking – summarizing your view – is concerned with the need and purpose of the invisible, but self-evident, original cause of creation, and is unique to humans; other thinking is concerned with understanding causality in creation, and is shared by humans and other living beings?

S: Yes. I think that this was how philosophy was originally defined. But, misguided by language-based ideas, or perhaps in order to effectively hinder a total identification with just objective causality [see Chapter 5, p.224], philosophy has come to be used on the basis of the language-based word 'I' or 'ego' or 'self' as human identity and on the basis of history – that is, time, tradition – instead of on the basis of our original identity, our ability to experience, and on the basis of our original experience of the whole, ever-present creation. The ego, interpreted in this way, sees itself, including its own body, as an outsider in creation, and so from this position it wants to control causality as an end in itself, without any interest in the purpose of the whole creation – creation in this view being seen basically as disorder, chaos. But the desire for control means 'mechanical control by power', and we can never use this control in relation to the universe...

P: Why not in relation to the universe?

S: Because we can never get to the original cause of the whole universe, to which our own planet also belongs.

P: And we can't even get to the origin of the planet we are on?

S: Yes, or even to the original cause of any object on the surface of our planet.

P: What about the Big Bang?

S: If this theory is right, then the event of the Big Bang is one relative cause of the universe, but not the original cause, because we still have to ask how reality was before the Big Bang.

P: So we can't use control in relation to the whole universe...

S: ...and we can't use control on the Earth's surface in relation to living beings. We can only have the illusion of it. Our basic need in relation to living beings is to be understood, and we can't bring that about by power. Not even God can. For the non-created parts of the whole, understanding requires distance. God can understand his parts without distance. So the lack of distance in the original reality gives rise to God's need, if he is to satisfy his need to be understood, to create creation, where an enjoyable common life and the experience of distance are possible for the parts, so that both we and he can be understood – because his parts can't understand either each other or the whole in the same immediate way that the whole can understand its parts. To both understand and be understood is real understanding, and this is a precondition for love to be experienced satisfactorily. God understands us, but we can't even have an idea about either God or the parts without creation. So God must give us first the idea that he and the parts exist. And that he does by creation. But he can't give through creation the same unified meeting between himself and his parts that he can give the parts between each other through the units of the created body.

Distance and light are required to give the parts an idea of the existence of the parts and the whole. God's technical problem with creation is how to give us this idea, how to give us the possibility of understanding that he is behind his activity, the whole creation. Through creation all God can do is have the parts meet each other – through the experience of a created body. That much he can force. But he can't force in a similar way a meeting between the parts and the whole, because that is the original, distanceless meeting, in the Being.

P: But he can't force us to understand that we don't actually meet each other directly, but only indirectly, through our created bodies? In other words, God wouldn't try to be authoritarian. He realises that he can't force us to understand that we are not the formally different parts that in creation we experience ourselves to be?

S: That's right, and it is only when we stop being dazzled in our thinking by these absolute, formal, bodily differences and start viewing ourselves as absolute likes, in the way I have been suggesting throughout these dialogues, that we have the necessary precondition – through the same ability to experience – for permanent understanding of the whole ever-present reality and for loving it as an undivided, inseparable whole. We must then come to an agreement through language that the creator has the same need – to be understood as like – behind his creation, so that we can start to check and understand creation in consciousness of his purpose – instead of trying to control creation and instead of, on the basis of the confused idea that we have the same ability to create that God has, trying to force creation to comply with and produce our own pluralistic purposes.

P: This confusion about who can create what – to put it simply – seems to me to have been central to our discussions.

S: Yes. The idea that human creativity is comparable with Nature's creativity is, directly or indirectly, basic to all traditions. It is directly basic to pantheism, which has neither the idea of an unchangeable original reality, nor the idea of one single God with whom to compare the creativity of human 'gods'.

It is indirectly basic to theology. Theology has the idea of an unchangeable original reality as part of its conception of one God, but God is seen as a part, and not as a whole with parts. This leads to the reflection – even if it is unspoken – that God is a part of 'something', that he must have his own reality before creation; or that behind God there is nothing, only empty space. Logically – although, again, this is not explicitly expressed – God has therefore to create the world – Heaven and Earth – and parts, partners, and has to place the parts as participants in his creation: in Heaven, or on the surface of the 'concrete' Earth in a heavenly garden of Eden. Against this background, the identification with knowledge and creativity, and the attempt in this way to be like God, is declared in theology as criminal – though again not explicitly.

P: You are referring again to the story of Eve and the serpent?

S: Yes. But nothing is said as to why it is criminal. The prohibition confirms – though, yet again, this is not explicitly expressed – the idea of the likeness of these two, in my view definitively incomparable, abilities: God's creativity and human creativity.

P: In other words, human creativity mimicking God's creativity would not be prohibited unless it was regarded as possible?

S: Yes. The confusing idea of likeness as creators makes us blind to the real likeness, which lies in the first and basic ability of humans, of all living beings and of God: the ability to experience, receive, take in. This comes before the second ability: the differing ability of every living being, including God, to act meaningfully in accordance with what they experience. The ability to receive is the real likeness, our common identity, because it is recognizable as the same, and is independent of everything that we experience and of all our reactions to what we experience.

The confusing idea of our identity as our ability to create – based on an identification with our creation-based knowledge and our creation-based creativity – is globally entrenched in every tradition and has been reinforced by the four hundred years old tradition of modern science. Because of this, we must – at the same time as coming to an agreement about the creator's purpose – come via language to a global agreement that our ability to create can't be compared with Nature's original, subjective creativity based on God's, the creator's, need to be understood by the parts of his existence.

These two agreements would solve the problem of ethics in a natural way, by creating the insight that all individual life is at the same time a common life in the same reality. It would also actualize our natural, common, original responsibility – what is called 'conscience' – in our common relation to the whole Nature. This would temporarily run alongside, until it gradually replaced, our traditional responsibility – which is also referred to as 'conscience'. But this latter 'conscience' is blind to the original meaning of creation. It involves instead – as a necessary substitute – our creating and following moral rules and other human-made commandments and prohibitions. And the transgressors of these have to be criminalized and punished, in order to avoid the negative consequences of this confused use of human creativity.

Chapter 3

The organic view of unity

Stefan Hlatky

FOR ALMOST TWO HUNDRED YEARS THERE HAS BEEN A POINTLESS confrontation between theology and atheism. Innumerable naive forms of theological belief have been opposed by an anti-belief, atheism, that tries to hold a non-existent, and therefore unassailable, position between an irrational, absolute denial of all belief and an equally irrational, absolute belief in the future of technology – that is, in the ability of humans to be original creators. This pointless confrontation must end. It needs to be replaced on both sides by a philosophical attitude, in the original meaning of the word 'philosophical', namely 'reflection on the truth concerning the original cause of the changing and perishable reality we experience'. It is essential that this happen if we are to escape from the impotence that thinking has suffered from since its derailment in 1828. [See footnote, p.10.]

Theologians and religious groups need to recognize that they gain nothing by committing themselves to interpretations that they themselves do not understand and also, therefore, cannot explain.

The representatives of atheistic anti-belief need to realize that thinking is not a free-standing treadmill that can be turned at will for one's own amusement or that of others, without the slightest consideration of what its natural purpose is. They must also realize that it is no solution in the long run to blame the psychological distress caused by disorientated thinking on the concept of God or on religions in order to bolster an argument for getting rid of these.

The belief in life, the belief in the living unity, and the religious thinking linked with that belief, are part of the innate human characteristic that distinguishes us from animals. If human language – the tool that religion uses to answer children's questions about the meaning of life – is impoverished by having its role restricted to that of making only mechanical descriptions and connections, this will still not get rid of this characteristic. We must realize that the greatest conceivable offence against children is to prevent them from developing their innate feeling for the living unity of existence.

This is the second part of an article prepared for an 'exhibition' held in Stockholm, Sweden, in 1976, to present Hlatky's hypothesis. Translated by Philip Booth.

The fact that the Church has contributed to the situation by indoctrinating people with a superstitious theology is a separate issue. It is no solution to compound this by exploiting language in every way to parody tastelessly the human capacity for belief and the concept of God, the symbol of the living unity. This locks children exclusively into their ability to orientate technologically* to the world.

What is the point of a hate campaign against God? And can it be right to destroy a child's belief in life and the love that goes with that belief by tying the belief, through language, to the idea of a meaningless, dead reality driven by chance?

With all their natural questions about life and reality, children constantly try to put a living image together. But the attempt is futile so long as it is the generally accepted practice in upbringing and education to gloss over their questions with a vague reference to the progress of technology. Technology offers only the mass production of data and 'truths' that relate to a dead, mechanical view of life. Given such 'progress', mental health can only deteriorate with each generation.

Technological progress since 1828 clearly exemplifies the 2,000-year-old saying: 'For what is a man profited, if he shall gain the whole world, and lose his own soul?' (Matthew 16:26, Sermon on the Mount). Technological progress is good for physical health and increases the yield of our physiological lives, but it cannot promote the psyche's, the inner person's, health. Mental health will inevitably deteriorate as long as we encourage children to have their thinking directed by a view of reality as dead and driven by chance, and as long as we deny the necessity of a God-based philosophy of life and any notion of the invisible unity of reality as living.

It may be true that the literal-minded, scholastic Church has lost the ability to interpret Christ's teaching in the Sermon on the Mount. But it does not testify to greater talent to make cheap fun of that inability and glibly to ridicule the ethical problem addressed in the Sermon on the Mount, which each of us must face. An opposition that offers only aggression and abuse is simply being destructive.

The Greek word *politik* means political science, and the task of politics is to solve the problem of how we live together as this relates to our existential needs. In this sense, politics is necessary and of practical use. But the belief that humanity's psychological problem can be solved by politics is a catastrophic mistake. It can only lead to further wars and to an increase in the lust for power and in competition and hatred between people.

What is religion?

All children realize that the senses are limited. So children are not satisfied, as animals are, by just their sensory experience of the environment. They explore and take an interest in everything, thereby demonstrating that, alongside their interest in satisfying their existential needs, they have the curiosity and the interest in understanding that are typical of humans. To begin with, this interest in understanding lacks direction. Children also need protection and care so that they do not harm themselves. Only when they have learnt to talk can they meaningfully begin to give expression to the human need to understand. They do this by asking adults questions about the causes of everything and about what cannot be seen or grasped with the senses.

This need and ability to understand the cause of everything is a natural, innate characteristic, and not an interest that adults create. The evidence for this is that all children, when they have learnt to talk, express the need, earnestly and with authority, in the form of a crystal-clear logic that often confounds adults and makes them feel embarrassed and inferior.

The word 'religion' comes from the Latin 're-ligio', which means 'to lead, tie or link back', referring to the acquisition of language. When children learn to talk, they are inescapably drawn into – that is, led, tied or linked back to – the adults' and previous generations' conception of reality. Thus language functions as a mental inheritance, alongside biological inheritance.

The word 'religion' in its original meaning points to the collective responsibility we have for language. The adults' generally established conception of the human being and of causality in reality is expressed in language, which thereby ties all children into this general conception. Children cannot challenge the adults' conception in its entirety until they themselves become adults. So when the adults' philosophy is confused, children lose as they grow up the logical, crystal-clear philosophical perspective they had at the beginning. This explains how mistaken ideas about fundamental philosophical questions can persist for hundreds of years.

While the mental inheritance is being handed down, children are simultaneously collecting experience from their own biological interactions with reality. When the mental inheritance – the philosophy – is confused, children constantly discover contradictions between the adults' explanations of causality and their own biological experience of existence. This disturbs children's sense of identity, which becomes insecure and unclear, and burdened with psychological problems caused by the confused ideas.

The problem of identity culminates in puberty, when children encounter, through their experience of sexual maturation, the psychological problem of the relationship between the sexes. This combines with children's realization that they must shortly take full responsibility for themselves, and provokes a sharp identity crisis. They are forced to undergo something akin to a new birth, in which they have to leave behind the insecure, unclear identity of childhood and assume a new identity. They have to try to be grown up, and to pretend like everyone else to be secure, lucid and mature. Like everyone else, they have to carefully hide themselves psychologically. They are ashamed that they feel a lack of identity, though this is a collective problem that we can only overcome together, and of which, if we should feel ashamed at all, we ought to feel collectively ashamed.

What is the organic view of unity?

The organic view of unity is an initiative[1] aimed at collectively and objectively testing the proposition that we and reality as a whole exist as a single, interconnected organism, a living body. The organic view of unity is based on the concept of *one* Nature as the expression of this whole – that is, on the concept of the universal unity of life. It thereby addresses the illogicality of the stance that both theology and atheism take in relation to the question of the original cause – which is to exclude the concept of the universal unity of life. They proceed instead from a concept of Nature as both dead and living.

Theology and atheism themselves differ. Theology talks of an invisible, living being who created the world at the beginning of time and who has since had technical control over the 'dead dust' and the living organisms. Atheism does not accept the idea of God as the technically controlling cause, but sees 'dead matter' (or at least what our sight judges to be 'dead matter') as performing this role. So atheism in effect sees dead matter as the (dead) creator or God, which, it is maintained, has created us and all other living organisms over time with the benevolent assistance of chance (Diagram 1).

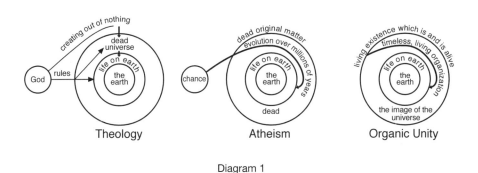

Diagram 1

The question of the original cause – a fundamental philosophical problem that is absolutely crucial for humanity – has thus given rise to the most naive culture-clash in world history. This has been going on for almost two hundred years now and is on the point of destroying the ability of human beings to survive.

What counts as evidence?

The evidence for the existence of an invisible reality is each person's own experience that the sense of sight is limited. It is precisely because everyone

---

[1] This is a reference to an open group that was formed in Stockholm in the 1970s to invite discussion of Hlatky's hypothesis. It called itself Verksamheten Vidga Samtalet (in English, Action to Broaden Dialogue). It was instrumental in putting on the 'exhibition' of which this article was a part.

knows that the ability to see is limited that everyone is interested in and thinks about the invisible. The reason humans can do this thinking already as children is that the capacity for reflection in humans is not confined to their existential needs, as it is with animals. Every person has the freedom, out of love for the truth, to philosophize, to reflect logically on humanity's natural situation and on the cause and meaning of the whole creation. The demand for evidence, the demand that others should show what it is impossible for anyone to see, demonstrates that some people are willing to believe only in what they can see. By believing only in what can be seen, these people restrict the unrestricted ability humans have to deliberate on the basis of all their experiences of existence.

Science cannot lead to philosophy

Scientific progress amounts to discovering more and more and thereby expanding our capacity to act in relation to the visible environment. Developing this capacity is both necessary and good. The mistake is to rely on this capacity alone and to believe that discovering more and seeing more is the same thing as understanding more. This belief marks the age-old collision point between science and philosophy.

In earlier times, philosophy was displaced by the hope that the ability to understand could be developed through meditation techniques and 'looking inwards'. Since 1828, it has been displaced by the exclusive store set by technical development and research, 'looking outwards'. In both cases the result is error: in earlier times, an excess of mystical, occult and magical theories; nowadays, an excess of technical, political, psychological and parapsychological theories.

If we fail to take account of the relative nature of the senses, and instead base our view of causality on what our eyes see, thus binding our view of causality to time and space – i.e. leaving out of account the invisible reality behind our

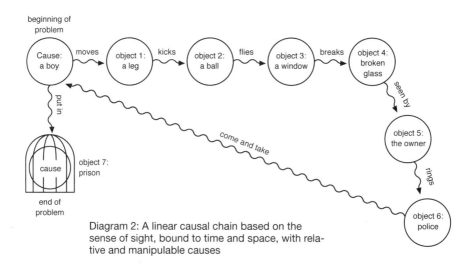

Diagram 2: A linear causal chain based on the sense of sight, bound to time and space, with relative and manipulable causes

perishable reality – then we will understand causality and the functional*
connection between everything in the following way (Diagram 2).

This basic view of causality locks us into the idea that everything is an object
in itself, that there are only separate objects (which we consider to be either 'living'
or 'dead' [see Dialogue 2, ' "Life" and "death" vs conscious and non-conscious',
p.57]. We imagine that there are functions – such as going, flying, seeing, loving,
or light, warmth, electricity, gravitation, etc. – that create between the separate
objects relations or connections that are either temporary or stable.

If we use this view to begin seriously looking for the real cause – that is, for
the original cause – we cannot escape the problem that all the parts that we can
distinguish as living or dead objects demonstrate some form of activity themselves. Over time, therefore, they show up as both passively acted-on objects and
as actively operating causes (Diagram 3).

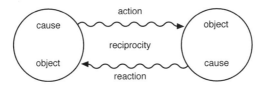

Diagram 3: Every object both is acted upon by, and acts upon, other objects

This raises the dualistic problem of reciprocity – action and reaction – and, the
same problem multiplied, the pluralistic problem of everything acting on and
reacting to everything else. This makes the whole question of causality and truth
relative. It also leads to an extremely complicated, frightening and irrational chaos
(Diagram 4).

In order to avoid confusion, and in order not to be panicked by the feeling
of helplessness engendered by this view of the question of causality, everyone's
psychological instinct for self-preservation forces them to carefully restrict their
efforts at understanding. They explore only certain causal connections, and
completely ignore or exclude others. They are forced to prioritize and specialize.
From individually selected causes, so-called viewpoints, they develop explanations
that explain nothing about the philosophical question of cause – that is, the
single, original, absolute cause.

Distinguishing between philosophy and technology

All of us can readily understand what philosophy and the human characteristic
connected with it are. We just need to keep in mind that the senses are limited,
and to realize that the evaluation of the question of causality that we make on
the basis of sight and the comparative thinking connected with sight represents
only one type of objectivity. The natural purpose of this type of distance-based

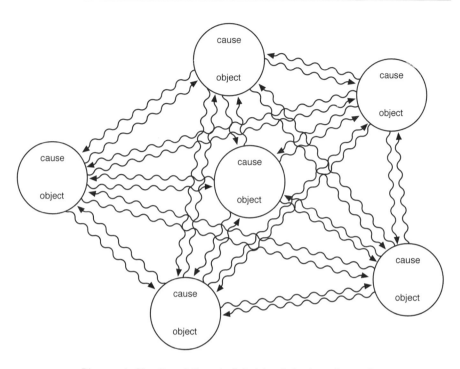

Diagram 4: Chaotic, relative, dualistic/pluralistic view of causality

objectivity – technological objectivity – is the development of our ability to act.

Then we need only to allow the logic that we all used in childhood to be valid. This is the purely life-based objectivity that children have before they are confused by what they are taught about human identity. And by 'life-based' is meant that it is based entirely on both our immediate, subjective and our distance-based, objective experience of life. The natural purpose of this pure human logic is to understand the objective cause and meaning of the whole of life.

Since the time when, with the development of modern science, it became humanity's goal to actually find the original cause in the manifold – as some original, indestructible part [see references to Democritus in the Dialogues] – technological and philosophical objectivity have become completely mixed up. That is why it can seem very difficult at first to distinguish between the two. To do that we must discard what we have been taught, and go by what we built our logic on in childhood and which we still experience as the self-evident – that is, all the natural insights that arise out of our own experience of existence.

If we want understanding and communication between people to grow, so that we can put a stop to people's increasing isolation, we must collectively renew an interest in the self-evident. We must build up philosophy alongside technological understanding. This requires us to stop ignoring or being irritated by the self-evident – which are our present ways of dealing with it, because of the one-sided interest in the learnable and the complicated to which we have been accustomed since childhood.

The ABC of philosophy

Philosophy has been put to use in every century because humans have always understood that they cannot see the source or cause of either themselves or everything they see around them. It was realized that everything we can perceive with our senses is changeable and destructible, and that something changeable, destructible and impermanent cannot be that cause. No permanent understanding can be built on the impermanent.

Proper philosophy must begin, therefore, by adopting a commonsense*-based stance as to what an object – that is, something permanent – is, and as to what therefore objectivity is. The term 'objectivity' derives from the fact that our whole experience of reality is founded on experiences of objects and functions (Diagram 5).

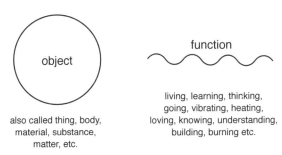

object

also called thing, body,
material, substance,
matter, etc.

function

living, learning, thinking,
going, vibrating, heating,
loving, knowing, understanding,
building, burning etc.

Diagram 5: Object and function

It is self-evident to every 'child-mind'* – that is, to a mind not confused by purely language-based ideas – that for a function to be able to arise, there must exist an object, a permanent something. In other words, a function, i.e. activity, cannot exist by itself, but only in conjunction with an object that functions, i.e. is active. This self-evident insight explains why we have problems understanding causality if, on the basis of our senses or our memory, we experience functions – for example, a sound, a smell, a feeling or an idea, or more 'tangible' functions such as lightning, smoke or a cloud – as detached 'objects' in themselves, without knowing where they come from (Diagram 6).

This creates the insecurity and anxiety we feel until we discover the cause of any function. To discover the cause of a function is what 'to satisfy our understanding' means. But if we content ourselves with surface, mechanical, sensory-based explanations – which means understanding based on impermanent causes – we gain only an illusory understanding and an illusory feeling of security. We then live in the belief that we have understood, but we cannot escape the problem that our understanding is superficial and does not ultimately satisfy us.

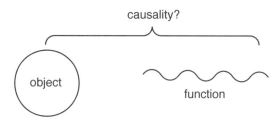

Diagram 6: Causality is incomprehensible if an object and its function are detached

If no interest is then taken in philosophy – in understanding the permanent, original cause – the anxiety that stems from an unsatisfying understanding persists, and with it an intellectual impotence. This impotence drives people to want to discover more and more of the endless possibilities that mechanical understanding offers. But the problem still cannot be escaped that all mechanical causal explanations bind understanding to the same impermanent, changeable image of reality.

This is how things stand nowadays. We should be aware, therefore, of the 'A' of philosophy: the self-evident, but easily forgotten, insight that only what corresponds to our conception of an unchangeable, permanent object – something that we cannot find in our visible image of the world, where everything changes and renews itself – can have existence, can be something. A philosophically conceived unchangeable object may be able to change its form, but it can never become more or less, or become anything other than what it is (Diagram 7).

Diagram 7: An existent philosophical object, something, may be able to change its form, but can never become more or less or anything else

Philosophically, the concept of 'object' is the exclusive alternative to – that is, the opposite of – the concept of 'space' or 'empty space'. 'Object' is occupied space, reality, that which exists, that which is something. 'Space' is the theoretically conceived opposite of 'object' and corresponds to the concept 'nothing' (Diagram 8).

Philosophically considered, 'object' cannot stop being, disappear or become nothing. Nor can it start out of nothing to become something and then grow by becoming more 'object' out of nothing. Thus reality fundamentally must be one and the same permanent object – viewed as an inseparable relation between

Diagram 8: Object vs space

the whole and its parts – which is unchanged throughout time. It is not, however, like a dead, rigid object that cannot express any function. Rather it is like our experience of a mobile object, such as water or a living body, with a changeable, relative relationship between the parts, but without this changeability altering anything about the whole state of the object or the object's unity (Diagram 9).

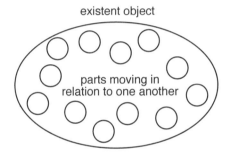

Diagram 9: Reality: an existent object, a whole with relation to its parts

Next we should be aware of the 'B' of philosophy: the self-evident, but easily forgotten, insight that function cannot exist by itself. Function cannot exist like an object, nor can it appear alongside or detached from the object that expresses the function – though we often believe the opposite when we do not take the relative nature of the senses into account (Diagram 10).

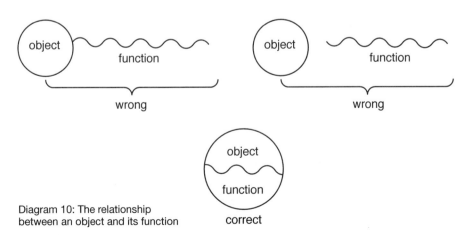

Diagram 10: The relationship between an object and its function

This is why it is futile for scientists to try and work out what movement, warmth, electricity and the other forms of energy are in themselves. It is impossible to find the explanation for life by trying to set our eyes on what life itself is – as impossible as discovering the function 'walking' in the absence of someone who is walking. Function can be the expression of an object only for as long as the object expresses and thereby sustains the function continuously in time.

The logical conclusion is that function must be conceived of as the expression of an object's inherent, *permanent* nature – in philosophical terms, the 'ability' or 'quality' of an object. This means that a permanent, original object also has a permanent, original nature that is in no way changed by the object's starting or ceasing to be active, that is, whether it is a temporarily active or a temporarily inactive object.

For philosophy, though, it is necessary to understand the difference between two forms of activity. One is consciousness in itself, which is understandable if we know its need, that is, its intention. The other is the activity initiated by consciousness in order to satisfy the need in relation to the environment. The understanding of the first is a philosophical question, the understanding of the second is the natural purpose of memory-based thinking. (It is impossible to represent the relation between these two diagrammatically.) (Diagram 11)

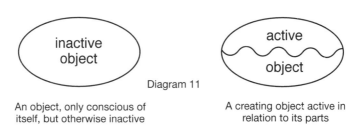

Diagram 11

An object, only conscious of itself, but otherwise inactive

A creating object active in relation to its parts

Next we should be aware of the 'C' of philosophy: the self-evident, but easily forgotten, insight that function, because it is not something in itself, cannot be transmitted from object to object except by direct contact. This is self-evident proof of the fact that in the whole reality the objective relation – between the whole and its parts – and the functional relation – what we call Nature – must be an unbreakable, permanent unity (Diagram 12).

God and the conscious mind[1]

These self-evident philosophical reflections about the relationship between object and function were current in all old cultures. Thus people have always

---

[1] This term Hlatky later replaced with 'consciousness',as sometimes used in this article. Later still he replaced it with 'conscious part' or 'part with the ability to experience'.

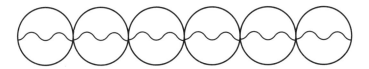

Diagram 12: Function can be transmitted from object to object only by direct contact: thus the whole reality, including Nature, must represent a permanent unity

been convinced that there must exist at root a permanent, original object, and that the understanding of this object can explain all the changing phenomena that we experience with our senses. The same conviction also characterizes modern science, and explains why scientists search for this permanent, original object so feverishly.

In earlier times it was regarded as self-evident that this permanent object must at least have the same nature that we have. That is, it must be a living being that is conscious of itself. It is illogical to think that the cause of ourselves lacks the nature that we ourselves experience. So this philosophically conceived permanent object came to be interpreted as a human-like, living being, and acquired the name 'God'.

With the same philosophical objectivity, it was considered self-evident that there must also exist a permanent object that is the cause of what the changeable form of each human body expresses. This object was called the conscious mind, and was thought of as a unitary sense behind the five sense-channels (Diagram 13). This term for the human being's permanent identity fell away in the Christian tradition, and is only hinted at in the functional concept 'soul'.

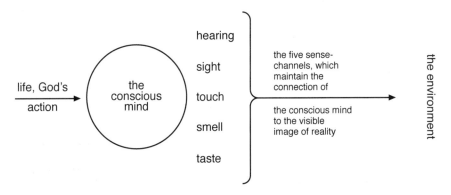

Diagram 13: The place of the conscious mind in relation to God, the senses and the environment

Because of the lack of technical knowledge of the surrounding image of reality, religions constantly made the same mistake when interpreting the relationship between God and the conscious minds. They began from the limited experience that sight gives of relations between objects in the surroundings, and so imagined God alongside the conscious minds (souls), with functions acting as the links (Diagram 14).

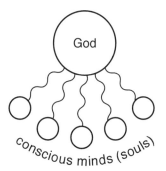

Diagram 14: The mistaken view of God's relationship to the conscious minds

The organic view of unity aims to correct the faulty conception shown on Diagram 14 by combining philosophical objectivity with the knowledge of our image of reality that modern science gives.

If we allow philosophical objectivity to be valid, it becomes quite self-evident that everything that the whole reality expresses must have a permanent, living cause – God – and that what our life expresses must also have a permanent, living cause – the conscious mind.

Viewed logically, the relationship in fact must be an objective relationship between an indivisible whole, which is living, active and mobile within itself, and its parts. There must be an indivisible inherent nature that holds both for the whole object and for all the parts in it (Diagram 15).

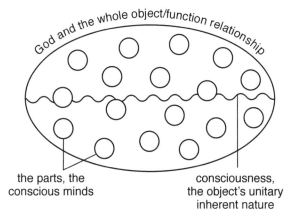

the parts, the conscious minds

consciousness, the object's unitary inherent nature

Diagram 15: Organic view of unity's view of the relation between God, the parts and consciousness.

To use a modern comparison, we can think of the whole reality as a living organism in which we as conscious minds inhere as parts, in a way that is similar to the way cells inhere as parts in our living body. The fact that we, in our capacity as conscious minds, are parts of reality's invisible permanent existence – the whole object – means that we cannot see or touch either the object that we are or the whole object. All attempts in this direction are simply a waste of time, and they block our understanding by involving our brains in clearly irrational issues. The fact that we cannot see or touch the object itself does not prevent us from understanding what is essential about the object: its inherent nature or essence, that which we ourselves experience – that is, our ability to experience.

We experience this – God's and our nature or essence – expressed in several ways. We experience it in relation to God as the active, superordinate, unitary Nature of the whole universe. We also experience it as 'an expression of life': this occurs when we see – that is, indirectly experience with our sight – the expression of another conscious mind. Finally, we experience it as our own consciousness, our own awareness, our own experience of being. This last is our primary, direct experience of the nature that we have in common with God.

If we base a discussion of the object-question on these experiences, and bear in mind our common dependence on Nature, we can begin to understand ourselves and the common reality in which we live. We can never experience any other nature or quality of the original reality, which includes ourselves, than consciousness. Certainly we can theoretically conceive of the opposite of being conscious: being dead – because we see 'dead' animals and 'dead' human beings and we generally think of the whole universe as 'dead', that is, as not having consciousness behind it. But we cannot experience this opposite state.

Scientific research offers evidence

The organic view of unity takes into account the philosophical significance of scientific research. This was not possible in philosophical discussions of the past. It became possible when the age-old philosophical idea that the senses are limited was confirmed experimentally with the help of technical instruments, and the law of energy was formulated.

The law of energy, simply put, states that matter is energy (Einstein's $E=mc^2$). Interpreted philosophically, this means that what we experience, on the basis of our senses of sight and touch, as objects and causes are not objects and causes in the philosophical sense, but energy or function.

In films or television and, most recently, in lasers, technology has given us analogies to this that we can actually experience. Here functional phenomena are experienced as convincing realities, in a similar way to the way we experience things in reality itself. The whole experience that we have watching a film at the cinema is a sense- and memory-induced 'dream', provoked by the phenomenon of light on the cinema-screen. A similar illusion occurs, even without the cinema, when we day-dream.

Part of the reason that we have not noticed the philosophical significance of the law of energy is that the whole of our upbringing and education is based on the belief that all the objects that exist are to be seen in the image of the universe. In addition, it is generally considered that as individuals we can see only a microscopic part of the total function compared with what all the experts together can see, which in turn is only a microscopic part of all the invisible function that exists. So it is considered quite pointless even to try to adopt a stance on the basis of the little that *one* individual can see.

We should turn around this disempowering view of the situation. We should realize – basing our view on the true significance of the law of energy – that we can easily conceive of the object (God), even though we can never set our eyes on it. In addition, we are all fully conscious of the function that we need to take into account in order to understand ourselves and the whole reality.

Thanks to the success of scientists in literally seeing through our whole image of reality without finding anything permanent in it, we can nowadays apply philosophy in an objectively anchored belief in God and in an objectively anchored belief about ourselves. We can thereby begin to develop a common understanding of objects and function, both visible and invisible, in the whole reality.

We need schools and research in order to learn how to act purposefully in the world. We need philosophy in order to be able to apply correctly – while constantly remaining conscious of the Nature to which we are all bound – what we learn in schools and through the discoveries of research.

Experience of life nowadays

That the human sciences – psychology, education and sociology – are so fragmented that each person nowadays has a different theory is because, locked into the sense of sight, we localize consciousness in the brain, i.e. in the function of memory. We start from the idea that consciousness arises gradually in the brain, projected there by impressions from the environment – though also influenced, of course, by physiological needs and genetic inheritance. This view is represented diagrammatically in Diagram 16.

Children, therefore, never acquire a conception of their true identity. Locked into a one-sided belief that the environment – especially in the form of our own species – makes the child what it is, they try on that basis to work with their 'consciousness' to acquire a better identity. This operates like a closed loop that constantly confirms the theory and locks them into it more and more: that is, they try to influence their environment, especially their relationships with other people, so as to acquire a better identity for themselves, so as to be able to improve their environment further, so as to be able to acquire an even better identity, and so on. Added to this are the dubious and confusing theories suggesting, for example:

1. that we have freedom of thought;
2. that we can change reality, and are on the point of freeing ourselves from

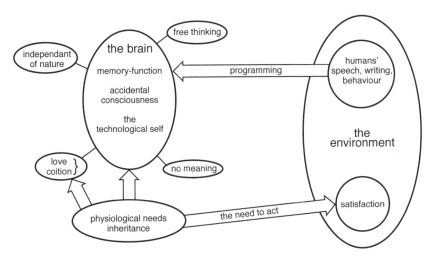

Diagram 16: The modern scientific conception of the human being and his/her relation to the environment

Nature as a result of learning to control it;

3. that there is, therefore, no defined meaning to life, but only those meanings that we ourselves invent;

4. that love begins when one falls in love with somebody;

5. that expanding one's consciousness means either broadening one's conception of what one's environment is, or doing research and increasing one's knowledge of a limited environment.

If we are brought up with the idea of a fundamentally dead reality, the interest in an unlimited consciousness of the whole cannot even arise. So we have a situation in which trained scientists, trying to understand in its entirety this reality that they think of as dead, completely restrict themselves to the sense of sight and spend thirty or more years studying in order to be able to see what can be seen only inside scientific institutions. Those who lack this opportunity cannot think of anything to do other than to ignore the question of causality and to wait until the scientists have solved it.

Experience of life in the future

We need to persuade those who manage our mass media to become interested in ending the present culture-war by initiating a general exchange of opinion on the basic, age-old philosophical concepts of

(1) God, the living cause

(2) the conscious mind, the human being

(3) the soul, the personality.

This exchange should start from objectively considered ideas and should take the relativity of the senses into account. Then the whole question of causality and

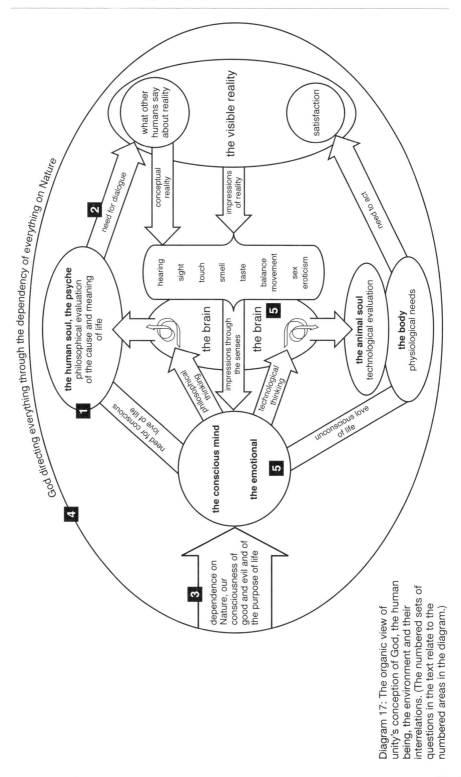

Diagram 17: The organic view of unity's conception of God, the human being, the environment and their interrelations. (The numbered sets of questions in the text relate to the numbered areas in the diagram.)

the human sciences could both be rapidly enlivened again.

What is required is that we collectively realise that a philosophically convincing belief in God is the natural state of every human being. If we have a philosophically convincing belief in God, then we experience our true human identity. Such a belief is also a prerequisite for our being able to understand one another when we talk together about conditions in reality. This ability animals do not have. If there is no interest in the cause and meaning of conditions in reality, then each person spontaneously, from early childhood, wants to experience him- or herself as the cause, even though we know that this cannot be right. This gives rise to the double identity – that is, an acquired identity superimposed on the natural identity – which blocks understanding, communication and agreement, as well as the benefit of love that accompanies these.

Diagram 17 seeks to highlight how the evaluation of the human being's experience of existence is changed by a living, organic view of unity, and what general questions this raises.

1. *(See relevant area of Diagram 17)*

Is it sensible to believe that conceptual reality is a reality separate from Nature; in other words, that human beings can have their own reality, alongside the reality in which we all live?

What does 'to torment one another psychologically' mean?

Do not all mental troubles arise out of fixations on ideas?

Why do we become fixated on ideas?

Which Nature is superordinate: our conceptual reality, or the Nature that rules in reality?

What are the consequences if each person has their own unique reality disconnected from Nature?

What is the difference between day-dreaming and involvement in reality?

How can it be possible to do violence to each other with words, i.e. combinations of sounds?

2. *(See relevant area of Diagram 17)*

Animals cannot speak to each other about Nature, but humans can. What is meant by 'idea'?

What kinds of ideas do we create in children's Nature-conscious minds when we teach them to talk?

There are many languages, but can we, with respect to meaning, invent any language we like?

Is it not in fact Nature that governs language?

Do we gain anything by ignoring the fact that Nature governs language?

Why do we need to talk to each other?

3. *(See relevant area of Diagram 17)*

Is it the brain – the data-machine – that determines how Nature should be? Does not everyone know that Nature is determined?

Do we have an undetermined freedom to think about the determinedness of Nature in any way we like, or is it a freedom with responsibility?

Is the determinedness of Nature altered by our thinking any way we like?

Who starts to suffer and to become disturbed when we think mistakenly: Nature or we ourselves?

4. *(See relevant area of Diagram 17)*

Can we conceive of the whole reality if we do not conceive of it as one?

When do we begin to conceive of something as one?

Do we think about the human being when we think about all the parts of the human body?

Do we not have to give a name to everything we want to talk about?

Is it plausible to conceive of the whole reality as a mechanical function?

Can any mechanical function first create itself with the fantastic, purposeful precision that the construction of the whole reality displays, and then also make that intelligent being, the human, who is supposed to direct reality?

5. *(See relevant area of Diagram 17)*

Is it plausible to think that the brain, which has been shown to be a biologically constructed data-machine, can programme and direct itself?

Why, then, does everyone speak of the heart in relation to being touched emotionally, without anyone thinking of the pump that keeps the blood in circulation?

Is there any reason to think and strain one's brain if one considers that everything is as it should be?

We have built up an enormously fine medical system for caring for the body. Why does everyone complain that the person has been neglected? Who has done the neglecting of the person?

Chapter 4

Are we alike or unlike?

Stefan Hlatky

Introduction

A T THE END OF THE 1960S THE HUNGARIAN-BORN LAWYER STEFAN Hlatky put forward a philosophical theory about the existence of God which he called the organic view of unity. He arrived at his theory by applying to the philosophical domain the findings of natural science concerning the relationship between energy and matter. He was thereby able to throw new light on the age-old philosophical problems.

The basic idea of Hlatky's theory is that the whole reality is a living existence, an organism, that is conscious of itself. We have its same quality of consciousness and are part of this conscious existence in a similar way to the way cells are part of our body. Existence itself, i.e. God's and our own permanent existence – the Being – is not available to our senses. What we perceive with our senses as the universe is like a 'hologram', a moving, three-dimensional image- or energy-projection.

The exhibition aims to show that – with the help of modern natural science – the shortcomings of the old philosophies can be corrected, and we can arrive at a completely logical understanding of the situation of the human being.

In Part I the exhibition presents the organic view of unity. Part II describes the basic characteristics of the five major world religions and of science, and outlines their respective standpoints in relation to the basic questions of philosophy:

THE CAUSE	What is the original cause?
MEANING	Is there a superordinate meaning?
THE HUMAN BEING	What about us is perishable, what permanent?
SOCIAL GUIDELINES	How do we organize a society that is satisfactory for everyone?

Hlatky's aim is not to create a new society or to introduce a new philosophy. It

---

This article was prepared as part of an 'exhibition' about the human being and the worldviews of human beings held in Stockholm, Sweden, in 1980. Its introduction has been left as it stands for the sake of historical completeness. Translated by Philip Booth.

is rather to try and break the state of conflict and resignation that exists in relation to questions about life and society, and through objectivity and logical reasoning to bring about a unification of philosophy, a unification that accords with the new findings of natural science as well as with the basic ideas of the old cultures.

Part I
WHAT IS PHILOSOPHY?

The whole and the part

As far back in history as one can see, humans have been interested in the question of identity – that is, in understanding themselves as a part of the whole, a part of the whole reality. Understanding this was regarded as a prerequisite for understanding the meaning of the whole of life, if it has a meaning.

What we see of the universe are stars and planets dispersed in space apparently without connection, and therefore the question always arose as to whether there is an invisible whole behind the multiplicity. This question has led to two opposing hypotheses. The one is that there must exist a God who has created our fragmented, perishable reality and is outside it and separate from it. The other is that our perishable reality must have a permanent form that exists as an indestructible connected unity beyond the range of our senses. This indestructible reality has been given different names: 'the being', 'the permanent being', 'the permanent order'.

The need for truth and mental health

It was already considered in the oldest known cultures that this philosophical interest – the interest in the invisible whole and the meaning of life – is a distinct need, the need for truth, which categorically distinguishes humans from animals. People were conscious of the fact that we are not compelled to meet this need, whereas, by contrast, we cannot escape the physiological needs that we have in common with animals. Since the need for truth is not forced in the same way, human beings can easily forget it. This is the problem of so-called 'free will': humans can choose to meet the need or to ignore it.

The psyche was taken into account in the oldest cultures as much as it is today. The starting-point of thinking then, however, was that a contradiction-free understanding of the whole of life, of the whole truth, and, arising from that, an experience of universal citizenship, are as important for mental health as fresh air, pure water and nourishing food are for physiological health. A life in which the human being's need for truth is satisfied was denoted in different cultures by different names: wisdom, individuality, bliss, eternal bliss, righteousness, peace of mind, freedom, salvation, complete consciousness, cosmic consciousness,

God-consciousness, love-consciousness, etc. Of course, the meaning of these concepts could vary, depending on what conception of the whole was held.

The two parallel cultures

On the basis of this view of the human being, a categorical distinction was made between two different cultures. One culture, the 'worldly' culture – in today's terminology, the technological culture – dealt with the ability of humans to acquire knowledge and to explore and direct 'this world', the visible, perishable world with which we have a tangible, objective relationship. The other, the 'philosophical' (or spiritual) culture, dealt with the invisible, permanent reality behind the visible world and beyond our influence.

1. The worldly culture and the question of power

The worldly culture's aim was to cultivate and preserve all the skills needed by humans to cope in the best way possible with their environment, with regard to physiological needs, reproduction and the question of territory – that is, with human beings' existential needs. This culture dealt with everything to do with power, i.e. action, strength, skilfulness, ownership, knowledge, arts and technology, as well as the acquisition of so-called supernatural (parapsychological) or magical (psychic) powers and skills.

2. The philosophical culture and the question of belief

The philosophical culture was organized cooperatively with the aim of cultivating and preserving the specifically human ability to use logical reflection to work out, understand and live in consciousness of the whole truth. This culture's primary goal was, starting from the visible, to arrive at a logical theory of the invisible original cause of everything. It was understood that, in relation to the question of the original cause, it is only possible to work with hypotheses and theories. The whole problem was called, therefore, the question of belief. The aim from the beginning was to reach a clear belief that was completely anchored in reality, so this search was not to be given up until a hypothesis that accorded with every experience had been found.

The problem of dissemination

It was whenever anyone succeeded in arriving at a tenable and contradiction-free theory that the hardest problem for the philosophical culture began. This was the problem of ensuring the general uptake of the theory, which required that the theory be disseminated and taught. The real benefit obviously comes when several people agree about a philosophy and they all strive to maintain that agreement on the basis of logic. The next important step was to establish the theory as part of general upbringing. It is necessary for children to obtain clear and logically coherent answers to the natural, philosophical questions that arise as they learn to speak, and for them thereby to acquire in a reality-anchored* way the whole theoretical reality of ideas that functions as a human being's 'own' reality. This created the need to harmonize the philosophical culture and the technological, 'worldly' culture, as well as the need to preserve the clarity of the theory for the next generation.

In this way different theories have since time immemorial been passed down the generations, via language, as answers to philosophy's timeless questions. This passing down has continued without interruption, at first by oral tradition, then later also in writing. It has either been organized by priests or initiates around more or less authoritarian pronouncements – that is, in what we usually call religions – or it has taken place in freer forms, as for example within Hinduism; or it has gone on as a splintered search for the truth without being guided by philosophical ambition, as, for instance, in the numerous Greek schools in the centuries before the establishment of Christianity.

The difficulty that led to errors

Judging by the evidence, people were conscious that it is clarity and logical coherence which give philosophy its general validity and power to convince – that is, give it a natural authority, which cannot be replaced by either 'supernatural' or 'worldly' authority. The fact there are few signs of this insight in all the mysticism, superstition and authoritarian belief of the past is due to many things, but above all to the difficulty of communicating the philosophy.

Before the advent of modern mass media and energy-driven means of transport, this difficulty was, practically speaking, insuperable. Not only were people geographically isolated, but there were great chasms between people as regards education and, linked to this, the use of language. Everything was based on dialogue, there were only a few books and few people could read and write. To convey a philosophy in its entirety while maintaining its clarity was for these reasons alone almost impossible. In order to reach the general public a good many simplifications and popularizations had to be made, and if the philosophy was to be preserved, it had to be bound to a belief in authority and to associated cult ceremonies.

Geographical separation contributed to cultures developing in different ways. Differences then created breaches, competition and enmity between cultures. In addition, popularizations often led to a loss of clarity in the philosophy within one and the same culture. As consciousness of the truth diminished, the leaders of the philosophical culture were forced to present the inherited teachings in an increasingly authoritarian, power-conscious way that was incompatible with the aim of philosophy. This altered the relationship between the representatives of the philosophical and worldly cultures. Natural cooperation came to an end, to be replaced by rivalry for power, and this brought with it further conflicts and breaches that benefited neither party. The result was deeper and deeper error, until some other culture would take over, or until people would see reason and would reconstruct the logic that had given the original philosophy its strength.

Natural science's view of philosophy

An historically unprecedented change took place at the end of the sixteenth century, starting in Europe. This was modern science. People began to pin their faith on the development of technical instruments, which they hoped to use to correct gradually the shortcomings of the old philosophies. The commitment to this approach soon became complete. It rapidly spread over the whole Earth when developments in printing and other mass media, together with various energy-driven apparatuses, created new possibilities for communication and the dissemination of knowledge.

At the beginning of this technological development it was regarded as natural that philosophy and technology should work together, and so both cultures were considered necessary. But it was acknowledged that science itself excludes philosophical speculations, because scientific discipline demands that the subjective, i.e. emotion or feeling, should not be taken into account. Scientists are allowed to concern themselves only with the objective, the measurable, i.e. 'the movement of matter' (which they have divided into organic – biological and inorganic – mechanical).

Technology becomes an end in itself and philosophy is discarded

In recent centuries, however, the interest in the development of technology has led to the technological culture being developed as an end in itself. This began early in the nineteenth century, when the hope was cherished that the whole truth could be arrived at by the scientific method alone. At the same time, the philosophical culture – and thus the belief in a living cause – began to be pointed to as the reason for all humanity's errors. And then, so that no one could question the purpose of this completely one-sided development of only one culture (the technological), the idea of God and the idea that life has meaning were discarded. The philosophical culture thus became totally excluded from upbringing and education.

Energy and matter

From a philosophical point of view, the most important discovery modern science has made is that what we perceive with our senses as matter is not matter in the true sense, but only one form of energy among other forms of energy such as movement, light, heat, electricity, etc. This was already clear from Einstein's famous formula of 1905, $E=mc^2$.

It became possible a few years ago to illustrate more practically that what we perceive as matter really can be an illusion when three-dimensional images, holograms, were constructed with the help of laser-beams. The same thing can be illustrated even more easily using concave mirrors, as in the 'Mirage' on show in this exhibition. [The 'Mirage' consists of two semi-spherical concave mirrors placed one on top of the other to form a sphere, with the reflective sides of the mirrors facing inwards. The top mirror has a hole in the middle of it, through which one can place an object in the bottom of the formed sphere. The image of this object is then projected by the concave mirrors in such a way that the object appears to be located in the hole at the top of the sphere.]

The old cultures often understood about the relativity of sense-experience. There are clear references to the fact that what we see is an illusion, an appearance, and not reality's actual existence (e.g. maya in Hinduism, or Plato's cave simile).

They could not, however, describe their theories in the objective way that science can today, and therefore could not draw any clear conclusions about the structure of reality. In place of the modern theory that energy can change into different forms, they thought that matter could convert into different forms, from finer to coarser. From this idea came the notion of the various elements: earth, water, air, fire and ether.

It was imagined that two material realities existed alongside each other. One was regarded as consisting of 'fine', subtle matter, which is therefore invisible and intangible: for example, spiritual beings, souls, astral bodies, etc. The other, which we perceive with our five senses, was thought to be constructed out of coarser material, and is therefore visible and tangible.

Modern energy theory requires us to completely abandon the idea, still surviving within religions, that matter has various forms. We must not, however, then make the mistake that many scientists make when they reject the idea of matter altogether and instead conceive of energy, functions and patterns of functions, as the original reality.

Energy means power, activity, work. It cannot be found by itself, but only as a potential or active quality in something that exists. The fact that our whole visible image of reality is energy means that it is no more real than the previously mentioned 'Mirage'-image, or the images on a TV screen. This also explains why everything we can see is perishable and destructible.

According to modern science, kinetic energy (c) can appear in potential forms (m). This creates what we think of as dead things. This 'materialized energy', which in 'materializing' becomes visible, cannot be the original cause of what occurs in reality. The cause, which has the ability to express continuously our whole image of reality, must be a unitary existence that is invisible and intangible as a whole but is in a material sense permanent.

The organic view of unity

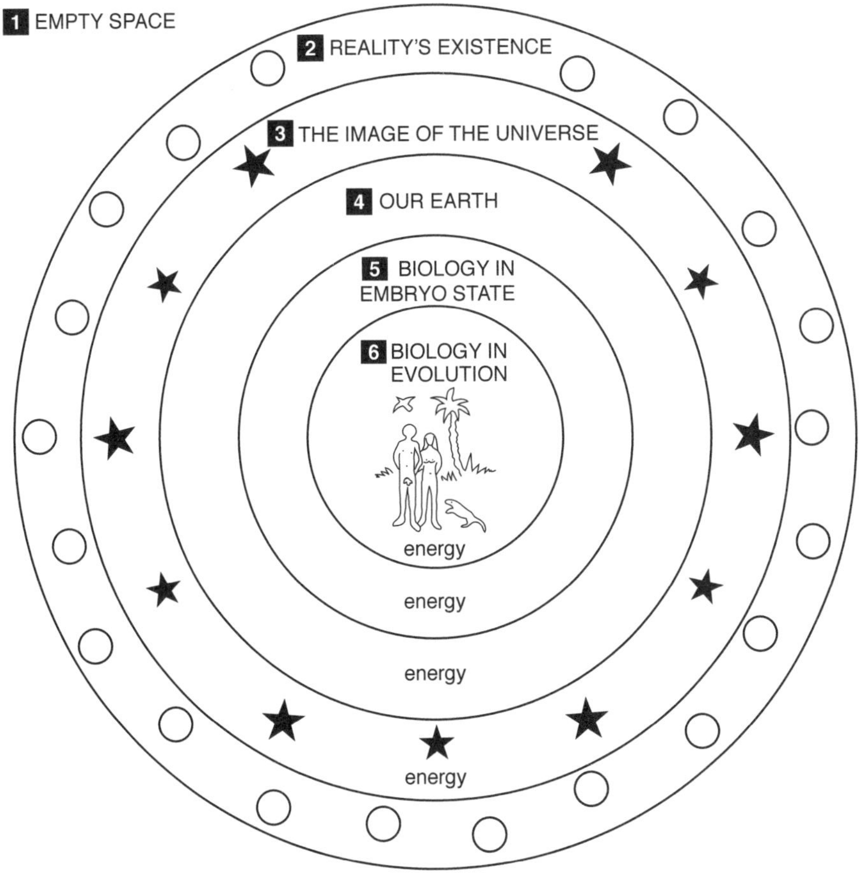

Diagram 18: The cause. (The diagram should be imagined as a sphere. The numbers on the diagram refer to the numbered sections 1 to 6 below.)

The cause

1. Empty space

Everything that exists occupies space. Thus empty space is 'nothing', in contrast to the existent, which is 'something'. Unfortunately, empty space has often been thought of in the same way as the existent is thought of – that is, as a three-dimensional 'something'. Democritus, for example, who introduced the atom theory and materialism, thought of empty space as being just as existent as atoms.

'Something' – an existent whole – can only be imagined as limited. 'Empty space', on the other hand, cannot be thought of as limited, and so the idea of 'empty space' leads to irrational notions of infinity. 'Something' can be discussed and understood. But to conceive of and understand 'empty space' is clearly impossible.

When we are trying to understand reality, we should therefore devote our attention to the existent. 'Empty space' should be seen only as space. Knowing how great a volume existence has, or how much space existence needs, is not essential. What is essential for the understanding of reality is its quality, that is, what nature or property it has.

2. Reality's existence

Reality's actual matter, that which is 'something', must be uniform and unchangingly permanent, independent of time. Time is as unreal a concept as empty space. The idea of empty space leads to *one* notion of infinity, whereas the idea of time gives rise to *two* notions of infinity – the past and the future. Existent reality cannot possibly have begun or come into being. Nor can it cease to be or vanish. This is because something cannot arise out of nothing, and what is cannot become nothing. By contrast, it is the nature of function, of all activity, that it begins, goes on for a while and ends. It is this that gives us the experience of time and the practical need to calculate time. Function cannot be permanent or exist in the way the existent exists.

Reality is always in the present and is always the same. It must as a whole be a living being, since only this can explain all the function that goes on inside it. The alternative is that reality is a dead object. But a dead object cannot do anything by itself. It cannot cause or control its own activity. Nor can it act meaningfully. If reality were a dead object, it would be unable to display the minutely connected order that we see it manifests. So if the function in the whole reality – what we experience as Nature – is activity in a living being, we must take as our starting-point, not science's movement of matter, but 'the movement of the senses' – that is, emotion, feeling – if we are to understand the whole function.

It is everyone's experience that 'the movement of the senses' is the basic cause of every activity that living beings express. 'The movement of the senses', which characterizes consciousness, is what we call feeling or emotion – that is, our ability to be qualitatively touched by creation. All scientific explanations are incomplete in the same way, because feeling is not measurable and so cannot be included in them.

The idea that the whole reality is a living, conscious existence brings us to the notion of 'God'. This is the name given to the whole existence, and the same or similar name that all earlier cultures used to denote the original living cause. According to the organic view of unity we, in our capacity as experiencing conscious minds, are parts of God's existence [the conscious minds are represented by the circles in Diagram 19], which throughout its whole has the same nature as we have. The difference is that God's experience of himself encompasses us, who are parts of his existence, whereas our experience of ourselves cannot encompass God, the whole.

However, because of our ability to philosophize – i.e. logically to reflect on and understand the original cause – we have the possibility of encompassing God in our experience in a convincing way. Given this conception of God's existence, it is easy to understand the meaning of life, as seen from both our side and God's. The full benefit of love requires mutual understanding between likes, and this we see as the greatest benefit that life offers. The same must also be true for God. Thus the meaning of both our life in creation and God's life in the Being – which basically are the same life – coincide.

God cannot show himself or talk to us in the way we can talk to one another, because the whole cannot have the same relation to the parts as the parts have to each other. That is why the possibility of understanding God is offered to us in an indirect way through the whole image-projection. Thus it can be said that the image of the universe is God's talking to us, which we, with our ability to think logically, can interpret and understand.

3. The image of the universe

The whole universe is like a hologram, that is, like an enormous cinema film with three-dimensional pictures. It is not reality's existence. The continuous shining of billions of stars in combination with the rotation of the Earth reminds us every night that we live inside a gigantic, three-dimensional body, which we experience from the inside. Everything in our image of reality is function. It can therefore begin and end and recur at certain intervals. That is why a scientific theory of the beginnings of the universe can be considered as having a realistic basis. But such a theory is still only a statement about the periodicity of the universe. Science offers no explanation of either cause or meaning.

4. Our Earth

Every morning the image of the universe is turned off for us by our sun when it starts to illuminate events on Earth. It is here that we experience conditions in reality at close quarters. This takes place partly through the exchange with our environment that the satisfying of our physiological needs involves us in, and partly through our life together with other biological creatures, which compose a unitary household that we call an ecosystem.

5. Biology in embryo state

Since nothing in the ongoing image-projection can exist unchanged, but has to be renewed continuously, all life on Earth proceeds from a beginning to an end. We experience the beginning as a germ state, and this can easily create the belief that the beginning of life is contained in the seed. This in turn leads to the idea that the rest of reality consists of dead matter. Within Christianity the irra-tionality of drawing a boundary between dead matter and life was dealt with by the explanation offered in Genesis that God intervened directly to create every-thing living out of dead dust.

When Wöhler demonstrated in 1828 that there is no boundary between dead (inorganic) and live (organic) matter, this was interpreted as proof that there is no God. The mistake was then made of writing off the concept of a living cause and with it the entire philosophical culture, and the whole reality began to be regarded as fundamentally dead, as functioning mechanically.

6. Biology in evolution

All bodies develop from a seed state into a fully grown state, and exist for a certain time as an active part in the total ecosystem. In order for the whole continuous development to be maintained, there has to be the same rate of breaking down as there is of growth. Things are so ordered that the whole of Nature's household is sustained by its eating itself up all the time. If one forgets that the ecosytem is a closed system, one can become stuck on the concept of evolution and believe that the whole system, with humans currently at its apex, aims at a further evolution towards unknown life-forms.

The fact that everything sheds its seed and thereby forms the starting-point for new generations has led in the past to the insoluble problem of what comes first: the chicken or the egg. Such insoluble problems – which are characteristic of dualistic thinking – arise when one tries to understand function, the perish-able, as an object in itself. Nothing can be solved with dualism. One has to have the idea of one reality behind the dualistic reality we experience. With the chicken and the egg, there is an infinite regress, unless one has an original reality. Note that objective science cannot say how things come into, how they appear in, this reality.

All understanding requires that we associate a function with an existing source expressing that function, e.g. sunshine with the sun, birdsong with a bird. So if we are to experience reality in an ordered way and not just as a chaos of functions, we must have some kind of source, an experience of some form or some living being, for any function that we experience. We need associations with visible forms in order to be able to satisfy our existential needs and to relate to our surroundings.

Within philosophy, on the other hand, where it is a question of understanding the original cause, it is crucial to grasp that all these forms we see are useful illu-sory forms or images. But they are not existence itself, the permanent.

The human being

[1] The human being's real identity is the conscious mind, which is an inherent part of reality's existence, conceived of as God's existence (See Diagram 19). However, since existence itself is invisible and intangible, we can never demonstrate or prove our real identity objectively. We can only assume that we are a conscious mind on the basis of our subjective experience of being.

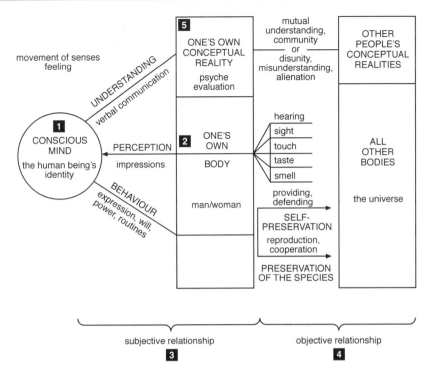

Diagram 19: The human being
(Numbers on the diagram are referred to in the paragraphs in the text.)

[2] Our body is a part of the whole energy-projection that we experience as reality's image. Through our body the whole reality's image is revealed to us at the same time as we, through our body, are indirectly revealed to others.

Everything in reality's image is dualistic, bi-polar – e.g. light/darkness, warmth/coldness, positive charge/negative charge, living/dead, construction/destruction etc. This tells us that the image is not the permanent, unitary reality. This same polarity is expressed in the fact that the whole biological process that builds up Nature's household is driven by the relationship between two sexes, male and female.

When the philosophical interest in understanding the permanent reality behind the perishable, bi-polar image is forgotten, human beings cannot come to an understanding of their real identity. They cannot then have feeling for others as like themselves, i.e. as having the same identity in the permanent reality, the Being. Instead, they begin to experience their identity in the dualistic image. This means they identify themselves with their body: either with its physical aspect, or with its mental aspect (their thinking or various skills), or with its sexual gender, interpreted as the source of emotional relationship (love). [I.e. the idea of relationships as involving 'giving and receiving love' (see, for example, Dialogue 3, 'Can love be one-sided?', p.74.)] This creates alienation, on the one hand between the two sexes, and on the other between individuals on the basis of dissimilarities in appearance, abilities and intellect.

Nature-mediated consciousness

We are basically conscious of life in the same Nature-determined way that animals are. [3] This consciousness of Nature comes to us partly through the nervous system, as subjective impressions of the conditions in our body, and partly through our senses, as objective [4] impressions of the conditions in our surroundings.

Animals can only live in the now. They can only be aware of the ongoing impressions of current reality. They cannot ask themselves the question 'Why?', or be interested in background explanations, i.e. the whole truth. They simply follow their existential needs without being able to philosophize or reflect on the meaning of what they have to deal with. Thus animals are the species within Nature's household that evaluate reality in determined, goal-directed ways. Individual animals follow the evaluation of reality that holds for their species as if programmed to do so – that is, without themselves knowing that this is what they are doing. The evaluating that animals do is thus not 'individualized', which is why Nature's household functions so perfectly if we leave human beings out of account.

The human being's own reality

[5] The human being's Nature-mediated consciousness becomes 'individualized' through the learning of language. When children learn to talk, they have to associate all their experiences with verbal symbols. In this way, each child develops their own language-dependent ideational or conceptual reality, which they must have if they are to be able to take part in general language communication.

It is through this ideational or conceptual reality that the human perspective arises. Thus humans have a double experience of everything. They have one experience that is practical, reality-based* – which they have in common with animals – and a second that is theoretical, memory-based. This conceptual 'reality' is our own to the extent that we ourselves create it, cultivate it and bear responsibility for it. Thanks to it, we can communicate all our subjective and objective experiences to each other. This opens up the possibility for us to understand and enjoy mutuality through being able to recognize our own experience of reality in others. We can then also work out the needs of other species and what their experience of reality, based on those needs, is.

In this way, all humans become conscious of the global unity of need-governed Nature, that is, of the subjective likeness of every living thing, behind the absolute objective unlikeness when viewed practically (it is not possible, for example, to find two oak leaves that are completely alike). [As Hlatky puts it, we are 100% alike and 100% unlike.] The discovery of mutuality makes it possible for us to enter into the experience of others. To the extent to which we can recognize our needs and problems in other living beings, we can acquire the same feeling for their lives as we have for our own.

This is how, alongside the Nature-mediated, objective understanding, there arises the subjective understanding that makes it possible for human beings to experience undivided love.

When this philosophical goal for the human capacity for reflection is forgotten, humans cease to experience their theoretical perspective on life as a (philosophically) objective perspective on the subjective – that is, on a living reality. Instead they experience it either as a subjective perspective on the objective – that is, on a non-living reality [this is a reference to pantheistic theories, see Dialogue 1]; or, as happens, for example, within scientific institutions, as a (technically) objective perspective on the objective (i.e a non-living reality).

In this way, human beings block the possibility they have of undivided love, because the unsolved philosophical questions then appear negatively as disturbances. They show up as a feeling of meaninglessness in relation to the perishability of everything, as anxiety in relation to death, and as disorientation around the question of identity, with this last creating a feeling of alienation. Alienation, indeed, is the absence of the Nature-given prerequisite for love: the experience of mutuality.

Part II

THE HISTORICAL BACKGROUND

A short summary of the great cultures' and science's ideas as they relate to: the cause, the human being, meaning and social guidelines

The great cultures (background)

Hinduism (background)

The word Hinduism is a geographical term that refers to the area around the Indus river in northern India. The word Brahmanism comes from the name of the Indian priestly caste, the brahmins. In modern times the terms Hinduism and Brahmanism are used interchangeably for the social and religious system that the majority of the Indian peoples profess.

The roots of Hinduism go back to about 3000 BC. As a religion, however, Hinduism was not founded by a particular person, but grew continuously. It is also called the 'eternal religion' or the 'eternal tradition' in that it holds that human beings and incarnated gods – such as Rama, Krishna and Shankara – have appeared in every age in order to formulate the old truth in a new way.

Hinduism has no tightly constructed dogma. It carries out no mission in foreign lands and includes a multitude of gods, beliefs and ways to salvation.

All living beings in the universe are differentiated from birth by aptitude and duties. Within humanity there are also a number of different classes. At the top of this so-called caste system stand the brahmins, who perform sacrifices and teach the *Vedas*, the sacred texts. They are followed by the kshatriyas: warriors who uphold the order of society. Then come the vaishyas: farmers, craftsmen and merchants. These three highest castes go through a special initiation ceremony and are therefore called 'the twice-born'. They have the right to study the *Vedas* by themselves. Beneath these three classes come the shudras: labourers who are supposed to serve the higher classes. At the bottom of the religious/social system are the pariahs: the untouchables, such as street-cleaners, etc. It is considered that the social organism will only be able to function if the different classes work together without conflict.

The *Vedas* are the oldest Hindu texts, dating from *c.* 1500 BC and later. They contain among other things formulae and sacrifice-texts for religious ceremonies. The *Upanishads*, dating from *c.* 700 BC and later, are philosophical texts about Brahman, the innermost being of the universe who is the basis of everything. The *Bhagavad Gita*, from *c.* 300 BC and later, is a philosophical teaching poem that emphasizes devotion to a personal God.

The individual can choose from among the countless manifestations of the 'highest being' the one that satisfies their spiritual maturity. For the wise, it is a question of expanding their consciousness and recognizing that they are one with the original reality. If this appears to be too advanced, the individual may conceive of a personal God or creator, Brahma. Devotion to God then takes the place of wisdom. For the person who is not mature enough for this, God is represented by a statue in a temple. Rituals then replace meditation and righteous action replaces love.

Hinduism is still the dominant religion in India, where about 90% of the population are adherents. Worldwide there are 780 million Hindus (1995).

Buddhism (background)

Buddhism is a particular form of the Indian religion, Hinduism. The founder of Buddhism, Gautama Buddha, lived in India about 500 BC.

The name 'Buddha' – the enlightened one – refers to the enlightenment that he achieved sitting in meditation beneath a wild fig-tree. Here he obtained clarity about his earlier forms of existence, the reincarnation of other beings and the causes of suffering. The causes of suffering include: enjoyment of the senses, desire for life, and ignorance.

This insight freed the Buddha from further reincarnations and opened the way to Nirvana, a condition of eternal peace. Instead of entering Nirvana immediately, he began to preach his teaching about suffering and the overcoming of suffering.

The Buddha denoted certain parts of the Indian religion of that time as meaningless – for example, the caste-system, the custom of sacrifice, and the position of the brahmins (priests). He retained, however, the old Indian conceptions of karma and reincarnation. The Buddha recognized no personal God, but talked of an impersonal world-law.

The Buddha's adherents were divided into two groups: lay people, living in families, who had a secular profession and observed five moral precepts; and orders, made up of monks and nuns, who lived in strictly regulated ways, in chastity and poverty.

The original core of Buddhism, Hinayana – the Lesser Vehicle – is aimed at a small number of people. It is based on meditation and philosophically orientated insight. So there also gradually developed a popular form of Buddhism, Mahayana – the Great Vehicle – which puts the emphasis on active love of one's neighbour, cult ceremonies and devout worship.

The texts in the *Theravadas*, which are said to render the Buddha's word, were discovered about 200 years after his death.

Buddhism first spread throughout India and Sri Lanka. It later also took hold eastwards, in Cambodia, Korea, Thailand, Burma, Tibet, Mongolia, Vietnam and the Malay archipelago of Java, Sumatra and Borneo [now the Republic of Indonesia], and westwards, in Afghanistan and eastern Iran. In China, Buddhism achieved an importance equal to Confucianism. In Japan it was mixed in with the national religion, Shinto. Buddhism is followed nowadays (1995) by about 325 million people.

Universism[1] *(background)*

Universism, which is the system that is the basis of all Chinese thinking, originated in about 3000 BC. Heaven, the Earth and humans constitute the unitary universe, which is governed by an all-encompassing law. There is a connection between Heaven above and the physical, psychological and moral life of humans on Earth.

The most important figures in Chinese thinking are Confucius and Lao Tse, who are both thought to have lived about 500 years BC.

Confucius held the view that the human being's task consisted in externally directed activity – in the fulfilling of his social role. He was a moral philosopher who promulgated norms both for the life of the individual and for the governing of the state. He revised and extended earlier traditions, collecting them in five so-called canonical books, among them the *I Ching or Book of Changes*. Confucius' views were also passed on by his pupils in the form of dialogues and sayings. His teaching has in certain periods taken on the character of a state religion in China, with the idea of the emperor as Heaven's representative.

Lao Tse saw the human being's task as lying in internally directed contemplation, the aim of which is to experience the indescribable 'Tao' – the law of Nature and the eternal original source of all being. He is regarded as the author of the *Tao Te Ching*, the book about Tao. Confucianism and Taoism have existed side by side and have shaped social life in China for more than 2000 years.

Christianity *(background)*

Viewed historically, Christianity arose out of Judaism. It is best thought of as having at first been a Jewish sect. It had the same sacred texts as Judaism. Some generations after Jesus's death the collection of texts that now constitute the New Testament was added to the Old Testament. The books of the Old Testament were written during the millennium before Christ, the New Testament between 60 and 100 years after Christ's birth.

The centre of Christianity is the person, preaching, life, death and resurrection of Jesus. He was probably born in Bethlehem in ancient Judaea. It is thought that he occupied himself early in life with religious questions and acquired a deep knowledge of Judaism's basic texts. When he was 30 years old he began his public activity, which lasted between one and three years. The success that Jesus had in his activity disturbed the Jewish authorities. They took particular objection to his saying in the Sermon on the Mount that the correct attitude is more important than a life led according to the letter of the law. The conflict with the Jewish authorities eventually led to his being accused of blasphemy and to his crucifixion.

Jesus' disciples, however, insisted that Jesus had risen from his tomb, had shown himself to various people and finally had risen up to Heaven. The idea of

---

[1] This term is attributed by Helmuth von Glasenapp, in his book *Die Fünf Weltreligionen* (Eugen Diederichs Verlag, Köln 1963), to J.J.M. de Groot.

a bodily resurrection meant that a special importance was given to the person of Jesus beyond his teaching. This had a great effect throughout history on the spread of Christianity. Paul later introduced the view that obedience to the law of Moses cannot absolve human beings. Only belief in Jesus Christ and his sacrificial death leads to salvation and eternal life.

Jesus rejected all demands that he should become an earthly king: 'My kingdom is not of this world' (John 18:36). He spoke of himself as the 'Son of Man', which in Aramaic is equivalent to 'human being'.

Christianity, with its three main branches – the Eastern Orthodox, the Roman Catholic and the Protestant – has about 1.9 billion adherents today (1995). Europe became its centre, but it spread globally as Europeans explored new parts of the world from the end of the fifteenth century onwards.

Islam (background)

Islam or Mohammedanism means 'submission', which refers to the fact that believers should submit to God's will. Islam is closest to Judaism. Common features are that they distance themselves from polytheism and from the veneration of idols, and that they expect a Messiah and believe in the Day of Judgement.

The founder of Islam, Muhammad Ibn Abd-Allah, was born in AD 570 in the town of Mecca in what is now Saudi Arabia. At the age of 40 Muhammad came forward as a prophet of God. He saw himself as the last in a long line of prophets that included Noah, Abraham and Jesus. He emphasized that he was not divine, but only a human whom Allah had chosen for his mission. Muhammad had taken inspiration from both Judaism and Christianity when he began to develop his teaching.

The kernel of Muhammad's religious message consists of sermons about the coming judgement. His sermons met with such strong opposition from the influential circles of Mecca that he and his followers were forced to leave and move to Medina. The sacred text of Islam is the Qur'an, a compilation of Muhammad's teachings and revelations. The Qur'an's content was not up to the standard of philosophically schooled thinkers, and so was interpreted symbolically. Islamic theologians and philosophers have diligently discussed how the belief in human free will relates to God's omnipotence. The Qur'an acquired its definitive version soon after Muhammad's death in 632.

Islam has about one billion believers (1995). It is spread in a belt across North Africa, eastwards through Central Asia as far as China, as well as down through India to the Malay archipelago.

The spread of Islam was closely associated in the beginning with the aspirations for power of the Muslim state. According to the Prophet's original teaching, religion and state should form an indivisible whole. It is wrong to assert, however, that the conversion of a large part of the world to Islam occurred only with the help of the sword. From its very beginning Islam won many converts through the power of its ideas and through the social advantages it conferred.

The great cultures: the cause

Hinduism (the cause)

In a philosophical sense the multiplicity of the external world is maya, an appearance. This appearance is a meaningful, permanently maintained reality-illusion. Behind this illusion there exists an original being – the absolute, Brahman. In the popular mind the original being is thought of as a supernatural personality which thinks, feels and behaves like a human being, even if it or he has many heads and arms and its powers exceed those of humans.

Just as wakefulness and sleep follow each other in humans, so, it is thought, there is a series of world-creations and world-destructions: Brahma-days, followed by periods of total rest, Brahma-nights.

Dharma, the eternal law, expresses itself partly as the natural order – by rivers flowing towards the sea, plants developing from their seeds, etc., and partly as a social order for all living beings.

According to the widely held Samkhya philosophy, there is 'primal matter', which is in an undeveloped state when the world is at rest. The primal matter is made up of three constituents or 'gunas': *sattva* (lightness and light), *rajas* (movement and pain) and *tamas* (heaviness and darkness). During the rest period these three gunas are in equilibrium, but at the world-creation they begin to interact at the initiative of the original being. First there arises the finer matter and then gradually all the coarser matter, and together they form the 'world-egg'. The original being penetrates and fertilizes the egg and releases out of itself the creator-god, Brahma, to establish the world according to the eternal law, dharma.

The original being expresses itself in the form of three figures: Brahma, Vishnu and Shiva – a trinity that represents the original being in its functions as creator, sustainer and destroyer of the universe.

'In the beginning, my dear, this [universe] was Being alone, one only and outside this, nothing. Some say that in the beginning there was non-being alone, one only and outside this, nothing; and from that non-being, being was born. Aruni said: 'But how, indeed, could it be thus, my dear? How could Being be born from non-being? No, my dear, it was Being alone that existed in the beginning, and outside this, nothing. It (Being, or Brahman) thought: 'May I be many; may I grow forth.' [...] So He created the universe out of himself, and when He had created the universe out of himself, He went into every being. Everything which is has its self in Him alone. Now, that which is the subtle essence – in it all that exists has its self. That is the True. That is the Self. That thou art, Svetaketu.'

(From the *Chandogya Upanishad*)

Buddhism (the cause)

Buddha does not deny that there are greater or lesser gods, but none of them is omnipotent or has created the universe. Even the highest, Brahma, is subject to the eternal law of change. This law governs him, just as the law of day and night, summer and winter, death and reincarnation, governs the world of life on Earth.

All phenomena in our world are perishable. There are no eternal material atoms, no original substance and no immortal souls. The process of the world has neither beginning nor end, and there is no boundary to the world's space. A series of world-creations and world-destructions is assumed and, following from this, it is assumed that there exists an infinite number of world-systems.

Humans and the world they experience consist of countless factors, 'dharmas'. Dharmas do not arise and vanish by chance, but are subject to strict regulation by law. They constitute the infinitely numerous forms of expression of the world-law, which manifests itself partly in the purposeful construction of the cosmos and partly also, through karma, in the moral order of the world.

Examples of dharmas are: earth, water, air, fire, life-force, perceptions, consciousness. Everything that can produce an effect is called a dharma. They are best characterized as forces. Dharmas have existence for a short time and then disappear. Their appearance depends on the presence of other dharmas, in the way that the appearance of a plant presupposes that there are a seed, soil, moisture, air, etc. The only dharmas that are indestructible and not dependent on other dharmas are empty space and Nirvana.

'The perfect person does not concern himself with the cause of the world, nor does he regard the present as temporally fixed, or fix his heart on rebirth in a special sphere.' (From *Purabheda Sutta*)

'There is, monks, an unborn, unoriginated, uncreated, unformed. If, monks, there were no unborn, unoriginated, uncreated, unformed, there would likewise be no escape from the born, originated, created, formed.' (From *Udana*)

Universism (the cause)

The whole universe is seen as a giant organism in constant transformation, in which the different parts act on one another the whole time. The question as to what or who is the cause of these events is not clearly answered, but the main view is that it is an impersonal god-principle, alternately called 'Shang Ti', 'Heaven' or 'Tao'.

Shang Ti – the ruler above – is at Heaven's fixed point, the polar star, and observes all the events in the world. He is the originator of everything that happens, but is himself inactive. He has, however, no qualities that could allow any emotional relationship with humans. Shang Ti is foremost a personification of the order that manifests itself in Nature.

Tao means 'way'. It is seen partly as the law of Nature and partly as the original being. Tao's upper side is characterized by substance, essence, which is beyond our imagination and can only be intuited. Tao's under side is characterized by its involvement in the world of the senses, which can be the subject of human investigation.

Out of the polar division of Tao into Yang and Yin – the three forming a trinity – emerge Heaven and Earth. Heaven is a masculine Yang-being and Earth a feminine Yin-being.

Yin and Yang in cooperation bring forth the seasons of the year and the organic world, which then reproduces itself with the help of seeds and seminal fluid. Heaven – Yang – is soul and is in movement. Earth – Yin – is body and is at rest.

'XXI
In his every movement a man of great virtue
Follows the way and the way only.
As a thing the way is
Shadowy, indistinct.
Indistinct and shadowy,
Yet within it is an image;
Shadowy and indistinct,
Yet within it is a substance.
Dim and dark...
... From the present back to antiquity
Its name never deserted it.
It serves as a means for understanding how everything came to be.
How shall I understand that things are like that with everything that is
    called beginning?
By means of this [the way].'

(From the *Tao Te Ching*)

Christianity (the cause)

According to the Old Testament, God is the only perfect being, who exists of himself from eternity to eternity. God is, furthermore, unchanging, and the universe and all that is in it is dependent on him.

God is a personal spirit-being, who is boundless, omnipresent, omniscient, all-wise and omnipotent, the creator of the world and originator of its order, and the world's law-giver and judge. In the Old Testament God is described as omnipotent, 'the Lord', who rules over his creation and punishes and forgives humanity. In the New Testament Jesus speaks of God as 'the Father in Heaven' who loves humanity. In his teaching about God he emphasizes God's goodness: 'There is none good but one, that is, God' (Matthew 19:17).

According to the usual interpretation, which is based on the story of creation in Genesis, the world has been created by God out of 'nothing'. The world is created in time, i.e. before the creation of the world only God existed. God sustains and rules the world. He guides it with mercy, wisdom and power according to his purpose.

In the New Testament the creation is described differently. Here the Greek *logos*, 'the word', is talked of. 'In the beginning was the Word, and the Word was with God, and the Word was God. The same was in the beginning with God. All things were made by him; and without him was not any thing made that was made' (John 1:1-3).

The Christian church talks of God's Trinity – the Father, the Son and the Holy Ghost – but emphasizes monotheism, i.e. the belief in *one* God. Jesus is regarded as identical with the Son.

> *'1. In the beginning God created the heaven and the Earth.*
> *2. And the Earth was without form, and void; and darkness was upon the face of the deep. And the Spirit of God moved upon the face of the waters.*
> *3. And God said, Let there be light: and there was light.*
> *4. And God saw the light, that it was good: and God divided the light from the darkness.*
> *5. And God called the light Day, and the darkness he called Night. And the evening and the morning were the first day.'*
>
> (Genesis 1:1-5)

Islam (the cause)

Allah is an eternal, unique being who was neither born nor conceived. He is the creator of everything and the omnipotent ruler of the universe. Allah is invisible, without form and not bound to any place. Seven properties belong to his existence: life, knowledge, sight, hearing, will, omnipotence and speech.

Only Allah can, in the absolute sense, act out of himself. Everything living and lifeless is dependent on him and subject to his will. It is he who brings forth everything. He is also the originator of all good and evil deeds. He is not bound by any norms: 'He pardons whom he will and punishes whom he pleases' (Qur'an, Surah 3). In Islam there is no concept of an evil force independent of Allah. What appears to us as lawfulness has to do with the fact that Allah generally allows Nature to follow a determined course. But if Allah wishes to, he can do away with this course of Nature at will.

The world has been created from nothing by Allah's command 'Be!' According to the Qur'an, he created seven heavens and seven earths. The heavens lie in storeys on top of one another. A usual formulation is that above these heavens are a further seven seas of light and finally Paradise itself with its seven compartments. Beneath our Earth are six hells.

The creation of the world was completed in six days. In the first days, Allah created the Earth; in the following days, he created everything that exists on Earth; and in the final days, he created the heavens.

The Qur'an distances itself strongly from the Christian doctrine of the Trinity, the 'Godhead-in-Three'.

'In the Name of Allah, the Compassionate, the Merciful

Allah is One, the Eternal God.
He begot none, nor was he begotten.
None is equal to Him.'

(From the *Qur'an*, Surah 112)

The great cultures: the human being

Hinduism (the human being)

The world is peopled by an infinite number of living beings: plants, animals, human beings, spirits, demons and demi-gods. Between humans and animals there is a difference only of degree. Each being consists of a spiritual soul – *atman* – and a more or less material body.

The soul, which exists timelessly, without beginning or end, continuously establishes new bodies of different kinds, in accordance with karma, the good and evil actions it has performed. During its migration from the dead body to the new body the soul is surrounded by an invisible body made out of 'fine' matter, which contains the organs for perception, memory, imagination, will, etc. During the night, in the state of deep sleep, the soul enters the 'All-One' and returns on waking to the world of multiplicity.

Human beings in their capacity as souls are imperishable, but they have been placed in the perishable, material world that does not have real existence. Because they believe themselves to be their perishable body, they experience fear and suffering. Only when they free themselves from their ignorance about the character of the material world, when they challenge their suffering and ask questions about the nature of the Absolute, Brahman, do they begin to be humans in the real sense, i.e. make use of their human ability.

The caste-system with its ranking order only has validity for the existence that is related to the world, and is connected to karma, the consequences of actions in earlier existences. However, everyone, irrespective of which caste they belong to, can attain spiritual perfection or salvation. But then there is another ranking order which indicates how near to, or how far from, salvation any individual is. Salvation – becoming free from the cycle of reincarnation, *samsara* – can only be attained by eradicating one's ignorance and by renouncing one's desires.

'Know the Self to be the master of the chariot; the body, the chariot; the intel-
lect, the charioteer; and the mind, the reins.

The senses, they say, are the horses; the objects, the roads. The wise call the Self – united with the body, the senses, and the mind – the enjoyer.'

(From the *Katha Upanishad*)

Buddhism (the human being)

All the parts of the world-system up to Brahma's heaven are subject to a periodically recurrent appearance and destruction. At the beginning of our world's appearance a situation of Paradise rules on Earth. Humans are sexless light-beings who need only subtle food and do not need to work.

Over time desire arises, and this fall of man leads to people beginning to use more substantial food, to cultivate the earth, to build houses and to choose a king. Thus arise the castes. The moral decay continues for thousands of years, ending in a great part of humanity taking each others' lives in a great war. Some peaceable people, who have retreated into the woods, now lay the foundations for a new and better culture.

There is no indestructible soul, but in its place is a changeable number of elements enveloped in a physical body. These elements do not stop with death, but continue on the other side to effect the break-up of the physical body and to create the basis for the life of a new individual, who is heir to the deceased's good and evil acts.

What seems to us to be a unitary personality is a cluster of dharmas of various kinds that have combined into an apparent whole.

The connecting link between the old and the new existence are desire, the impulses of will and the thirst for life. Reincarnation can occur in any of the universe's myriad worlds. Where and when reincarnation is to take place people themselves determine by their actions – karma. Karma is a comprehensive balance-sheet kept by the book-keeping device inherent in creation's lawfulness.

The starting-point of the path to salvation is reached through the insight that everything earthly is perishable and full of suffering. By refraining from evil, by performing good deeds, by purifying one's heart and by clarifying one's thinking through meditation, one reaches enlightenment and Nirvana by degrees, and reincarnation comes to an end.

Twin-verses:
'All that we are is a result of what we have thought. It is based on our thoughts, built up on our thoughts. If anyone speaks or behaves with bad intention, suffering follows him just as the wagon-wheel follows the ox's foot.
All that we are is a result of what we have thought. It is based on our thoughts, built up on our thoughts. If anyone speaks or behaves with good intention, happiness follows him like a shadow which never leaves him.'

(From the *Dhammapada*)

Universism (the human being)

The human being is the result of cooperation between Heaven and Earth. Heaven gives the spiritual, subtle Yang-element and Earth gives the coarse Yin-element. The soul is seen as an individual being that can continue to exist for a shorter or longer time after its separation from the body. The strong emphasis on reverence for the spirits of ancestors is based on the idea that the deceased are in some way still present.

Harmony rules in the universe, and so this must also be the case for humans. Hence humans are seen as good by nature, while all the evil in them is the result of inadequate insight. In order to avoid misconceptions that disturb the harmony, humans must acquire insight and knowledge by studying the past and by imitating moral examples.

The belief of the masses, however, is defined by the idea there are countless good and evil spirits, which float around everywhere and can bestow blessings or cause harm.

> 'XVI
> *Knowledge of the constant is known as discernment.*
> *Woe to him who wilfully innovates*
> *While ignorant of the constant,*
> *But should one act from knowledge of the constant*
> *One's action will lead to impartiality,*
> *Impartiality to kingliness,*
> *Kingliness to heaven,*
> *Heaven to the way,*
> *The way to perpetuity,*
> *And to the end of one's days one will meet with no danger.'*
>
> (From the *Tao Te Ching*)

Christianity (the human being)

According to the Old Testament story of creation, God first created humans in his own image. After that he formed the human body out of the 'dust of the ground' and breathed the breath of life into it.

First God created Adam, the first man. He then created Eve, the first woman, from one of Adam's ribs. They lived a blissful life in Paradise. They had perfect control over their sensuality, i.e. they had no physical desires that were at variance with the 'spirit', nor were they ashamed of their nakedness.

Before God formed humans on Earth, there also existed, created by God, invisible, personal spirit-beings endowed with understanding and will, who can take on a visible body for particular purposes. These beings, who are God's servants, are called angels.

The likeness of the human to God consists in the fact that the human, in contrast to the animal, is endowed with an immortal, spiritual, intelligent soul and possesses free will. The spirit, the nature of which is eternal, can exercise control over the life of the soul. The spirit is the centre for the ethical, moral and religious life of the human. The soul exercises control over the body.

The idea of reincarnation existed in Christianity, but was abolished at the Church Council of 553.

From the moment that God created the angels, they possessed complete knowledge of God. But God put them to the test. One group of angels did not pass the test. Blinded by arrogance, they deserted God and tumbled down into the underworld. Although they can leave their abode from time to time in order to tempt humans and to lead them astray into sin, they cannot do anything unless God allows it. The will of the 'devils' is no longer free; they can only choose between different evil deeds.

One of the fallen angels, Satan, entered Paradise by taking up dwelling in a serpent. He seduced Eve into eating fruit from the forbidden tree, the tree of knowledge. Eve then persuaded Adam to eat the forbidden fruit. Because of this sin of eating from the tree of knowledge, they were driven out of Paradise. The sin was inherited by all Adam's descendants.

> *'26. And [God] hath made of one blood all nations of men for to dwell on all the face of the Earth, and hath determined the times before appointed, and the bounds of their habitation;*
> *27. That they should seek the Lord, if haply they might feel after him, and find him, though he be not far from every one of us:*
> *28. For in him we live, and move, and have our being; as certain also of your own poets have said, For we are also his offspring.'*
> (Acts of the Apostles 17:26-28)

Islam (the human being)

Living beings are divided into various categories. The most perfect are angels, whom Allah created out of light. They are sexless beings who neither eat nor drink. The most important angels are Gabriel, who for twenty-three years communicated the content of the Qur'an to the Prophet; Michael, who bestows rain and food; and Izrail, who is the angel of death.

Allah created the original human, Adam, from clay and water and breathed the breath of life into him. After creating Adam, Allah caused the whole of mankind to arise out of Adam's spine and to make a declaration of faith. He then led them back again into Adam's spine and collected the souls in a shrine on his throne. There they wait until the time comes for their birth, when they can be united with the bodies allotted to them. With death the soul and body are separated, to be united again in the resurrection on the Final Day of Judgement.

Shaitan (Satan) or Diabolos was originally an angel. He was ejected from Paradise because, out of pride, he would not prostrate himself before Adam, who had been created from clay. Together with his under-devils, he tries to entice humans to do evil, until he himself will be annihilated on the Day of Judgement.

The first human couple were Adam and Eve, and the same stories are related about them as in the Bible. Humanity was not burdened with original sin by the Fall, because Adam repented and obtained forgiveness.

Adam was the first prophet to instruct humanity on the basis of divine revelations. Other prophets followed him, Muhammad among them.

> *'Does there not pass over a man a space of time when his life is a blank?*
> *We have created man from the union of the two sexes so that We may put him*
> *to the proof. We have endowed him with sight and hearing and, be he thankful*
> *or oblivious of Our favours, We have shown him the right path.*
> *For the unbelievers We have prepared fetters and chains, and a blazing Fire.*
> *But the righteous shall drink of a cup tempered at the Camphor Fountain, a*
> *gushing spring at which the servants of Allah will refresh themselves...'*
>
> (From the *Qur'an*, Surah 76)

The great cultures: meaning

Hinduism (meaning)

In the *Bhagavad Gita* it is said that the purpose of all living beings – i.e. the purpose of the parts that inhere in the wholeness – is to serve 'God's highest personality'. This service also gives joy and satisfaction to those inhering parts.

The teaching about karma and the transmigration of the soul is central. In the worldly existence the aim is to obtain a good form of reincarnation through good deeds. But even the happiest form of existence comes to an end some time, so those who learn to recognize the transitoriness of worldly striving focus instead upon achieving permanent salvation. This salvation can be reached in different ways. One such way is through love and devotion (bhakti) to the personal Godhead, in order to be freed by its 'grace' from everything that binds one to the perishable world.

According to the truly philosophical schools, human beings must themselves, however, arrive at an understanding of the perishable nature of the material world, of *maya*. Through this understanding they can curb their suffering, thereby preventing new karma, and can destroy their karma from earlier existences. What is required is, on the one hand, insight into the unity of the Godhead and the soul, and on the other, insight into the dissimilarity between the soul (which is permanent) and what we call matter (which is perishable). This insight must not be merely theoretical, but must involve intuitive knowledge for which study of the sacred texts and regular meditation exercises are a necessary preparation.

When a person has attained this salvation or insight, their actions come to coincide with the will of 'the highest consciousness', and this has the effect of making them happy.

The situation of the saved person after death is described in different ways: sometimes as a merging into the Godhead, but more usually as a continued individual existence in a non-earthly life.

'I am the One source of all: the evolution of all comes from me. The wise think this and they worship me in adoration of love.
Their thoughts are on me, their life is in me, and they give light to each other. For ever they speak of my glory; and they find peace and joy.'

(From the *Bhagavad Gita*)

'In reality you are always united with God. But you must know this. Beyond this there is nothing more to know. Meditate, and you will understand that spirit, matter and Maya (the force that unites spirit and matter) are only three different sides of Brahma, the Only Reality.'

(From the *Svetasvatara Upanishad*)

Buddhism (meaning)

Buddhism is intended as a path to salvation for individuals. The well-being of the whole is a joyful consequence and a beautiful by-product of the right behaviour of the individual, but there is no original purpose for which the 'wheel of the law' is set in motion.

Life is suffering, because everything is perishable and even the happiest person is subject to illness, ageing and death. Suffering can disappear only if desire and the other passions that bring about reincarnations can be destroyed. This can occur only gradually over many existences. Progress towards salvation is stepwise: first the gross moral mistakes are removed from worldly life, and then, through spiritual asceticism, the finer forms of passion are also eliminated.

What leads to salvation is neither exaggerated self-torment nor surrender to enjoyment of the senses, but rather the middle way: a moderate denial of the world.

The path to the abolition of suffering is the Noble Eightfold Path: right understanding, right thought, right speech, right action, right livelihood, right effort, right mindfulness and right concentration.

When one has acquired complete freedom from passions, one has reached the goal. One is then a Buddha – a sublime, perfect human being. One still wanders, of course, upon the Earth, but with death one enters the eternal peace of Nirvana.

Compared with the world, which is in constant movement, Nirvana is a quiescent existence. For the wise it is the only true, blessed reality, which persists when all the perishable dharmas are away.

'The greatest happiness that a man can imagine is the bond of marriage that ties together two loving hearts. But there is an even greater happiness, and this is to surrender oneself to the truth. Death will separate husband and wife

*again, but death will never do any harm to him who has united himself with
the truth.'*

(From *Wedding Feast in Jambunada*)

Universism (meaning)

The big life-questions about the cause and meaning of everything are put in
the background by both Confucius and Lao Tse. Confucius instead emphasizes
behaviour, while Lao Tse stresses that Tao, the concept of the ultimate limit, lies
beyond both words and silence.

Harmony with the cosmos, the universe, is the basis of a happy life.
Therefore, the human being's foremost endeavour must be to get to know the
world's process, so as to be able to conform to its order. An important aid in this
is the *I Ching or Book of Changes*, the symbols of which are interpreted intuitively.
In addition, astrology, number- and colour-symbolism and meteorological
phenomena can be studied.

In their ethical attitude human beings must follow the lofty example of
Heaven. Anyone who fails to follow the world-law, but strives for selfish goals,
encounters misfortune.

In order to experience peace of mind and to gain insight, a person within
Taoism can use meditation and contemplation in order to keep sense-impressions
and consciousness of one's own personality at bay and thereby reach a state of
transcendence. There thinking becomes like a mirror for the 'world-spirit', and
the person can experience the 'highest bliss'.

In popular belief the deceased are rewarded in a Heaven or punished in a Hell
– a notion, however, that is alien to the great Chinese thinkers.

*'The Master said, A gentleman, in his plans, thinks of the Way; he does not
think how he is going to make a living. Even farming sometimes entails times
of shortage; and even learning may incidentally lead to high pay. But a
gentleman's anxieties concern the progress of the Way; he has no anxiety
concerning poverty.'*

(From *The Analects of Confucius*, Book XV)

Christianity (meaning)

God's purpose with creation is to make his perfection known to the created
beings. The human being's task, according to the Old Testament, is to honour
and serve God in humility and obedience.

According to the account of creation in the Old Testament, the world is
created for humans' well-being. The Earth and the heavenly bodies, the animals
and the plants have no purpose of their own, but exist only for the sake of
humans. Humans occupy a unique position: they are the crown of creation, and
everything that takes place in the world takes place for their sake.

According to Jesus, the aim of the human being's life is to live in love of God and one's fellow human beings.

Through the disobedience to God of Adam, humanity's first ancestor, the whole of humanity became sinful and lost eternal life in Paradise. In the New Testament Paul introduces the idea that, because of original sin, humans cannot break the influence of evil by their own force. Freedom from sin can occur only through God's grace, which God expresses by allowing his son, Jesus, to suffer a vicarious expiatory sacrifice for the whole of humanity. When a person believes in Jesus, there ensues a complete change of mind – salvation – so that the person renounces all sinful acts and can partake of eternal life.

As judge, God rewards all good and punishes all evil. The punishment in many cases is already carried out during life on Earth. When the soul becomes separated from the body through death, it is judged and receives payment for its actions. The righteous receive, according to their deserts, a greater or smaller share of bliss: 'In my Father's house are many mansions' (John 14:2). Those who reject true belief go after death to Hell. There they undergo different punishments, in proportion to their sins.

> '31. Therefore take no thought, saying, What shall we eat? or, What shall we drink? or, Wherewithal shall we be clothed?
> 32. (For after all these things do the gentiles seek:) for your heavenly father knoweth that ye have need of all these things.
> 33. But seek ye first the kingdom of God, and his righteousness; and all these things shall be added unto you.'
>
> (From Matthew 6:31-33)

Islam (meaning)

The human being constitutes creation's true aim. For humans Allah has spread out the Earth like a carpet and stretched the sky upwards like a roof. Animals and plants, too, have been created entirely for the sake of humans, to give them food and clothing, to carry their loads and to serve them in other ways.

To the question as to why Allah created the world, Allah replies with the following words: 'I was a hidden treasure and I loved to be known, and therefore I created so that I might be known.'

The human being's task is to submit to Allah and to obey his will as it has become known through the Qur'an.

Thoughtfulness is considered a form of piety, and knowledge and reason are described as what Allah created first of all.

On the Day of Judgement, Allah will allow the good humans to partake of the delights of Paradise and will make the evil ones suffer the eternal torments of hell-fire.

'But those who believe and do what is good – and we put no more on a soul than it can carry out – they belong to the kingdom of heaven and will remain there eternally. And from their hearts we shall remove all resentment and all worldly enmity.'

(From the *Qur'an*, *Surah 7*)

The great cultures: social guidelines

Hinduism (social guidelines)

The caste order prescribes in detail what the members of each caste should do and what they must avoid. The system of rules is not general, but differs from caste to caste.

There are separate initiation rites for male members in the three highest castes. They have to learn, for example, secret 'mantras' (holy words), which they must repeat every day throughout their lives. Young brahmins leave their parents after the initiation and must learn ceremonies and study the sacred texts under the guidance of a teacher (guru).

According to one tradition, there are four life-goals: 1. fulfilment of duty; 2. wealth, material happiness; 3. sexual satisfaction; 4. salvation, freedom from reincarnation.

Fulfilment of duty refers to duties towards parents and the authorities, as well as to the kindness and helpfulness one should show towards other people. This social attitude, however, amounts more to a collecting of credits for the individual's own sake than to a sharing in and sympathy for the needs and suffering of others.

Each individual's fate is a necessary consequence of their actions in a previous life. Those who live a worthy life on Earth are reincarnated as a brahmin or as a warrior, whereas those who live an unworthy life are reincarnated as social outcasts, or as dogs or pigs, etc.

To help on the path to salvation, different exercises can be performed. These exercises are called yoga 'union' and take different forms. For example:

Karma-yoga (the path of action), which is based on practising good actions. Good actions do not lead to salvation itself, but are a necessary preparation for subsequent paths

Bhakti-yoga (the path of devotion to God), where the individual strives to be united with the Godhead through service, adoration and devotion, with, among other things, the help of songs and mantras that give expression to fervent love of God

Jnana-yoga (the path of knowledge), the aim of which is the achievement of understanding and, through understanding, the developed, real experience that the individual's innermost self is united with the divine Brahman.

'Treat others as you yourself wish to be treated.'   Krishna

Buddhism (social guidelines)

Correct behaviour is governed by Buddha's ten precepts, of which the first five hold for the believing laity:

1. Not to kill any living being (which is why Buddhists are vegetarians)
2. Not to steal
3. Not to lie
4. Not to be unchaste
5. Not to drink intoxicants

For novice monks and more committed laypeople there are five further precepts:

6. Not to eat anything during prohibited hours
7. Not to seek entertainment
8. Not to adorn oneself
9. Not to lie down in excessive comfort
10. Not to accept money (for oneself)

In Buddhism there is no God who has issued these prohibitions and who punishes humans if they break them. The Buddhist precepts are, therefore, purely moral precepts, that is, instructions that are intended to make it possible to live in conformity to the world-law, the moral world-order. Those who follow the world-order gradually leave the shore of *samsara* on this side for the shore of Nirvana on the other.

The supreme way to acquire religious merit is benevolence. This is to be found in the wise – that is, those who have knowledge of the world-law and are free from all desire. This spiritual equanimity makes it impossible to harbour feelings of anger or hate.

Leadership within the religious life has always lain in the hands of the monks, who live in monasteries, consecrate their lives to meditation and sometimes give instruction to lay people.

In the beginning, Buddhism was a teaching for the wise and set greater store by the quality than by the quantity of its adherents. However, it could only satisfy the religious needs of the masses to a limited degree. In order to meet these needs, ceremonies, cult procedures and forms of devotion were later developed. But in its innermost core the character of the philosophy has been preserved.

Buddhism has not required of its adherents that they break off connections with other religions. Other forms of belief are regarded as valuable, even if imperfect, preliminary stages to the highest truth preached by Buddha.

'Take care of your friends and trusted ones, by treating them as you treat yourself.'

Buddha

Universism (social guidelines)

The ruler of China – the Middle Kingdom – was seen as Heaven's representative and as responsible for the order in the world. At the same time it was crucial that the emperor himself followed Heaven's order and also led his subjects according to it. The Chinese thinkers, therefore, proceeded carefully to outline the detailed requirements and the moral principles for the ideal regent, at the same time creating guidelines for the citizen. The regent should be both lenient and firm, frank and polite, strict and just, etc.

The whole problem of the function of the state and life within the state took on a religious dimension; the subject owes the prince love and loyalty, like the son in relation to the father within the family. The family is the basic social institution, but the reverence and veneration practised within the family should also be broadened to encompass the whole Earth.

Because rites were considered indispensable for governing people, rules were created for the cult of the ancestors: burials, wedding, etc. The offering of sacrifices plays a large role in these rites, since sacrificing was seen as a deeply rooted need in humans.

Both Confucianism's and Taoism's texts have a pronounced philosophical character, and were studied mostly by an intellectual upper class.

'What you do not want done to yourself, do not do to others.'

Confucius

'Towards him who is good towards me, I am good, and towards him who is not good towards me, I am also good.'

Lao Tse

Christianity (social guidelines)

In Christianity, as in Judaism, it is the human being's duty to obey God's law as it is summed up in the Ten Commandments:

1. Thou shalt have no other gods before me.
2. Thou shalt not take the name of the Lord thy God in vain.
3. Remember the sabbath day, to keep it holy.
4. Honour thy father and thy mother: that thy days may be long upon the land which the Lord thy God giveth thee.
5. Thou shalt not kill.
6. Thou shalt not commit adultery.
7. Thou shalt not steal.
8. Thou shalt not bear false witness against thy neighbour.
9. Thou shalt not covet thy neighbour's house.
10. Thou shalt not covet thy neighbour's wife, nor his manservant, nor his maidservant. (Exodus 20:3-17)

In the New Testament the commandment of love and its application between human beings is particularly emphasized.

Jesus summarized his ethical teaching in two commandments from the Old Testament: 'Thou shalt love the Lord thy God with all thy heart, and with all thy soul, and with all thy mind. [...] Thou shalt love thy neighbour as thyself.' (Matthew 22:37-39).

Human beings are intended to 'reign' over creation, and because of this they have a special responsibility that distinguishes them from the rest of creation.

Jesus created no new theological system, but rather gave the old truths clear expression in parables. As opposed to behaving simply according to laws, he emphasizes a pure attitude of mind. He also emphasizes that God's kingdom is not of 'this world': 'For what is a man profited, if he shall gain the whole world, and lose his own soul?' (Matthew 16:26).

'Therefore all things whatsoever ye would that men should do to you, do ye even so to them.'

(Jesus, Matthew 7:12)

Islam (social guidelines)

The five pillars of Islam are:

1. The declaration of faith: there is no other God than Allah, and Muhammad is his prophet.
2. Ritual prayer: this takes place five times a day, and those praying must turn their faces towards Mecca.
3. Fasting: this lasts for the whole month of Ramadan, from sunrise to sunset every day.
4. Alms: these are contributions that are collected according to certain criteria, in cash or in kind, for religious or social purposes.
5. The pilgrimage to Mecca: this should be undertaken by every orthodox Muslim at least once in their life, if they are in a condition to make it.

The Islamic law, Shari'a, means literally 'right way'. It is principally the Qur'an that constitutes the basis for questions of law. The Qur'an was later supplemented by the tradition known in Islamic law as *hadith* or *sunnah*. Sunnah is a moral code based on stories about how Muhammad is supposed to have behaved in different situations.

In Shari'a law there are many different doctrines used in Islamic countries. One example is the thesis of the *jihad*, the holy war. This doctrine is to defend the holy Islamic territory from external and internal enemies.

Within the family the husband, because of his strength and his ability to procure life's subsistence needs, is the guardian of the wife and the child. The woman's freedom of action and property rights are preserved as long as she fulfils the requirements of married life and looks after home and child. It is permitted for a man to have up to four wives, if he can look after the rights of them all. The man has the right to request a divorce, but if he chooses a divorce without cause, he has failed in his duties and can be punished by a court of law.

Natural science

The historical background

The basis for what we nowadays call the natural sciences was already laid 500 years before Christ by the Greek natural philosophers. The Greeks believed in the existence of a cosmic order, into which they strove to fit everything that they experienced and observed. The task of natural philosophy was to try to find the law and the order behind the multiplicity of Nature.

The Greek natural philosopher, Aristotle (*c.* 350 BC), is regarded as one of the earliest scientists, in that he systematically studied different species and natural phenomena and the connections between them. According to Aristotle, the Earth is the centre of the universe. Around the Earth are eight crystal spheres. The outermost is *nous*, reason, which Aristotle identifies with God. This picture of the universe, with the Earth at its centre, was taken over by Christianity and survived up to the sixteenth century.

It was as a special branch of natural philosophy that materialism was developed, beginning with Democritus around 400 BC. The starting-point was the hypothesis that reality consists fundamentally of small, indestructible, material particles – atoms – and that all the qualities in Nature arise through the displacement and movement of atoms. According to this conception, everything functions by blind, mechanical necessity.

Democritus' materialism soon fell into oblivion. Philosophy as we now know it – which was introduced by Socrates and Protagoras – and, most of all, Christianity came to dominate the world-outlook up to the sixteenth and seventeenth centuries. During the twelfth and thirteenth centuries, however, there was a renewed interest in the study of visible natural phenomena as a subject in its own right. To begin with, this endeavour found support in the Christian philosophers of the Middle Ages. Thomas Aquinas emphasized sense-experience as a path to knowledge. The aim of all branches of science, in his view, is to penetrate the whole of life and logically illuminate it so that humanity can see the world-spirit, the first Mover, God, who has given everything its meaning and form.

The conclusions reached, however, by early scientists – Copernicus and Galileo, for example – began to be more and more at variance with the Church's traditional world-picture, which had the Earth at the centre of the universe.

Johann Kepler, in about 1600, demanded that science should search for causes that are not only hypothesized, but can actually be physically demonstrated. Only in questions of quantities, that is, relationships of size, can humans attain full knowledge. The qualitative properties of Nature – colours, sounds etc. – appear different to different individuals. The quantitative relationships are the same for everyone, and so science must stick to these, according to Kepler. Kepler is therefore regarded as the founder of 'exact' science.

The above-mentioned scientists were by no means atheists. Rather, they saw knowledge of the surroundings – science – as a thing in its own right.

Francis Bacon, in about 1620, emphasized the fact that science had made extremely limited progress since the days of antiquity. He began by saying that people ought to 'throw aside all thought of philosophy, or at least to expect but little and poor fruit from it, until an approved and careful natural and Experimental History be prepared and constructed' [quoted by H. Butterfield, *The Origins of Modern Science*, G. Bell & Sons Ltd 1965, p.99]. Bacon believed that many people had become stuck on the wrong track through searching for original causes in their scientific work. This belonged rather to philosophy, and to bring the question of the original cause into science in his opinion led science astray.

From that time onwards, modern science seems to have developed more as a general movement, very dependent on the increasing correspondence between scientists. The experimental method came into fashion among groups both inside and outside the universities.

In the early seventeenth century a completely mechanical interpretation of the universe was put forward, attempting to show that the universe functioned like a clock. A consequence of this mechanistic world-picture was that God appeared remote and indifferent to human affairs. Under the influence of the scientific way of thinking an atheistic, materialistic trend developed in the latter half of the eighteenth century.

New findings gave scientists the hope that they would be able to explain the whole material world, including the human body, purely mechanistically, without recourse to some invisible God. Democritus' mechanistic view of reality was taken up again. The concept of a background invisible existence that is responsible for all natural phenomena gradually fell away. This marked the start of modern materialism. The gap between belief and science grew wider and wider, and the natural sciences began to acquire an authority of their own.

This mechanistic conception implies a 'unitary view' of Nature, in that all natural phenomena, it was declared, depend on one principle: the movement of particles. The law of the indestructibility of energy, proposed in about 1840, was regarded as lending considerable support to this mechanistic view of unity. It saw all the events in Nature as expressions of energy, which can appear in different forms – mechanical work, light, heat, electrical energy or magnetic energy.

Friedrich Wöhler produced in 1828 an organic substance – urea – out of inorganic matter. Following this it was thought that all living processes could be described in ordinary physical and chemical relations, without the help of any special 'life-force'.

As a result of Charles Darwin and the theory of evolution, the human being was deprived of its special place among other living beings, and came to be seen as a link in life's long chain of development. How consciousness arises as a consequence of the movement of matter remained, however, an open question.

During the first three decades of the twentieth century, physics underwent a sweeping revolution and two entirely new branches developed: quantum mechanics and relativity theory. These two areas of physics – sometimes together called 'the new physics' – brought in their train a radical change in natural science's picture of the world.

In 1905 Albert Einstein put forward his special relativity theory, the most important result of which is expressed in the formula about the equivalence of energy and mass: mass can transform without residue into energy, and vice versa. In his general relativity theory, Einstein describes the force of gravity as an effect of the 'curving' of space around heavy masses, that is, planets and stars.

Since 1930 the natural sciences have increasingly pursued the idea of energy as the basic scientific principle.

The cause

One theory about how the universe has come into being has become so generally accepted amongst astronomers as to be called the 'standard model'. In broad outline, it centres on what is sometimes called the Big Bang theory. It proceeds from the idea that all the matter of the universe originally collected in a very dense 'original atom' that exploded between 20,000 million and 15,000 million years ago. The resulting gas, under the effect of gravitation, formed a cloud, which in its turn compacted into galaxies and stars. This means that everything that happens in the universe is thought of as having its basis in the original explosion, though it is not possible to explain why this has all developed into the reality we live in today.

There is a competing theory, which philosophically seems far more acceptable, namely the 'steady state' model. According to this theory, the universe has always been roughly the same as it is now. As it expands, new matter is continuously created to fill in the empty space between galaxies. On this view, the question as to what the universe was like in the beginning becomes meaningless – there has never been a beginning.

Physics, the basic science, already abandoned materialism at the beginning of this century when Einstein formulated his formula $E=mc^2$. The universe is not built up out of solid, indivisible blocks; rather, all matter can be transformed into energy. Not all physicists, however, have given up the search for the foundation-stones of the world. Some still continue to hunt for elementary particles.

These particles, which are the constituent parts of the atom, sometimes behave like hard balls. But under other conditions they are like a force field or vibrations, which expand into something entirely lacking physical attributes. As to what vibrates, no one has any idea. In other words, no one is sure what our reality is actually composed of.

The human being

According to the view that the natural sciences hold today, the appearance of life on Earth is a natural consequence of a long process of chemical development. Life on Earth arose out of dead matter, as a natural and inevitable result of the conditions that existed almost 4000 million years ago. As Professor Lima-de-Faria (Lund University, Sweden) has put it, life has no beginning: it is an integral part of the structure of the universe. Its development has now been traced back to close to its 'beginning', and scientists have come up against the carbon atom. This is 'ultra-simple' and stone-dead, but nonetheless it is seen as the original source of life itself.

The process of biological development has led – through the preservation of those mutations and other copying errors in the genes that confer an advantage in the struggle for life – to the sequence of living organisms: bacteria, algae, higher plants, animals and humans.

Just as in the seventeenth century, Nature has been explained as being something like a big clock. The human being is explained as functioning like a machine. The life of the soul is a function of complicated neurophysiological, electrochemical processes. Nowadays this is science's official standpoint.

Meaning

Each person may believe what they wish, as natural science does not claim to prove or refute any particular article of belief or anything that is essential to belief, but only to scrutinize critically everything it encounters in the natural world.

This modern view of human life and life's purpose is captured in such views as: the universe is dead and life is only an infinitely small, insignificant part of the universe; the purpose of life is to maximize enjoyment and to minimize suffering; human beings are their bodies and nothing more.

Social guidelines

A scientific way of looking at things has gradually taken over the Church's role as the interpreter and explainer of reality and of the human being's direction. The development of technology, and the belief that it can bring humans happiness, has set new goals for human endeavour. Economic growth and striving for material well-being now come first.

Chapter 5

Science, religion and philosophy

Stefan Hlatky

Introduction

I F, WITH REGARD TO THE TERMS 'PHILOSOPHY', 'RELIGION' AND 'science', we are to strive for a clarity that has general validity and for a single under-standing, in place of a great mass of contradictory views that are difficult or impossible to communicate, we must begin by defining the term 'philosophy'. As long as we are not in agreement about the meaning of this word, the terms 'religion' and 'science' must also remain unclear. I would like to begin with a historical review.

1 Two kinds of understanding

'Philosophy' is a composite of the Greek words *philein* and *sophia*, and means 'love of wisdom'. We know that in earlier times humanity considered there were two ways of developing understanding. One way was knowledge and, linked to knowledge, skill; the other was belief and, linked to belief, wisdom. Corresponding to these, intelligence and reason were also referred to as two different qualities.

That there are two types of understanding has never been doubted. Throughout history, however, there seems to have been a difficulty in differenti-ating these as two disciplines of thought. The difficulty lies in the fact that, without giving the matter proper consideration, people tend to superficially compare human consciousness – with which humans are able to reflect logically, and which thereby gives them the possibility of believing – with the consciousness of animals, and then view human consciousness as free and independent. In this comparison the point is made that humans experience and know far more than animals, who,

---

Lecture given to staff and students at the ETH (Eidgenössische Technische Hochschule)-Zentrum, Zürich, Switzerland, on 8 March 1986. Translated by Philip Booth.

in developing experience and knowledge, are tied to the purposes and goals determined by their biological needs. The realization that human will and thought have an obvious relative freedom leads, if it is not properly considered, to the conviction that the purpose and goal of human consciousness is to develop experience, knowledge and skill, so as to be able to keep on improving our understanding of the whole of life. This idea occurs within the framework of the conviction that understanding is a consequence of experience, knowledge and skill. It is forgotten that the starting point has to be belief, and that experience, knowledge and skill can never free us from the necessity for belief.

2 *Change, relative and absolute existence*

We need knowledge and skill because life manifests itself to us as ever-changing. Like animals, we must understand to some extent the laws of change in order to be able to act meaningfully and appropriately in relation to this property of life. However, the knowledge necessary for dealing with this change is needed by us for two quite different reasons. The first is so that we can change things, and the second is so that we can preserve things – because creation expresses itself to us not only as change, but also as the relative being or existence of bodies or objects that we seek to preserve.

This relative being or existence of all physical things – which constitutes for us the visible and tangible material contents of life, of creation, and which is therefore also the starting-point for objective knowledge – has, through the ages, lured human beings into losing sight of their total, real situation. It has led to the idea that the Being, the permanent reality – which is behind physical creation and from which we and the whole creation come – that is, the whole of causality, can be researched and visibly and tangibly experienced.

In this way the age-old philosophical belief in an invisible absolute God was exchanged for the belief in an investigable absolute Being, i.e. for the possibility of complete knowledge, 'absolute consciousness'. Belief thus came to be seen as a lack of experience. The only belief that was deemed necessary was the belief in those who had greater experience.

3 *Inner and outer science*

What makes the tradition of human thought so complicated is the fact that research – that is, the leaving behind of the conditions that normally hold in order to study the conditions beneath creation's surface – is possible in two directions: one inner, the other outer. These give rise to two different types of science.

We know that both types were developed in ancient times among closed circles of initiates. Inner science – by which is meant the study of the events lying beyond normal sense-experience that the initiates characterized as transcendental or mystical – was always fully developed and passed on via tradition. But it was considered that the natural limitation of the senses represented an insuperable obstacle to the extent to which the external world could be investigated. Nonetheless, the initiates also developed outer science to the natural limits of the senses, and conditions both on Earth and in the skies were systematically studied.

There is much evidence to suggest that it was very well known that outer science can easily tip over into a power mentality, into a meaningless demonstration of skill. For this reason much of this knowledge was kept secret. On the other hand, the difficulty with inner science was the same as that found nowadays in the area of quantum physics, namely that the conditions that exist beyond the limits of normal sense-experience cannot be compared with everyday physical conditions, and therefore also cannot be described using normal language and logic, which are based on sense-experience. If one wants to discuss these conditions, a language and a logic corresponding to them has to be developed. Thus initiates always had their own language, which was impenetrable to the laity, just as nowadays quantum physicists have to employ a special mathematical language.

4 Parallel traditions

This situation meant that a tradition of science and philosophy (knowledge and wisdom) could not be established and passed on via a single, clearly logical tradition, but only via two parallel traditions: one that was closed, 'turned away from the world', reclusive (among initiates and generally in closed institutions) and one that was open, 'turned towards the world', which was developed as religion (which sought to present interpretations of the closed tradition's findings from both inner and outer science to the public). The open religious tradition, however, instead of being passed on through logical arguments – the method of philosophy – was handed down through comparisons, examples of lives to be imitated, rituals, dogmatic statements, moral laws, and so on.

How far, on the other hand, people were able to maintain and hand down logical thinking in the different closed traditions is difficult to reconstruct today. We can only draw some conclusions on the basis of the shifting tensions between the closed traditions and the open traditions. It can be assumed, however, that in the closed traditions the effort was always made to reconcile all the experiences gained from both inner and outer science with everyday experiences of life, and to interpret all these experiences logically in relation to the timeless philosophical questions – if only in order to protect the traditions against logic-based attacks.

5 Belief in God or belief in human beings?

This aim of achieving a meaningful description that encompassed all experience was quite clearly defined in the different types of open and closed traditions as the choice of wisdom. The traditions could not, however, agree on whether, in order to reach this goal, they ought to choose a belief in God or a belief in the possibility of exploring the Being (as they conceived it), i.e. inner science. They could only agree that outer science cannot lead to wisdom, to an understanding of creation. According to the choice they made, either the traditions were essentially monotheistic, or they were based on the possibility of developing consciousness through inner research, where belief was seen as necessary in relation only to human beings (see end of Section 2).

The theories that proposed the development of consciousness – that is, pantheistic theories – presented inner science, as opposed to outer science, as the search for wisdom, and in so doing obscured the concept of science.

Because the monotheistic tradition could be successfully disseminated to the public only through authoritarian statements, it too was forced to require belief in human beings. In so doing, it obscured the concept of belief.

6 *Creation or development?*

The concept of creation, too, was very confusing in the monotheistic tradition. Those who considered life just from the point of view of the material surface could imagine God's creation as occurring only in the same way that human beings are able to make and destroy material things. Thus they were forced to ascribe omnipotence to God and thus to present him as incomprehensible. In fact, in so doing they made belief in God impossible. Only belief in the traditions' commandments and in the givers of the commandments remained possible, as it is impossible to believe meaningfully in something that is incomprehensible.

The theories of development, which regarded the internally explorable background of creation as the original cause, discarded the belief in a permanent existence and recognized only change. They held that because change follows given laws, it is possible to control the changeability by understanding those laws. They held that only given laws exist, but no creator of the laws. The belief that given laws exist leads to the idea of achieving increasingly higher consciousness of these laws, which thus leads to wisdom. The path to this wisdom, according to this theory, can be accelerated if one submits oneself to the guidance of those who are more conscious (in the hierarchy of levels of consciousness).

In practice, the difference between monotheism and the pantheistic theories of development was a very fine one. Both considered that human beings must conform to the given laws if they wish to strive for wisdom, that is, God-consciousness, correct belief – rather than allow themselves to be led astray by their own free will. Also the laws were formulated in similar ways by reference to the golden rule ('Do not do to anyone else what you do not want done to yourself'). Because of this fine line, no religious tradition in history has ever been organized in either a clearly monotheistic or a clearly pantheistic way. The golden rule could not be derived either from God or from the transcendental experience of reality in such a way that it could be understood by people as logically binding, that is, as clearly in accordance with their everyday experience of life.

In spite of the constant mixing of these two types of tradition, monotheism and pantheism remained irreconcilable, because theoretically they are just as mutually exclusive as are monotheism and atheism.

7 The Greek thinkers

The Greeks seem to have been the first to break with the closed tradition and to make philosophy (the subject of the never-changing, existent Being) and science (ideas about ever-changing creation) a public matter.

Their schools of natural philosophy did not agree, however, about either the purpose or the method of philosophical reflection, but rather were variously influenced by all the traditions of the then known world. Attempts were made to localize Being in the 'elements' of inner, transcendental science (ether, fire, air, water and earth), which were originally thought of as spiritual. The unity of changing creation was associated with *logos*, 'reason' or 'word', a concept that is hard to translate, or with meaningless, mechanical necessity, *ananke*, or, closer to the theological view, with a universal reason or mind, *nous*. A purely monotheistic view was held only by the Eleatic school, who tried to demonstrate logically the necessary existence of a unitary Being and the impossibility of change.

The most influential Greek thinkers proved to be:

DEMOCRITUS: his Gordian solution to the problem of existence and change (Being and creation) provided the basis for the modern theory of atomism

PYTHAGORAS: his assertion that the whole of reality can be described in numbers, i.e. in a mathematical language, is a view still held by modern science

PROTAGORAS: he introduced the concept of *homomensura* ('Man is the measure of all things'), laying the cornerstone of modern concepts in political consciousness and thought

SOCRATES AND PLATO: Protagoras' fiercest opponents, they studied the connection of human language and human consciousness to reality. Plato proposed his transcendental experience of a hierarchically constructed reality of ideas as the original cause of creation. For this view, which repeatedly influenced Western thinking, one could consider him the father of psychology

ARISTOTLE: Alexander the Great's tutor, later Plato's pupil and colleague, who is regarded as the first scientist (in the sense of outer science). He was the first to study systematically the different species and phenomena of Nature with the aim of explaining the whole of creation meaningfully using just physical concepts – that is, excluding concepts derived from the experiences of inner science. Deviating from Plato, he saw change as deriving originally from *nous* – universal, uninvestigable reason – which he equated with God.

Alexander the Great, in line with the ideas of his father, Philip II, wished to unite all the known traditions into one single tradition. He founded a number of public schools that were equipped with, for those times, huge libraries. The Romans, who took over his kingdom, further developed this idea of a unitary philosophy.

Outer science, and objective reflection on the timeless philosophical questions based on it, thus began to blossom in the whole Mediterranean area – the then West – with the aim of unifying the old traditions based on transcendental, esoteric science.

The problem at that time was that only the external, objective sciences were studied and given shape. An objective structure could not be developed for the philosophical questions, as general thinking on these questions was bound to the mystical concepts of the religious tradition, which could not be explained objectively.

8 The appearance of Christianity

There is much to suggest that Christ's aim, in view of this situation, was to translate as far as possible the reclusive tradition of Jewish monotheism, of which he was probably an adherent, into everyday, objective language. He wanted to provide the publicly conducted objective science with the meaningful framework that the disunited philosophers of that time were struggling to find, and thereby to prevent science from developing as an end in itself, i.e. without philosophy. Because of this aim of uniting the two different types of tradition, he came into conflict with the tradition that was open to Hellenism, the Sadducees, and perhaps also the tradition that was closed to Hellenism, the Pharisees. His followers defended his new approach, which they called Christianity, against the Greco-Roman tradition and the teachings of the philosophical schools. Christianity proved superior.

Christianity's superiority was not, however, clear-cut if looked at objectively. The new tradition could not solve the original questions about Being, creation, the act of creation itself, time, consciousness and the soul without making dogmatic assertions. This lured Church leaders into excluding the public once more from the tradition, and into developing the mystical inner science in monasteries.

In AD 529 the philosophical schools in Athens were closed, and the responsibility for the public tradition of knowledge and belief was taken over by the majority Christian community.

9 Scholasticism

In the twelfth century, however, private teachers began to collect large groups of students around them, and with the establishment of the first university they started to break down the monopoly of the Church. Simultaneously, through the stimulus of Arab philosophers, particularly Averroës' commentary on Aristotle's teaching *On the Soul (De Anima)*, there were lively discussions about Aristotle's philosophy. The Church sought to prohibit training in Aristotle's philosophy, until Thomas Aquinas, through the influence of his teacher, Albertus Magnus, came upon the opposite idea. Rather than excluding Aristotle, Aquinas very skilfully unified Aristotle's physics and metaphysics with the dogmas of the Church, and depicted Aristotle as the greatest authority in philosophy. At the same time, however, Aquinas separated philosophy from theology, seeing them as two sciences guided by two different sets of principles.

The principles of philosophy, according to Aquinas, are to be understood by the light of reason, i.e. by logical reflection, while the principles of theology are to be understood through revelation. He did not, however, draw clear boundaries between philosophy and theology. Certain theological truths could be logically proven, e.g. that God exists, that the soul is immortal, while other truths, e.g. about God's Being, the Trinity and the sacraments, are accessible only through revelation and the belief in revelation. He placed the experience of revelation as theological knowledge above philosophy, regarding it as an original, dogmatic knowledge, the background to which is a mystical Being that cannot be investigated either technically or logically. Logical thought in this view is dependent on revelation, not revelation on logical thought.

Aquinas thus did what all other religious traditions in history, divided with Christianity into eastern and western, have always done: he restricted the role played by logical reflection about creation and change. The critical difference, however, was that the old traditions never came up with the absurd idea of wishing to prove logically or objectively such truths as the existence of God and the immortality of the soul.

It was disastrous for Christianity that it introduced Aristotle's views on physics, but even more disastrous that it regarded his metaphysical way of thinking, which excluded meaning, as philosophy, as a striving for truth (which should involve meaning as well as cause). This last error, which has still not been corrected, was to result in outer research being developed as an end in itself, i.e. without philosophy. This development continues nowadays at an ever-increasing pace, because it was thought from the first, and still is thought, that it will in the end yield answers to the philosophical questions.

10 *The beginning of rationalism*

This hope of obtaining a scientific answer to the philosophical questions was suddenly awakened throughout Europe when the microscope and telescope were invented at the turn of the seventeenth century, and the new or modern science, which had already superseded Aristotle's dualistic view in the fifteenth century, now took on a definite, 'precise' form. Experience of life was divided into primary (measurable, mathematically describable) objective qualities and secondary (non-measurable) subjective qualities, and research was restricted to the primary qualities. This restriction to a quantitative view corresponded precisely to and realized Democritus' mechanistic world-view. The invention of the microscope and telescope meant that human beings could now also go beyond the senses' natural limits in an external direction. Thus they might arrive at Democritus' atoms and be able to test his theory about the Being and creation. To begin with, quantitative or mechanistic science was kept separate from the phenomena of life. God and the act of creation were not yet called into question.

11 Modern materialism

In the eighteenth century, however, people began to regard Democritus' theory as already proven and as constituting an argument against God and in favour of materialism.

When Wöhler discovered in 1828 that it was possible to synthesize organic material from inorganic elements, materialists construed this as clear proof of the atom-theory, that the changing life we experience was not created by a God, but rather comprises a closed system in which creative activity arises out of inorganic matter.

At the same time Hegel maintained, in opposition to the Eleatics, that reality is fundamentally made of opposites, in other words, that it is fundamentally changeable. However, contradicting himself, he tried to hold on to a certain measure of idealism, by maintaining that history had a purpose. Marx, in his historical materialism, developed Hegel's dialectic consistently, without idealism, that is, without belief in any generally valid given meaning. Darwin reinforced historical materialism. Then came Freud and the development of modern psychology as a logical extension of the Marxist–Darwinist theory.

This is how the exclusive belief in knowledge began, its aim to obviate belief in philosophy and all other forms of belief. Striving for wisdom and inner exploration were considered the unscientific, naive project of our ancestors. Knowledge had its own validity. Technology – skill – was thought of only as a means (though in the twentieth century it was to be strongly helped towards becoming an end in itself by the two world wars). Every effort was made from then on to promote the development of a quantitative science from which meaning and purpose had been carefully excluded since the seventeenth century. The aim was to reach as quickly as possible the point that Comte and the first positivists dreamed of: the answering of as many questions as possible so that most things could be predicted, influenced or prevented, and humanity thereby freed from the necessity for belief.

As long as atomism was believed in, this point in development acted as a vision, associated with the idea that indivisible building-blocks lie at the basis of creation. So concrete has this belief become that corpses have been frozen in the hope that they might one day be brought back to life.

12 The resurgence of methods of inner research

When the principles of quantum physics became known in the 1950s and 1960s, the belief in atomism could no longer be held. Interest in philosophy was reawakened, and the changes in consciousness that could be triggered by psychopharmacology also stimulated interest in internally directed methods of investigation. Following disappointment with the mathematical viewpoint, which came to nothing, an intensive search began for a new or old belief or for any meaning whatsoever by which to live. This search was disorganized at first, but then became increasingly structured through the activities of a growing number of teachers (psychologists and gurus). They, however, like the leaders of the old religions, are only interested in apologetics. The concept of a unified logic and philosophy is rejected from the outset as intolerant. Yet they all long for unity, and gather large crowds of followers around them.

Many people nowadays belong to one or more of these groups that seek to add something to life. In general, however, differences are the only outcome. This stems from the modern principle of emphasizing a person's individuality: the development of individuality excludes unity. This has allowed for the introduction of the spirit of competition, in opposition to socialism, and, because of the strength of the backlash against socialism, it has developed at neckbreaking speed. This is how things now stand. Everybody develops him- or herself and becomes an expert, or a follower of some expert, in something. Because of this we find it difficult to relate to one another in everyday life.

At the same time, the materialist world-view has come to be represented by money, with the result that politicians and economists have exchanged roles.

13 *Technology in place of philosophy*

A similarly unfortunate change has also taken place in science. From a philosophical perspective, the scientific discoveries of the twentieth century have been crucial; however, the philosophical readiness to draw conclusions from them has been totally absent. It appears that no one is willing to call into question the absolute position of science in relation to philosophy. Only the fact that there has been an exclusive identification with science for several generations can explain why the formulation of relativity theory and the establishment of quantum physics have made no philosophical impression, in scientific institutions or elsewhere. Their only impact has been scientific, technological, political and psychological.

Atomism had already been shown in 1905 (in Einstein's theory of relativity, $E=mc^2$) to be untenable. Materialism and the exclusively quantitative view of science, which stand or fall with atomism, were nevertheless not called into question. This calling into question can, of course, occur only in the spirit of philosophy, and here it is important to remember that the spirit of philosophy and the spirit of science are the same, namely absolutely logical thinking. Only the subject matter is different. The subject of philosophy, as mentioned earlier, is the unchangeable Being; the subject of science is ever-changing creation.

To adopt atomism is to take a stance in relation to the subject matter of philosophy. Atomism actually represents an assumption, a belief. In order, however, to test the validity of atomism without disturbing underlying beliefs, scientists excluded philosophical questions as early as the seventeenth century, at Francis Bacon's suggestion [see p.219]. Since then they have continued, in a gracious but determined way, to reject all philosophical questions from their work. But this attitude is unacceptable. It cannot be reconciled with the scientific spirit, as the point at issue is the testing of a philosophical assumption – atomism – that has been the central problem of science for four hundred years.

The proof that the Being cannot be broken down into its smallest particles and is not accessible to scientific study is not proof that the Being does not exist.

Despite the clear refutation of atomism, materialism was 'rescued' by the discovery of ever smaller particles, and the quantitative viewpoint by Max Planck's introduction, in 1901, of the concept of the quantum, which made it possible to continue developing a mathematics for calculating the new physical conditions discovered in the 1920s. A transition to this new science meant that the original aim of pursuing causality to its hotly sought after end-point had to be publicly abandoned. This made it necessary to specify a new, if possible just as hotly sought after, aim for research.

14 The new positivism

The solution to this problem is now sought in a new positivism by changing the places of knowledge and skill. Nowadays, technology or skill has become the end, and knowledge has become the means, subordinated to technology.

From a philosophical viewpoint, this exchange of roles means that the concept of an objective Being and the construction of an objectively unified causality – which had already been contaminated with subjective elements when medicine was accepted as a branch of science at the beginning of the nineteenth century – has finally been abandoned. The unity of all sciences is no longer striven for; instead they are allowed to develop in different directions determined by random politics. This means that the objective, logical spirit of philosophy that held firm sway for four hundred years, albeit restricted by the quantitative viewpoint, has now been discarded. The sciences, instead of doing away with the restriction they imposed on objectivity, have opened their doors to political chance.

The transition to the new physics and the new technology has provoked a confrontation between the new physics and rejuvenated inner research, a confrontation in which the public is also taking an interest. But the public can play only a limited part, because there are now two sorts of initiates, the 'objective' initiates of the new physics and the 'subjective' initiates of transcendental or parapsychological experience.

The purely 'objective' initiates reject the experiences of the subjective method as unscientific – as modern science has always done. Those initiates with a foot in both camps emphasize the equivalence of the two experiences, and not suprisingly wish to claim superiority for the subjective experience their own nervous system offers them over the objective experience that technical instruments provide. The purely 'objective' initiates defend the quantitative, technological point of view, because they regard the changing energy, which they see as the original Being, as lacking consciousness. Those with a foot in both camps, who regard the same formless, changing Being as consciousness rather than energy, talk of developing consciousness and attack the 'objective' initiates for their technological viewpoint. In addition, the relationship between the representatives of the old physics and the new physics is not completely without conflict. This is where science stands today.

15 *The timeless task of philosophy*

These incredibly complicated conflicts can be solved, in my view, only if we reintroduce philosophy as the science of sciences, and if we try to solve the timeless questions of humanity not through knowledge, but by reflecting on the new insights available to us.

The timeless task of philosophy is to unify all questions, conflicts, contradictions and the whole pluralistic reality that constitutes our experience of creation within the framework of a single conception that excludes nothing and requires no compromises. That is why the exclusive subject matter of philosophy is the absolute whole. Nothing can be left out, for 'whole' by definition means something from which it is impossible to subtract anything without it ceasing to be whole.

Because the philosophical conception should unify everything, this task was always regarded as difficult or impossible. But the fact is that the problem of philosophy is not unification, because what is unified does not need to be unified, and if reality were not unified, it could not be something whole.

The first problem of philosophy is that the absolute whole cannot reveal itself to us as a whole, because we are parts of it, parts that can no more be loose, disassembled, free parts that have lost their connection with the whole than can anything else in creation.

The second problem of philosophy relates to the fact that a free will is an essential requirement for human beings if they are to conceive of the whole and understand it. Without this freedom – which has always given humanity problems – typically human abstract thinking is in practice impossible. It is freedom of consciousness that gives human beings the feeling of consciousness of self. The practical purpose of this individuality is to enable us logically to conceive of and understand the whole as like us, as also existing consciously, i.e. as God. Here we need the philosophical method of thinking. We must do it of our own free will, for the whole cannot show itself to us in the way a part can. That is why no one, not even God, can force us to want to know that we are a part of God's existence, to know about God and an existent design that underlies ever-changing creation. By contrast, in relation to our experience of creation, there is no such freedom.

If people do not wish to believe in God, do not wish to understand God's design and then relate to God, then they must live without design, or, in order to experience meaning, they must find their own designs and relate to human designs. They must then either gather followers around them or themselves be followers of others, and in the process will find the freedom and also the dependency of human beings to be the eternal, insoluble problem of human relationships. Only this choice – to believe in God or to believe in human beings – is free.

Appendix A

Language

Every language that is spoken on the Earth forces children or those who want to learn it to associate their experiences of life and the environment with sound-combinations – so-called words – until it is possible, through word-combinations – so-called phrases, which embody opinions – to discuss all conditions in the whole of reality. In this way every language covers the whole reality. That is why any language can be translated into any other language.

This view of the capacity for language and this way of using language is not, however, generally referred to, either in general upbringing or in schools. All that is generally talked about is the inadequacy of language. This is because humans usually use language only to describe themselves, that is, all their feelings and their own view of all the conditions, and never to discuss our common relation to the whole common reality, the absolute unity. Because there is an endless number of conditions and relationships between conditions, which create different emotions, everyone sees that it is impossible to describe all of them. In this way the idea of the inadequacy of language gets built into human consciousness, and any discussion of the whole is declared to be a priori impossible. This misapprehension can only occur because the whole is not shown to us as obvious (i.e. it cannot be seen, but has to be thought), but is shown to us only as self-evident. That is because everybody knows that basically there exists only one reality. Not a single human being has ever found a reason to challenge the existence of the whole, in spite of the fact that no one has ever seen reality as a whole.

Appendix B

What is Dialogue?

Communication between people is formally always two-sided, but basically it can be both one-sided and two-sided:

1. There is the **BASICALLY ONE-SIDED USE OF LANGUAGE**, in which, starting from different starting-points, people try to arrive at some common denominator, i.e. they want to understand each other so as to agree about something. This use of language can be divided in the following way according to different starting-points:

a. **Teaching:** the transmission of knowledge from teacher to pupil, which is determined above all by the natural need for child-rearing.

b. **Technical conversation:** the transmission of information required for those daily routines in which we have to cooperate with each other.

c. **Persuasion:** an open or covert (indirect, political, diplomatic) attempt to create in others commitment to something (a fact, an idea, an aim); or its opposite, the attempt to put other people off something.

d. **Recounting:** what is generally, but mistakenly, thought to be dialogue, in which people describe to each other their experiences and thoughts, with the aim of creating connecting links that build up an illusory sense of community, of acquaintanceship, or, when developed further, friendship – in order to escape a fundamentally pervasive feeling of alienation.

e. **Entertainment:** the same as recounting, only more one-sided.

f. **Idle chatter:** routinely maintains acquaintanceship.

2. Then there is the **BASICALLY TWO-SIDED USE OF LANGUAGE**, the real dia-logue, in which people, definitively agreeing, as a matter of self-evidence, that they have the same common human nature, and thus experiencing each other as having the same starting-point, use language to preserve this idea of fundamental likeness, this same common starting-point, both across the generations and in the differentiated conduct of everyday life.

This use of language can occur only exceptionally as things stand today because of the double identity – that is, an acquired identity superimposed on the natural identity – that we regard as normal and from which we therefore make no effort to escape. Nowadays this double identity only tends to disappear, and then just temporarily, in situations of collective catastrophe, allowing the natural identity alone to operate for that period.

The basic mistake in modern thinking is the theory that we cannot recognize human nature: that we cannot know what we by Nature are. This theory conserves and accelerates insecurity and impotence, as well as feelings of alienation, loneliness, isolation and suspicion in relation to one another.

Glossary

This glossary contains terms as defined by Hlatky

abstract
describes a quality, activity or function, as separate from (though only, thanks to language, theoretically so) concrete existence. See **activity**, **concrete**, **existence**.

activity
to be contrasted (as abstract) with existence (as concrete). Activity is all that can be created. Activity is experienced as changeability, causality or relation. Existence cannot be created. For the relationship between activity and existence, see Dialogue 1, 'Concrete vs abstract, existence vs activity', p.12. See **abstract**, **concrete**, **existence**.

aware
to experience something outside oneself with the senses, as distinct from internal perception, which relates to conditions in our body, including memory, mediated by the nervous system.

axiom
a proposition that neither requires objective proof nor is capable of being objectively proven. An axiom can only be agreed upon or not. See **self-evident**.

the Being
the permanent, existent, living, conscious, invisible, original, non-created reality that is behind creation and is the cause of creation; God's existence, God's 'body', including his conscious parts. See **existent**, **part**, **creation**, **consciousness**.

cause
particularly, the original cause. Only a subject, a living being, can be an original cause of activity. The living whole, the Being, must be the existent cause of all the activity – what we experience as Nature – in the whole.

check
Hlatky's hypothesis should be checked against our total subjective, internal and objective, distance-based, external experience of creation. See Dialogue 4, 'Checking Hlatky's hypothesis', p.128. See **distance-based**, **objective**, **subjective**.

child-mind
the state of mind that children have before their thinking becomes confused by purely language-based ideas. The state of mind, therefore, that arises out of Nature-based thinking. Common sense. What in German is called *Vernunft* or *die gesunde Vernunft*. See **common sense**, **language-based**, **Nature-based**.

common sense

(as an adjective, 'commonsense') what everyone in common can experience with the senses, mediated by Nature. See **Nature, self-evident**.

concrete

describes existence, and is the opposite of abstract, which describes activity. See **abstract, activity, existence**.

conscious

having the ability to experience, primarily in relation to one's own body through the nervous system, and secondarily the formal experience of other bodies, the whole creation, through the senses. See **aware, consciousness, God-consciousness**.

conscious part(s)

the permanent, existent, living, conscious, invisible, original, non-created parts of the only original, non-created whole, God. See **the Being, existent**.

consciousness

primarily, the ability to experience, to take things in, and to be moved or touched by what one experiences. Secondarily, it is the ability to act purposefully according to that experience – which requires purposeful thinking, which in turn requires memory of earlier experiences. Not to be confused, therefore, with what one actually experiences, with the contents of consciousness, with the faculty of memory-based thinking itself. Consciousness is the ability to experience that is behind the five senses. It is God's and our original quality. The basic need of the ability to experience is to be understood as like, and thereby loved, by what one experiences as having the same basic quality. See **identity, like, love, quality**.

creation

the reality that God creates, within himself, out of his need to be understood by his parts, and with which we, the parts, through our created connection to a created body, are able to interact and thereby to have meaningful experience. Creation is technical, ongoing activity, God's activity. Creation is only illusorily existent. See **existent, conscious part**.

creativity

the ability – of Nature or of living beings – to create activity. Either we orientate to what Nature (interpreted as having God behind it) creates, in which case the meaning of human creativity is not problematic; or we relate to what is created by humans as an end in itself, i.e. created by humans in the absence of any consideration of, or in a confusion about, the purpose of Nature's creativity. See **activity, Nature**.

dialogue

See **Appendix B** for a definition of Hlatky's view and other views of what constitutes a dialogue.

distance-based

based on the illusion of distance that we have in creation, and usually used in reference to objective experience. See **objective**.

diversity, the

creation experienced as many different things separated by space, rather than as the unitary, indivisible order it must be. See **manifold, multiplicity**.

dualism
the theoretical, language-based division into two of something indivisible. Dualism is on a continuum: monism – dualism – pluralism. Generally used to refer to our experience of creation, where we experience dualism as contradictions, opposites: in terms of presence and absence (such as hot and cold, light and dark, life and death, something and 'nothing') or in terms of polarities (male and female, good and evil, positive charge and negative charge). Hlatky argues that we have to have the idea of the one non-created, indivisible reality, the Being, behind the dualistic reality we experience as creation, and that we can only understand creation as one meaningful order that is flexible on the surface but fundamentally unchangeable. See **Being, creation, pluralism**.

ethics
behaviour based on an understanding of the meaning of creation and our inseparable, common life in creation, as opposed to morals, which are rules for behaviour put forward in an authoritarian way in the absence of ethics.

evaluation
the conclusion or set of conclusions that each person comes to in their efforts to understand reality, and what they come to value, the judgements they make, as a result of these conclusions.

everything-covering language
through human language we are able to 'cover' – that is, describe, give a name to – everything. This enables to us to communicate our experience and memory of every thing so that we can discuss the whole causality. God's purpose in giving us this possibility is that we should use it to arrive at an understanding of him and his purpose with the whole creation – that is, the original cause and meaning of creation – and thereby an understanding of each other. See further definition of the purpose of language in **Appendix A**.

existence (absolute)
that which is permanent, unchangeable, non-created, non-creatable, concrete; God's Being including the conscious parts. The absolute existence is invisible and intangible. Its immanent quality is the ability to experience and conscious, purposeful expression, that is, activity, of which only the absolute existence can be the cause. See **abstract, activity, axiom, Being, concrete, conscious part(s)**.

existence (relative)
that which appears to our senses as concrete, visible and tangible existence, but which is at the same time found by our senses to be the opposite – impermanent, changeable, created, creatable, abstract – and found in our experience of living beings to be transitory. See **abstract, concrete**.

existent
permanent, unchangeable, non-created, concrete. Objects in creation are illusorily existent. See **concrete, existence**.

existential
usually in 'existential needs': needs that are related to the survival of living bodies: light,

warmth, air, water, food, movement, reproduction etc. See **need**.

form

a form is something we experience from the outside as relatively existing (a cup, a pen, etc). See **existence (absolute)**, **existence (relative)**, **Being**.

formally

in its form, that is, as seen from the outside, without regard to other qualities.

function

activity, or cooperating activities.

functional

related to, demonstrating purposeful activity.

God-consciousness

the parts', the participants' consciousness of God behind his creation – as interpreted in Hlatky's or some other hypothesis.

identity

from the Latin *idem*, meaning 'the same'. Identity describes what is the same, what is unchanging about something. To talk of 'changing identity' is therefore a contradiction in terms. Only the Being has an identity: both as an absolute, unchangeable existence, whose essence is the same unchangeable cause, the ability to experience and act, which is the basic quality of life. See **Being**, **consciousness**.

language-based

purely language-based ideas or thinking: purely theoretical thinking divorced from our total current experience of creation and possible for humans only because of human language. It becomes anchored in language-based memory, what we call 'history', and gives rise to the identification with time and transitoriness. To be distinguished from Nature-based or reality-anchored ideas or thinking, with Nature interpreted as God's expression, God's activity. See **Nature-based**.

like

alike, the same as. God and his conscious parts are like in their ability to experience. Arising out of what they experience – God in the Being, the parts in creation – both have the need to be understood as like, and thereby to be loved. Likes cannot be compared with one another: like cannot be compared with like. The idea of like precludes any hierarchy. See **love**, **conscious part**.

logic/logical

logic relates to the meaning or purpose of the activity of a living being (as only living beings can have a meaning to their activities). An activity is logical if it meets the need it is intended to meet. Logic could be defined as the meaningful connection of a living being's need with the technical means of satisfying that need: e.g. when I am thirsty, it is logical to have something to drink. See **meaning**, **need**.

love

the basic need of God and of the conscious parts to be understood as likes, which gives rise on God's part to the need to create creation, and on our part to the need to understand and relate meaningfully to creation, on the basis of the natural, bodily needs, which are principally the same for every living being. Love is the feeling that accompanies our understanding that another living being is like us. Such understanding is thus the precondition for love. See **need, preference, undivided love**.

manifold, the
the same as the multiplicity and the diversity. Oneness experienced as dualism: the manifold and the interaction of it all. Used by Kant: Oxford English Dictionary '...the sum of the particulars furnished by sense before they have been unified by the understanding.' See **diversity, dualism**.

meaning
the purpose and the aim of an activity.

meaningful
describes activity that aims to satisfy a natural need. We feel alienated when we don't know the meaning of a human being's activity, i.e. activities that originate with humans but which do not meet a natural need and which aim to demonstrate unlikeness, 'originality'. Alienation is then our identity, because we don't recognize the meaning of Nature. We want instead to change Nature, out of a view that it is basically random or chaotic. See **need, natural**.

mechanical/mechanistic/technical/technological
relate to the ability of humans to acquire knowledge of constructive and destructive causality, independent of any need, and to explore and direct creation, the visible, perishable world with which we have a tangible, objective relationship. A mechanical or mechanistic view of life – which is characteristic of modern science – means a view that excludes the idea that the visible and tangible picture expressed by creation and represented by the manifold has a conscious meaning. See **creation, manifold**.

morals/moral rules
See **ethics**.

multiplicity, the
the same as the manifold and the diversity. See **diversity, manifold**.

mystical
something we do not know the origin of, and which we cannot therefore explain.

natural
in accordance with Nature's meaning and purpose. See **meaning, Nature**.

Nature
God's activity, creation's inherent quality. See **creation**.

Nature-based
Nature-based ideas or thinking: ideas or thinking based on our total internal, subjective and external, objective experience of Nature interpreted as God's activity. To be distinguished from 'purely language-based' ideas or thinking. See **language-based, objective, subjective**.

need
that which gives rise, on the basis of a living being's experience, to activity. The activity is aimed at fulfilling the need. Here we have to understand the difference between the need for love, the existential needs, and the artificial needs of human beings. The need for love gives rise to God's need to give out creation and it gives rise to the human need to understand, communicate and agree about God's need behind creation. The existential needs are the needs of the body and are principally the same for every living being on Earth, which makes it possible for us to love the other species as likes. Humans' artificial needs can be meaningfully connected to existential needs or can be independent of them. Identification with independent artificial needs makes the experience of natural love problematic. See **creation, existential, love, natural**.

objective
'what lies in front of' a person. 'Objective experience' is what one experiences outside oneself and is distance-based. To be distinguished from subjective: 'what lies behind or inside'. Both objective and subjective experience must be taken into account, as an indivisible unity, in philosophy. See **distance-based, philosophy, subjective**.

obvious
what is visible or plain to the senses. See **self-evident**.

organic
as in the organic view of unity, which Hlatky originally called his hypothesis. Organic, referring to the absolute whole, the Being, refers to a living whole, not exactly as in creation, where such a whole is made up of differing living parts organized towards an end, but rather a whole in which there is a distanceless, mutual relationship between the whole and like, living parts. The opposite is the mechanical view of unity, which is based on the idea that the unity is fundamentally non-living. A mechanical unity, a totality, is simply the sum of non-living, similar or dissimilar parts, without a mutual relationship between the whole and the parts. See **mechanical, totality, whole**.

part
'whole' and 'parts' are two indivisible sides of the same thing. The term 'whole' presumes parts, and the term 'part' presumes a whole, and both presume a meaningful relation between the whole and its parts. See **whole, conscious part(s)**.

philosophical reflection
relates basically to the question of the original cause of creation, as a precondition for understanding creation's meaning. It is based on axioms and is different from the thinking required to understand causality – cause and effect – within creation. See **axiom, creation, meaning**.

philosophy
is concerned solely with understanding the original cause and meaning of creation. See **meaning**.

pluralism
the view that there are many causes of what we experience in creation, and not a single original cause. The belief, for example, that what we experience as matter in creation is the cause implies in practice a belief in an endless number of causes, that is, absolute pluralism. See **dualism**.

predilection, preference
unavoidable, since creation offers us more than one way to satisfy some of our needs, but not to be regarded as the basis for love. But in the absence of love for the whole creation – that is, if we don't love God for his creation – we have to choose between what we prefer and what we do not prefer. We then experience what we prefer as a salvation from the negative feeling we have basically for creation, and we confuse it with love. We are then identified with our preferences and can never get rid of the basic negative feeling. See **needs**, **undivided love**.

psyche
is equivalent to the soul. It is the sum of evaluations of causality within creation, which we build up during our life with the help of our memory – through thinking steered by our common, natural needs and our personal, artificial needs – and which underlies the behaviour patterns we display. See **need**.

quality
property, capacity, nature, characteristic. A quality cannot be experienced objectively, as something in itself separate from the object that expresses the quality. The basic quality of God and his parts is the ability to experience. See **consciousness**.

reality
either the original reality, or the reality that we experience day to day, that is, creation – as specified. 'The whole reality' refers to both these together. See **creation**.

reality-anchored, reality-based
reality-anchored thinking is thinking anchored in reality – and not purely in memory, i.e. in time – in the same sense as 'thinking anchored in Nature'. To be distinguished from 'purely language-based thinking'. See **language-based**, **Nature-based**.

self-evident
axiomatic, not requiring nor being capable of objective proof or of argumentation, because it describes something that is evident only to the self, through immediate experience. It relates to common sense, since self-evident describes what is common – internally/subjectively and externally/objectively – to everyone. 'Obvious', by contrast, relates to what we perceive outside ourselves. See **axiom**, **common sense**, **objective**, **obvious**, **subjective**.

soul
See **psyche**.

subjective
'subjective experience' is experience of being conscious and experience of our body, including our memory and psyche, mediated by the nervous system. It is immediate and direct, whereas 'objective experience' is distance-based. See **distance-based**, **objective**, **psyche**.

technical/technological
See **mechanical**.

totality
something that is the sum of its (non-living) parts. See **whole**.

undivided love

love for the whole creation, that is, not fundamentally dividing creation into good and bad, lovable and not-lovable. This still leaves room for preferences, which are a practical necessity. See **predilection/preference**.

whole

a living entity that is made up of different living parts organized towards an end and in which there is a distanceless, mutual relationship between the whole and its parts. A whole is something from which nothing can be subtracted without its ceasing to be a complete whole. A totality, by contrast, is merely the sum of its parts, without an end in relation to its parts. When something is taken away from a totality, it remains a totality, albeit reduced in its extent. 'Whole' refers to something organic, 'totality' to something mechanical. See **organic**, **mechanical**, **part**, **totality**.

Index

Words in bold also appear in the Glossary (n indicates a footnote)